Understanding and Using WordPerfect 5.0

Patsy H. Lund
Lakewood Community College

West Publishing Company
St. Paul   New York   Los Angeles   San Francisco

Cover Design: Bob Anderson, Computer Arts, Inc.

CREDITS:

- WordPerfect MENUS FROM SOFTWARE REPRINTED WITH THE PERMISSION OF WORDPERFECT CORPORATION.
- WordPerfect KEYBOARD TEMPLATE (REDUCED IN SIZE) REPRINRTED WITH THE PERMISSION OF WORDPERFECT CORPORATION.

COPYRIGHT © 1989 by   WEST PUBLISHING CO.
                                  50 West Kellogg Boulevard
                                  P.O. Box 64526
                                  St. Paul, MN 55164-1003

All rights reserved

Printed in the United States of America

96 95 94 93 92 91 90 89   8 7 6 5 4 3 2 1 0

Library of Congress Cataloging-in-Publication Data

Lund, Patsy H.
  Understanding and Using WordPerfect 5.0 / Patsy H. Lund.
    p. cm. -- (The Microcomputing series)
  Includes index.
  ISBN 0-314-47353-X
  1. WordPerfect (Computer program) 2. Word processing. I. Title.
II. Series.
Z52.5W65L87 1989   88-34362
652'.5--dc19   CIP

CONTENTS

PART 1 FUNDAMENTALS 1

UNIT 1 INTRODUCTION TO WORDPERFECT 5.0 3

Supplies Needed 3
Objectives 3
Assignments 3
WordPerfect 5.0 4
    The Template 4
    Menus 6
    The Quick Reference Card 6
    The User's Manual 6
Understanding and Using WordPerfect 5.0 7
    Conventions 7
Review Questions 7
Documentation Research 8

UNIT 2 CREATING YOUR FIRST DOCUMENT 11

Supplies Needed 11
Objectives 11
Important Keystrokes 12
Assignments 12
Using Appendix A 12
Formatting a Data Disk 13
Making a Copy of the Student Data Disk 13
Guided Activity: Loading WordPerfect 5.0 13
Loading WordPerfect 5.0 into a Hard Disk System 14
The Cursor 15
The Status Line 15
Carriage Return 16

Word Wrap	16
Default Values	16
Hard Space	16
Soft Page	17
Hard Page	17
Guided Activity: Creating Your First Document	17
Saving Documents	18
Naming Documents	18
Guided Activity: Saving a Document	18
The Importance of Saving Documents	19
Cursor Movement Keys	19
Horizontal Movement	19
Vertical Movement	20
Go To	21
Saving a Document while Exiting WordPerfect 5.0	21
Guided Activity: Exiting WordPerfect 5.0	22
The Help Function	23
Guided Activity: Using the Help Screen	23
Retrieving a Document	23
Guided Activity: Retrieving a Document	24
Review Questions	25
Documentation Research	27
Review Exercises	27

UNIT 3 TYPING AND PRINTING A BUSINESS LETTER   29

Supplies Needed	29
Objectives	29
Important Keystrokes	30
Assignments	30
Document Identification Line	30
Guided Activity: Creating a Business Letter	30
Editing a Document	32
Guided Activity: Editing a Business Letter	32
Toggle Keys	34
The Insert Key	34
The Rewrite Feature	34
Guided Activity: Using the <TAB> and <INS> Keys	35
Menu	36
Guided Activity: Printing a Business Letter	36
Undelete	38
Review Questions	38
Documentation Research	39
Review Exercises	40

APPLICATION A   41

Contents v

UNIT 4 SIMPLE EDITING FUNCTIONS 47

Supplies Needed 47
Objectives 47
Important Keystrokes 48
Assignments 48
Enhancement Features 48
    The Bold Feature 48
    The Underline Feature 48
    Capitalization 48
    Centering Text 49
Guided Activity: Creating a Letterhead 49
The Flush Right Feature 51
Guided Activity: Inserting the Current Date Flush Right 51
The Block Feature 51
Guided Activity: Using the Block Feature to Enhance Existing Text 52
The Move and Copy Features 54
Guided Activity: Copying a Block of Text 55
Guided Activity: Moving a Block of Text 56
The Block and Switch Features 57
Guided Activity: Using the Block and Switch Features 57
Guided Activity: Printing a Revised Business Letter 58
Reveal Codes 60
Guided Activity: Revealing Codes 60
Making Backup Copies of Your Documents 61
Review Questions 61
Documentation Research 63
Review Exercises 64

UNIT 5 FORMATTING TEXT FOR PRINTING 65

Supplies Needed 65
Objectives 65
Important Keystrokes 65
Formatting Text for Printing 66
Formatting a Document for Printing 66

<u>SECTION 1</u> 67
Assignments 67
The Font Menu 67
Guided Activity: Using the Size and Appearance Submenus 69
Guided Activity: Using Superscripts 70
Guided Activity: Using Subscripts 71
Review Questions 73
Documentation Research 73
Review Exercises 74

SECTION 2 — 75
Assignments — 75
The Format Menu — 75
Guided Activity: Using the Format Line Submenu — 78
Guided Activity: Changing the Margins — 79
Margin Release — 80
Guided Activity: Right Justification — 80
Guided Activity: Line Spacing — 81
Guided Activity: Changing Tab Settings — 82
Guided Activity: Using Tab Settings — 83
Guided Activity: Creating Headers — 86
Guided Activity: Changing the Page Number — 87
Guided Activity: Inserting a Page Number at the Bottom of Each Page — 88
Guided Activity: Centering a Page Vertically — 89
Guided Activity: Creating a Document Summary — 91
Guided Activity: Displaying a Document Summary — 92
Review Questions — 94
Documentation Research — 95
Review Exercises — 95

SECTION 3 — 96
Assignments — 96
The Styles Menu — 96
Guided Activity: Creating a Style — 98
Guided Activity: Using a Style — 100
Guided Activity: Using the Styles Library — 100
Review Questions — 101
Documentation Research — 102
Review Exercises — 102

UNIT 6 CONTROLLING THE PRINTER — 103

Supplies Needed — 103
Objectives — 103
Important Keystrokes — 103
Assignments — 104
Printing — 104
The Print Menu — 104
Guided Activity: Printing Two Copies of a Single Page — 107
Guided Activity: Printing a Block of Text — 108
Guided Activity: Stopping and Restarting a Print Job — 109
Guided Activity: Printing a Document Stored on a Data Disk — 110
Guided Activity: Cancelling a Print Job — 111
View Document Feature — 112
Guided Activity: Viewing a Document — 113
Review Questions — 113
Documentation Research — 114
Review Exercises — 115

APPLICATION B — 117

PART 2 INTERMEDIATE EDITING FEATURES — 123

UNIT 7 DISCOVERING MORE WORDPERFECT FUNCTIONS — 125

Supplies Needed — 125
Objectives — 125
Important Keystrokes — 126
Assignments — 126
The Date and Time Feature — 126
    The Date Menu — 126
Guided Activity: Inserting the Date Automatically — 127
Indenting — 128
Guided Activity: Typing a Paragraph — 129
Guided Activity: Indenting Text from the Left Margin — 129
Guided Activity: Indenting Text from the Right and Left Margins — 129
Guided Activity: Creating a Hanging Paragraph — 130
Repeating a Character or Feature — 131
Guided Activity: Using the Repeat Feature — 131
Search and Replace — 133
    Search — 133
    Replace — 133
Guided Activity: Searching Up and Down — 135
Guided Activity: Automatic Search and Replace — 136
Footnotes and Endnotes — 137
    The Footnote/Endnote Menu — 137
Guided Activity: Creating Footnotes — 140
The Tab Ruler — 142
Guided Activity: Displaying the Tab Ruler — 143
Split Screen — 144
Review Questions — 144
Documentation Research — 146
Review Exercises — 146

UNIT 8 FILE MANAGEMENT — 149

Supplies Needed — 149
Objectives — 149
Important Keystrokes — 149
Assignments — 150
File Management — 150
Guided Activity: Using List Files to Retrieve a Document — 152
Guided Activity: Using List Files to Print a Document — 153
Guided Activity: Using List Files to Look at a File — 153
Guided Activity: Using List Files to Rename a File — 153
Guided Activity: Using List Files to Delete a File — 154
Locked Documents — 154
Review Questions — 155
Documentation Research — 155
Review Exercises — 156

UNIT 9 SPELLER AND THESAURUS   157

Supplies Needed   157
Objectives   157
Important Keystrokes   157
Assignments   158
The Speller   158
The Check Menu   158
The Not Found Submenu   159
The Double Word Submenu   160
Guided Activity: Spell-Checking   161
The Thesaurus   162
Guided Activity: Using the Thesaurus   163
Review Questions   164
Documentation Research   166
Review Exercises   166

APPLICATION C   167

PART 3 SPECIAL FEATURES   173

UNIT 10 SELECTING, SORTING AND MERGING   175

Supplies Needed   175
Objectives   175
Important Keystrokes   175
Assignments   176
Records, Fields, Lines, Words, and Keys   176
Sorting and Selecting   177
Guided Activity: Sorting a List   179
Merging   179
The Secondary File   179
Guided Activity: Creating a Secondary File   180
The Primary File   181
Guided Activity: Creating a Primary File   182
Merging and Printing   184
Guided Activity: Merging and Printing a Personalized Letter   185
Guided Activity: Sorting Merge Records   186
Guided Activity: Selecting and Sorting Records   188
Guided Activity: Addressing Envelopes   189
Guided Activity: Printing Envelopes   191
Mailing Labels   191
Formatting Mailing Labels   191
More On Merging   192
Review Questions   193
Documentation Research   193
Review Exercises   194

UNIT 11 MACROS   195

Supplies Needed   195
Objectives   195
Important Keystrokes   195
Assignments   195
Macros   196
Guided Activity: Creating a Permanent Macro to Print a Document   196
Guided Activity: Creating a Macro to Store Margin Settings   197
Guided Activity: Creating a Macro That Contains Text   199
Guided Activity: Retrieving a Macro   200
Guided Activity: Creating a Macro Chain   201
Guided Activity: Using a Macro Chain   202
Review Questions   203
Documentation Research   204
Review Exercises   204

APPLICATION D   205

UNIT 12 COLUMNS   209

Supplies Needed   209
Objectives   209
Important Keystrokes   209
Assignments   209
Text Columns   210
The Math/Columns Menu   210
Guided Activity: Creating a Newspaper Column   212
Guided Activity: Creating Parallel Columns   213
Review Questions   215
Documentation Research   216
Review Exercises   216

UNIT 13 TABLES OF CONTENTS, LISTS, AND INDEXES   219

Supplies Needed   219
Objectives   219
Important Keystrokes   219
Assignments   219
Tables of Contents, Lists, and Indexes   220
Marking Text   220
Guided Activity: Creating a Table of Contents   222
Guided Activity: Creating an Index   225
Review Questions   226
Documentation Research   227
Review Exercises   227

UNIT 14 MATH — 229

Supplies Needed — 229
Objectives — 229
Important Keystrokes — 229
Assignments — 229
The Math Feature — 230
The Math Definition Menu — 230
Guided Activity: Setting Tabs — 232
Guided Activity: Defining Columns — 232
Guided Activity: Creating a Budget Worksheet — 233
Guided Activity: Turning Off the Math Feature — 237
Review Questions — 239
Documentation Research — 240
Review Exercises — 240

UNIT 15 GRAPHICS — 241

Supplies Needed — 241
Objectives — 241
Important Keystrokes — 241
Assignments — 241
Graphics — 242
Graphics Menu — 242
Guided Activity: Creating a Vertical Line — 247
Guided Activity: Creating a Vertical Line Between Columns — 247
Boxes — 249
Guided Activity: Creating a Box with Entered Text — 253
Guided Activity: Creating a Box with a Retrieved File — 255
Review Questions — 256
Documentation Research — 257
Review Exercises — 257

APPLICATION E — 259

APPENDIX A GETTING STARTED ON YOUR MICROCOMPUTER — A-1

APPENDIX B ANSWERS TO CHECKPOINT QUESTIONS — B-1

INDEX — I-1

QUICK REFERENCE

PREFACE

As microcomputer use increases in academic and workplace settings, so also does the demand for well-designed application software. WordPerfect 5.0 was designed in response to the practical need to produce a variety of professional documents quickly and accurately. It is a sophisticated software package with extensive capabilities. Each word-processing task, however, has unique requirements, and therefore only some of WordPerfect's features are needed to produce an individual document. Consequently, WordPerfect 5.0 is arranged so that each feature can be accessed individually, just when it is needed.

Understanding and Using WordPerfect 5.0 is also designed to meet the needs of individuals who have unique word-processing tasks. It is arranged to guide the user through a step-by-step process in understanding how to use each of WordPerfect's features. It examines both the fundamental and the sophisticated word-processing capabilities of WordPerfect 5.0. This text itself is an illustration of WordPerfect's capabilities; it was both written and formatted with the WordPerfect word-processing package.

Each unit contains:

Objectives, which list the skills you will acquire.

Important Keystrokes, that summarize the commands you will use.

Guided Activities, which present step-by-step instructions for using individual program features.

Computer screens, which illustrate the menus that activate specific features.

Checkpoints, which test your understanding of the Guided Activities. (The answers to the checkpoint questions are in Appendix B.)

Review Questions, which test understanding of the information contained in each unit.

Review Exercises, which provide practice for the procedures covered in the unit.

Additional features of <u>Understanding and Using WordPerfect 5.0</u> include:

Applications, which you can use to apply your acquired skills.

Quick Reference, on the last pages of the workbook, which lists the most frequently used commands.

Data Disk, available to instructors, with student and instructor files. The student files are needed to complete the Guided Activities and Applications. TLhese files should be transferred to a separate disk which is used to store the files you create in Guided Activities and application exercises. The instructor files include solutions to Guided Activities and application exercises.

Transparancy Masters, which include selected figures in the text.

Instructor's manual, which includes answers to review questions and a Test Bank.

ACKNOWLEDGEMENTS

The author of <u>Understanding and Using WordPerfect 5.0</u> would like to acknowledge the efforts of the following people in the production of this workbook. Many thanks to:

Rich Wohl, editor of The Microcomputing Series, for his confidence in my ability to write and produce this book.

Connie Austin, production assistant, for her assistance and patience; and all the other West staff members who helped complete this text.

George UpChurch, Carson-Newman College; Dennis Gehris, Bloomsburg University; Sally Preissig, College of Lake County; Betty Martin, Carruthersville High School; Cindy Gaudet, University of Southern Mississippi; Lynette Kluster-Shishido, Santa Monica College; Tae Won Jin, New Hampshire College; Lucia Rossi, Seneca College of Applied Arts; for finding time to review this manuscript.

WordPerfect Corporation, for producing a software package with the capability to write this text.

My family whose generosity and good humor meant a great deal to the successful completion of this project.

ABOUT THE AUTHOR

Patsy H. Lund earned her Bachelor of Arts degree from Metropolitan University in St. Paul, Minnesota, and her M.B.A. from the College of St. Thomas in St. Paul. Her professional experience includes microcomputer training on IBM and IBM compatibles and technical writing for curriculum development.

Patsy is a college instructor, with teaching experience in the areas of Computer Science, Data Processing and Accounting, at Lakewood Community College, White Bear Lake, Minnesota. She is also the Vice President of a microcomputer training and consulting firm in St. Paul, Minnesota. This text is one of several in this series she has authored, co-authored or edited.

PUBLISHER'S NOTE

This book is part of THE MICROCOMPUTING SERIES. We are proud to announce that this unique series is now entering its fourth year, and currently includes four different types of books:

1. A core concepts book, now in its second edition, teaches basic hardware and software applications concepts. This text is titled UNDERSTANDING AND USING MICROCOMPUTERS.

2. A series on introductory level, hands-on workbooks for a wide variety of specific software packages. These provide both self-paced tutorials and complete reference guides. Each book's title begins with UNDERSTANDING AND USING . . . .

3. Several larger volumes combine DOS with three popular software packages. Two of these volumes are called UNDERSTANDING AND USING APPLICATION SOFTWARE, while the third is titled UNDERSTANDING AND USING SHAREWARE APPLICATION SOFTWARE. These versions condense components of the individual workbooks while increasing the coverage of DOS and the integration of different application packages.

4. An advanced level of hands-on workbooks with a strong project/systems orientation. These titles all begin with DEVELOPING AND USING . . . .

Our goal has always been to provide you with maximum flexibility in meeting the changing neds of your courses through this "mix and match" approach. We remain committed to offering the widest variety of current software packages.

We now offer these books in THE MICROCOMPUTING SERIES:

Understanding and Using Microcomputers, 2nd Edition   by Steven M. Zimmerman and Leo M. Conrad

OPERATING SYSTEMS

Understanding and Using MS-DOS/PC DOS:
The First Steps, 2nd Edition
    by Laura B. Ruff and Mary K. Weitzer

Understanding and Using MS-DOS/PC DOS:
A Complete Guide
    by Cody T. Copeland and Jonathan P. Bacon

Understanding and Using MS-DOS/PC DOS 4.0
    by Jonathan P. Bacon

PROGRAMMING LANGUAGES

Understanding and Using Microsoft BASIC/IBM-PC BASIC
    by Mary L. Howard

WORD PROCESSORS

Understanding and Using DisplayWrite 4
    by Patsy H. Lund and Barbara A. Hayden

Understanding and Using Microsoft Word
    by Jonathan P. Bacon

Understanding and Using MultiMate
    by Mary K. Weitzer and Laura B. Ruff

Understanding and Using PC-Write
    by Victor P. Maiorana

Understanding and Using pfs:WRITE
    by Mary K. Weitzer and Laura B. Ruff

Understanding and Using WordPerfect
    by Patsy H. Lund and Barbara A. Hayden

Understanding and Using WordPerfect 5.0
    by Patsy H. Lund

Understanding and Using WordStar
    by Steven C. Ross

Understanding and Using WordStar 4.0
    by Patsy H. Lund and Barbara A. Hayden

SPREADSHEET PACKAGES

Understanding and Using Lotus 1-2-3
    by Steven C. Ross

Understanding and Using Lotus 1-2-3 Release 2
    by Steven C. Ross

Understanding and Using Lotus 1-2-3 Release 3
    by Steven C. Ross

Understanding and Using SuperCalc 3
    by Steven C. Ross and Judy A. Reinders

Understanding and Using SuperCalc 4
    by Judy A. Reinders and Steven C. Ross

Understanding and Using VP-Planner Plus
    by Steven C. Ross

DATABASE PACKAGES

Understanding and Using dBASE III (Including dBASE II)
    by Steven C. Ross

Understanding and Using dBASE III PLUS
    by Steven C. Ross

Understanding and Using dBASE IV
    by Steven C. Ross

Understanding and Using pfs:FILE/REPORT
    by Laura B. Ruff and Mary K. Weitzer

Understanding and Using R:BASE 5000
(Including R:BASE System V)
    by Karen L. Watterson

INTEGRATED SOFTWARE

Understanding and Using Appleworks (Including Appleworks 2.0)
    by Frank Short

Developing and Using Office Applications with AppleWorks
    by M. S. Varnon

Understanding and Using Educate-Ability
    by Victor P. Maiorana and Arthur A. Strunk

Understanding and Using pfs:First Choice
    by Seth A. Hock

Understanding and Using FRAMEWORK
    by Karen L. Watterson

Understanding and Using Symphony
    by Enzo V. Allegretti

COMBINATION VOLUMES

Understanding and Using Application Software, Volume 1:
DOS, WordStar 4.0, Lotus 1-2-3 Release 2, and dBASE III PLUS
    by Steven C. Ross, Patsy H. Lund and Barbara A. Hayden

Understanding and Using SHAREWARE Application Software:
DOS, PC-Write, ExpressCalc, and PC-FILE
    by Victor P. Maiorana

Understanding and Using Application Software, Volume 2:
DOS, WordPerfect 4.2, Lotus 1-2-3 Release 2, and dBASE III PLUS
    by Steven C. Ross, Patsy H. Lund and Barbara A. Hayden

Understanding and Using Application Software, Volume 3:
DOS, WordPerfect 4.2, VP-Planner Plus, and dBASE III PLUS
    by Steven C. Ross and Patsy H. Lund

ADVANCED BOOKS

Developing and Using Decision Support Applications
    by Steven C. Ross, Richard J. Penlesky and
    Lloyd D. Doney

Developing and Using Microcomputer Business Systems
    by Kathryn W. Huff

We are delighted by the popularity of THE MICROCOMPUTING SERIES. We appreciate your support, and look forward to your suggestions and comments. Please write to us at this address:

West Publishing Company,
College Division
50 West Kellogg Blvd.,
P.O. Box 64526, St. Paul,

PART 1
FUNDAMENTALS

Fundamentals, the first of three parts includes a description of the contents of the WordPerfect 5.0 program and a discussion of the program design. You learn to load the program and use WordPerfect 5.0 commands and menus to create, edit, and print a documents. You learn to move the cursor efficiently through your document and to add or delete text. You learn to use a Help screen to find specific information on WordPerfect 5.0 functions and menus. You also learn to exit WordPerfect 5.0.

Part 1 includes Applications A and B, which contain exercises to apply the skills you acquired. The documents you create in unit exercises and application sections will be stored on your Student Data disk.

UNIT 1
INTRODUCTION TO WORDPERFECT 5.0

SUPPLIES NEEDED

1. WordPerfect 5.0 user's manual
2. WordPerfect 5.0 Quick Reference card
3. WordPerfect 5.0 keyboard template

OBJECTIVES

After completing this unit, you will be able to

1. use the Table of Contents and the Index to find information in the user's manual;
2. use the template to identify the purpose of each function key;
3. use the Quick Reference card to become familiar with the features that specific keystrokes activate.

ASSIGNMENTS

1. Review Questions
2. Documentation Research

WORDPERFECT 5.0

WordPerfect 5.0 is a software package that is capable of performing both simple and complex word-processing tasks. It consists of ten 5-1/4" disks. You will use the two program disks for every activity in this text. The other disks will be used as needed for special activities. The package also contains a keyboard template, a Quick Reference card, and a user's manual.

The Template

The plastic keyboard template (figure 1-1) fits over the ten function keys at the left of the IBM PC keyboard. A template is also included for those keyboards that have the function keys located in a row across the top (figure 1-2).

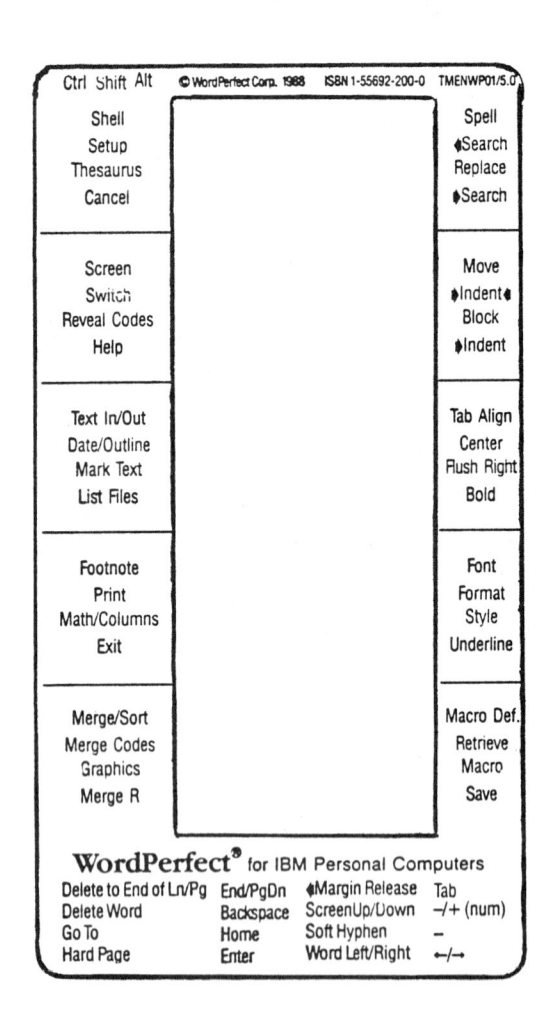

FIGURE 1-1 WordPerfect 5.0 Keyboard Template

Introduction to WordPerfect 5.0   5

| WordPerfect® for IBM Personal Computers
Delete to End of Ln/Pg — End/Pg Dn
Delete Word — Backspace
Go To — Home
Hard Page — Enter
♦Margin Release — Tab
Screen Up/Down — −/+ (num)
Soft Hyphen — −
Word Left/Right — ←/→
© WordPerfect Corp. 1988 TMENWP01/5.0
ISBN 1-55692-200-0 | Shell
Thesaurus
Setup
Cancel
F1 | Spell
Replace
♦Search
♦Search
F2 | Screen
Reveal Codes
Switch
Help
F3 | Move
Block
♦Indent♦
♦Indent
F4 | *Ctrl*
Alt
Shift | Text In/Out
Mark Text
Date/Outline
List Files
F5 |

| Tab Align
Flush Right
Center
Bold
F6 | Footnote
Math/Columns
Print
Exit
F7 | Font
Style
Format
Underline
F8 | *Ctrl*
Alt
Shift | Merge/Sort
Graphics
Merge Codes
Merge R
F9 | Macro Define
Macro
Retrieve
Save
F10 | Reveal Codes
F11 | Block
F12 |

FIGURE 1-2 WordPerfect 5.0 Keyboard Template (Top-row function keys)

The template identifies the purpose of each of the function keys located on the keyboard. Used in combination with the Alt, Shift, and Ctrl keys, these ten keys activate forty WordPerfect 5.0 features. The template makes it easier to remember those functions. To make it even easier, the template is color coded.

The color codes are defined as follows:

    BLACK Press the function key.

    BLUE Hold down Alt while pressing the function key.

    GREEN Hold down Shift while pressing the function key.

    RED Hold down Ctrl while pressing the function key.

Study the template and the features offered by WordPerfect 5.0. As you learn to use WordPerfect 5.0, associating each key with the function it performs will become automatic.

Menus

WordPerfect 5.0 is designed to access a menu each time a function key is pressed. Each menu offers a list of options that allows you to select a particular WordPerfect 5.0 feature. Menus simplify operations, save time, and reduce data-entry errors. WordPerfect 5.0 is designed to keep menus out of sight until they are actually needed, thus increasing word-processing efficiency.

The Quick Reference Card

The Quick Reference card lists WordPerfect 5.0's features along with the keystrokes that activate those features. It also lists the cursor control keys, which are used to move you quickly and easily through the pages of the documents you create.

The Quick Reference card is also color coded and provides information on starting WordPerfect 5.0, the color-coding system, saving documents, clearing the screen, and exiting the program.

The User's Manual

The WordPerfect 5.0 user's manual is an indispensable part of the WordPerfect 5.0 package for it documents all the program's features. It is, at first sight, an overwhelmingly large document, but you will learn to use it to look up those particular features that are relevant to your needs.

The manual is divided into four sections. The first section is entitled Getting Started. Use it to find basic information about WordPerfect 5.0 software and simple explanations of procedures you need to get started.

The second and largest section is the Reference section. It contains an alphabetical listing of WordPerfect 5.0 features along with an easy-to-follow explanation of how to activate each feature. Use this section regularly. It is arranged to help you find basic information with minimal effort.

The third section, entitled Appendix, contains information about program installation, printers, and a description of some of WordPerfect's special capabilities such as advanced macros and graphics.

The fourth section, the Glossary/Index, contains a glossary of WordPerfect 5.0 terms and a comprehensive index.

The WordPerfect Workbook

The WordPerfect Workbook is used in combination with the Learning disk. It consists of 32 lessons that teach you WordPerfect's features.

UNDERSTANDING AND USING WORDPERFECT 5.0

This workbook is divided into three parts. Part 1, Fundamentals, teaches you to create, revise, and print a document. After you have completed Part 1, you will be able to use WordPerfect 5.0 to produce memos, reports, business letters, and manuscripts.

Part 2, Intermediate Features, teaches you more about WordPerfect 5.0 techniques for editing printing documents. You will also learn to use the Speller and Thesaurus and to manage files.

Part 3, Special Features, teaches you about WordPerfect special features such as merging, math, keystroke programming (macros), and graphics.

Conventions

Several typographical conventions have been established to improve readability and understanding. They were established to clearly communicate each WordPerfect 5.0 function. They are as follows:

> When a keystroke activates a single command, it is designated like this: <KEYNAME> (e.g., <ENTER>, <SPACEBAR>).
>
> The keys that direct cursor movement are designated, for example, like these: <Up>, <Down>, <Left>, <Right>, <Home>, <End>, <PgUp>.
>
> When one key is used in combination with another, the first one must be held down while the other is pressed. Combination keys are separated by a hyphen (e.g., Alt-F4).
>
> When keys are pressed one after another but not in combination, they are separated by a comma (e.g., <Home>,<Home>,<Right> arrow).
> All functions begin with a capital letter (e.g., Exit, Save, Cancel).

REVIEW QUESTIONS

1. Explain how WordPerfect 5.0's keyboard template is used.

   Placed by function keys to help assist the user identify the special functions

2. Assume that you have used WordPerfect 5.0 to create a memo but have forgotten which key to press to use the Save feature. How can you quickly look this up?

   Use the template

3. Explain WordPerfect 5.0's color coding system.

   black - press function key, blue - "alt" key in combination, green - "shift" key in combination, red - "ctrl" in combination

8   WordPerfect 5.0

4. Which section of the user's manual (documentation) will you use to find information on starting the WordPerfect 5.0 program?

DOCUMENTATION RESEARCH

1. Locate the Glossary/Index section in the user's manual, then use the glossary to define the following terms:

   Defaults

   Megabyte

   Memory

   Bit

   Buffer

2. Locate the Reference section in the user's manual, then look up the description of each of the following:

   Initial settings

   Cancel

   Flush Right

   Indent

Capitalization

Justification

3. Locate the Getting Started section in the user's manual, then describe the following:

Keys to Know

Manual Conventions

The Template

Typing Zeros and Ones

UNIT 2
CREATING YOUR FIRST DOCUMENT

SUPPLIES NEEDED

1. disk operating system (DOS) disk
2. WordPerfect 5.0 disks 1 and 2
3. WordPerfect 5.0 Learning disk
4. two data disks
5. Understanding and Using WordPerfect 5.0 Student Data disk

OBJECTIVES

After completing this unit you will be able to

1. load the WordPerfect 5.0 program;
2. format a data disk;
3. create and name a one-page document;
4. save a document on your data disk in a designated drive;
5. retrieve a document;
6. use the "status line" to identify your position in a document;
7. use the cursor keys to move within a document;
8. use the <ENTER> key;
9. exit WordPerfect 5.0.

IMPORTANT KEYSTROKES

1. F10   saves a document
2. F7   saves a document and exits WordPerfect 5.0
3. Shift-F10   retrieves a document
4. F3   invokes Help screen
5. F1   cancels feature just activated
6. Ctrl-<Home>   move cursor to specific location
7. Cursor movement keystrokes:

   Horizontal Movement

   <Right> arrow key   moves cursor one character to the right
   <Left> arrow key   moves cursor one character to the left
   Ctrl-<Right> arrow keys   move cursor one word to the right
   Ctrl-<Left> arrow keys   move cursor one word to the left
   <Home>,<Right> arrow keys   move cursor to the right edge of the screen
   <Home>,<Left> arrow keys   move cursor to the left edge of the screen
   <Home>,<Home>,<Right> arrow keys   move cursor to the end of the line
   <Home>,<Home>,<Left> arrow keys   move cursor to the beginning of the line

   Vertical Movement

   <Up> arrow key   moves cursor one line up
   <Down> arrow key   moves cursor one line down
   <Home>,<Up> arrow keys   move cursor to the top of the screen
   <Home>,<Down> arrow keys   move cursor to the bottom of screen
   <Home>,<Home>,<Up> arrow keys   move cursor to the beginning of the document
   <Home>,<Home>,<Down> arrow keys   move cursor to the end of the document
   <PgUp> key   moves cursor to top of current page
   <PgDn> key   moves cursor to the bottom of current page

ASSIGNMENTS

1. Create **WORDWRAP**
2. Save **WORDWRAP**
3. Practice Cursor Movement
4. Exit WordPerfect 5.0
5. Retrieve **WORDWRAP**
6. Review Questions
7. Documentation Research
8. Review Exercises

USING APPENDIX A

Appendix A to this text contains information about your microcomputer and the disk operating system (DOS). It provides specific information about the keyboard, startup and shutdown procedures, specific commands, file naming, directory use, and document printing. By referring to this appendix, you will be able to use the WordPerfect 5.0 program to perform the tasks in this workbook.

Creating Your First Document   13

FORMATTING A DATA DISK

Your instructor will supply a copy of the DOS disk. Your first task is to use the DOS disk to format two disks, which will be used to store the documents you are going to create. Refer to Appendix A and follow the steps to format a disk. Be sure you format blank disks or disks containing information you no longer need. When the task of formatting is complete, use a felt-tip pen to label your disks "WordPerfect 5.0 Student Data."

MAKING A COPY OF THE STUDENT DATA DISK

Your instructor will lend you a copy of the Understanding and Using WordPerfect 5.0 Student Data disk. It contains the documents (files) you will edit as you follow the Guided Activities in this book. Copy the Understanding and Using WordPerfect 5.0 Student Data disk onto both of the disks you formatted. You will then have one disk to work with and one disk for backup. Follow the steps in Appendix A to Copy.

Be sure to return both the DOS and the Understanding and Using WordPerfect 5.0 Student Data disks to your instructor.

GUIDED ACTIVITY: LOADING WORDPERFECT 5.0

Refer to Startup Procedures in Appendix A to perform the following tasks:

1. Insert the WordPerfect 5.0 disk 1 into Drive A.
   Insert the WordPerfect 5.0 Student Data disk into Drive B.

2. Turn on the computer.

   Note: If your computer is already on, you must reboot it (Ctrl-Alt-<Del>). WordPerfect 5.0 needs a special command that is given from a file on the WordPerfect 5.0 disk 1.

   A prompt to enter the current date will appear, followed by a prompt to enter the current time.

3. Enter the date and time.

   An A> (A prompt) will appear.

4. Type **B:**

   Your screen will look like this: A>B:

   You have indicated that your documents will be stored on a disk in Drive B.

14   WordPerfect 5.0

5. Press the <ENTER> key.

   Your screen will look like this: B>

6. Type **A:WP**

   Your screen will look like this: B>A:WP

7. Press the <ENTER> key.

   The WordPerfect 5.0 copyright screen will be displayed. The message 'Insert diskette labeled "WordPerfect 2" and press any key' appears on the copyright screen.

8. Insert the WordPerfect 2 disk in Drive A.

9. Press any key.

   The message "Please wait" appears. In a few seconds a clear screen appears. The clear screen is the typing area on which you will create your document. Right now, it contains only a status line at the bottom of the screen.

✔ CHECKPOINT

   a. How does pressing <ENTER> after A>B: affect what appears on the screen?

   the A-prompt changes to the B-prompt

   b. Into which drive do you insert your WordPerfect 5.0 Student Data disk?

   "B"-drive

What You Have Accomplished

You have succeeded in loading the WordPerfect 5.0 program into your computer. You have also designated Drive B to store the documents that you will create. If you do not designate a separate drive on which to store your documents, they will be stored instead on the WordPerfect 5.0 program disk, on which there is little available space.

LOADING WORDPERFECT 5.0 INTO A HARD DISK SYSTEM

The procedure for loading WordPerfect 5.0 into a hard disk system differs from the procedure used to load it into a single or dual drive system. Assume that your hard disk has already been formatted and is storing the necessary DOS and WordPerfect 5.0 files. Follow the Startup Procedures for a hard disk system in Appendix A. A C> (C prompt) will appear. If WordPerfect Corporation installation suggestions were followed, type **CD\WP50** after the C>, then press <ENTER> to change to the proper directory. Type **B:** after the C>, then press **<ENTER>** to designate the drive on which to store your documents. Type **C:wp** at the B> to load the WordPerfect 5.0 program.

THE CURSOR

The **cursor** is a flashing line that shows where the next typed character will appear on the computer display acreen. It appears in the top-left corner of the screen each time you load the program.

THE STATUS LINE

The **status line** (figure 2-1) is displayed on the bottom line of the screen. The status line states (from left to right) the current document name, document and the page numbers, line position in inches from the top of the page, and column position in inches from the left edge of the page at which the cursor is presently located. The status line also displays messages from the program or from DOS.

Each document you create will be saved on your WordPerfect 5.0 data disk as a document file. In order to save a document you must name it. The procedures and rules for naming and saving a document are discussed later in this unit. The current document (the document you are currently working on) name appears in the status line. figure 2-1 shows the name to be given your first document.

The Doc (document) number indicates the number of the document currently being edited. Notice that the status line on your screen displays "Doc 1." Unless you are using the Split Screen Feature, which allows you to edit two documents simultaneously, this line will display "Doc 1."

The Pg (page) number identifies the number of the page currently being edited. The page number changes as you move the cursor through the pages of the documents you create. In figure 2-1 you are on Pg 1.

The Ln (line) number identifies the vertical position of the cursor on the page. This position is measured in inches. The first line on which you may enter data is one inch from the top of the page. The last line on which you may enter data is ten inches from the top of the page or one inch from the bottom of the page. In other words, WordPerfect provides automatic one-inch top and bottom margins. You will learn how to change these margins in a later unit. A standard page of text contains nine inches of typing space. Only 24 of those lines are displayed on your screen at one time. When you enter text beyond the 24, the lines of your document scroll off the top of your screen, one at a time. When you reach the end of a page, a line of dashes appears across the screen.

The Pos (position) number identifies the horizontal position of the cursor on the page. When you type a line, the position number changes as the cursor moves across the page.

```
┌─────────────────────────────────────────────────────────────────┐
│                                                                 │
│     B:\WORDWRAP                          Doc 1  Pg 1  Ln 1"  Pos 1" │
│                                                                 │
└─────────────────────────────────────────────────────────────────┘
```

FIGURE 2-1   Status Line

CARRIAGE RETURN

The purpose of a carriage return (<ENTER> key) within a word-processing program is different from a carriage return on a conventional typewriter. When you enter text on a screen and come to the end of a line, the program automatically wraps text around to the next line. Therefore, the only time it is necessary to press <ENTER> is when you want to begin a new line before you reach the end of the line you are currently on, as when you wish to begin a new paragraph. The <ENTER> key is also used to insert a blank line. If you press <ENTER> at the beginning of a line you will insert a blank line into the text. You should also press <ENTER> when you have reached the end of your document.

WORD WRAP

Word wrap is one of the most convenient features of electronic word processing. You no longer have to press a carriage return (<ENTER> key) at the end of each line of typing. WordPerfect automatically starts a new line when the cursor reaches the right margin. When a word is too long to fit at the end of a line, it automatically "wraps" around and becomes the first word of the next line. WordPerfect wraps the line depending on your program settings (margins, font) and the printer you are using. When you are following examples in this text, your lines may wrap at a different place. Press the <ENTER> key only when you wish to end a line and begin another before the cursor has reached the right margin or if you wish to insert a blank line.

DEFAULT VALUES

A **default** is the initial value (or startup setting) that a program assumes each time it is started. Default values are preset by software manufacturers, who make certain assumptions about the standards required by program users. Default settings are changed by embedding a code in an individual document at the exact location of the desired change. The changed setting affects only the document currently being edited.

HARD SPACE

Sometimes it is necessary to keep two or more words together on a line. When this occurs, insert a hard space by pressing **<Home>,<SPACEBAR>** between the words you wish to keep together.

SOFT PAGE

When a page is filled with text, WordPerfect 5.0 automatically inserts a page break. The page break informs the printer to start a new page. A line of dashes appears on the screen to indicate the end of one page and the beginning of another. The cursor jumps to the next page, and a new page number appears in the status line.

HARD PAGE

To end a page before it is filled with text, **press the Ctrl-<ENTER> keys**. A line of equal signs appears on your screen to indicate the end of one page and the beginning of another. The cursor jumps to the new page. If you want to delete this hard page break, move the cursor below the page break line and press **<BACKSPACE>**.

GUIDED ACTIVITY: CREATING YOUR FIRST DOCUMENT

Type the document shown in figure 2-2. Do not bother to correct typing errors now. Remember that you do not need to press **<ENTER>** at the end of a line. lines may or may not end where these do depending on the hardware you are using.

Type this document. Notice that when you reach the right margin, a new line is started automatically. If a word is too long to fit at the end of a line, it "wraps" round the screen and becomes the first word in the next line. This feature of the WordPerfect program is called "word wrap."

Press the ENTER key only when you wish to end a line and begin another, such as at the beginning of a new paragraph. Remember that your lines will not necessarily "wrap" at the same place as in this example.

FIGURE 2-2   First Document, **WORDWRAP**

✔ CHECKPOINT

c. Describe the purpose of the <ENTER> key in the WordPerfect 5.0 program.

carriage return when a new line is need   eg. end of paragraph

Position the cursor on the period at the end of the second paragraph then look at the status line.

18 WordPerfect 5.0

    d. What is the current position?

        2.5

    e. What is the current line?

        2.5

SAVING DOCUMENTS

The document you have just typed is now stored in the computer's internal memory (primary storage). If you shut down the computer, your document will be lost.

In order to save your work, you must command the computer to place it on your data disk (secondary storage) in Drive B. Your newly created document will be added to the directory of files already stored on your WordPerfect 5.0 Student Data disk.

NAMING DOCUMENTS

When you use the Save command, WordPerfect 5.0 asks for a filename. The rules for naming files are explained in detail in Appendix A. A document is always stored and retrieved by the filename you give it. As your store of documents increases, it becomes more important to give each file a meaningful name. In time, you will develop your own system of naming files so that they can be quickly retrieved.

GUIDED ACTIVITY: SAVING A DOCUMENT

1. Press the **F10** key to Save the document.

   This prompt will appear in the status line: "Document to be Saved:"

2. Type **WORDWRAP**

   Note: You may type the document name in upper- or lowercase or a combination of the two. WordPerfect will convert the name to uppercase

---

Document to be Saved: **WORDWRAP**

FIGURE 2-3 Saving **WORDWRAP**

3. Press **<ENTER>**

   The red light is now on for Drive B. This light indicates that your document is being saved on your WordPerfect 5.0 Student Data disk in Drive B. While the computer is in the process of saving your document,

Creating Your First Document 19

the document remains on the screen just as you typed it. When the red light for Drive B shuts off, WordPerfect 5.0 is ready for you to enter additional text. Notice that the document name now appears in the status line.

✔ CHECKPOINT

f. Identify the key that commands your computer to Save a document.

F10

The Importance of Saving Documents

It sometimes happens that a power failure or inadvertent keystroke destroys data that have been stored in the computer's internal memory. This potential problem is well worth your time and effort to avoid. Get into the habit of pausing every ten minutes to perform the Save function whenever you are working on a document.

Hint: Never remove a disk from a disk drive when the light is on; doing so may cause serious damage to either the disk or the computer.

CURSOR MOVEMENT KEYS

The cursor movement keys allow you to move the cursor easily to any position within your document. These keys are located on the numeric keypad on the right side of your keyboard. They consist of directional arrow keys, a home key, an end key, a page-up key, and a page-down key.

The cursor movement keys enable you to move the cursor to any position at which characters, numbers, or space have been keyed. Therefore, if you wish to move beyond the end of your document (where nothing has been keyed), you must use <ENTER> instead of the cursor movement keys.

Horizontal Movement

The <Left> arrow key moves the cursor one character to the left each time it is pressed. The <Right> arrow key moves the cursor one character to the right each time it is pressed.

When the <Left> and <Right> arrow keys are used in combination with the Ctrl key or immediately after the <Home> key, the cursor moves more quickly. The Ctrl-<Right> arrow keys move the cursor one word to the right; the Ctrl-<Left> arrow keys move the cursor one word to the left. The <Home>,<Right> arrow keys move the cursor to the right edge of the screen; the <Home>,<Left> arrow keys move the cursor to the left edge of the screen. The <Home>,<Home>,<Right> arrow keys move the cursor to the right (end) of a short or long line. The <Home>,<Home>,<Left> arrow keys move the cursor to the left (beginning) of a line.

20   WordPerfect 5.0

The <SPACEBAR> key moves the cursor one space to the right each time it is pressed.

Vertical Movement

The <Up> arrow key moves the cursor up one line on the document page. The <Down> arrow key moves the cursor down one line on the document page.

When the <Up> and <Down> arrow keys are used in combination with the Ctrl key or immediately after the <Home> key, the cursor moves more quickly through the document. To move to the top or the bottom of the screen, press the **<Home>,<Up>** or **<Home>,<Down>** keys. To move to the top of the current page, press the **Ctrl-<Home>,<Up>** arrow keys; to move to the end of the current page, press the **Ctrl-<Home>,<Down>** arrow keys. To move to the beginning or the end of a document, press the **<Home>,<Home>,<Up>** arrow keys or the **<Home>,<Home>,<Down>** arrow keys.

Remember that the <ENTER> key ends one line and begins another. Therefore, if you press <ENTER> at the beginning of a line, you will insert a blank line into your document.

✔CHECKPOINT

Use the vertical cursor movement keys to answer the following questions.

g. Move the cursor to the bottom left corner of the screen. What key or keys did you use?

Home & ↓

h. Move the cursor to the beginning of the document. What key or keys did you use?

Home & Home & ↑

i. Move the cursor down two lines without creating blank lines. What key or keys on the numeric keypad did you use?

↓ & ↓

How many times did you press the same key or keys?

twice

j. Move the cursor to the end of the document. What key or keys did you use? *Home & Home & ↓*

k. Move the cursor up one line. What key or keys did you use?

↑ & ↑

Use the horizontal cursor movement keys to answer the following questions.

l. Move the cursor one character to the right. What key or keys did you use? _→_

m. Move the cursor four words to the right. What key or keys did you use? _Ctrl + →_

How many times did you press the same key or keys? _4_

n. Move the cursor to the right end of the line. What key or keys did you use? _Home + →_

o. Move the cursor to the beginning of the line. What key or keys did you use? _Home + Home + ←_

Continue practicing with the cursor movement keys until you become proficient in moving the cursor through your document.

GO TO

The Go To keys, Ctrl-<Home>, move the cursor to a specific location in your document. The prompt "Go To" appears in the status line. Type a character after this prompt and the cursor will jump to the next occurrence of that character. Type a page number and the cursor will move to the beginning of the designated page. Press the <Up> or <Down> arrow keys and the cursor will move to the beginning or end of the current page.

SAVING A DOCUMENT WHILE EXITING WORDPERFECT 5.0

When you are ready to end a working session, you can both Save and Exit WordPerfect 5.0 with the same function key. You can Save and Exit from anywhere in a document; you need not move the cursor.

It is important to Exit WordPerfect 5.0 correctly. Do not shut down the computer before pressing the Exit key.

Hint: F1 is the Cancel key. It can be used to back out of those WordPerfect 5.0 features such as Exit, Retrieve, Block, and Search that display a message at the bottom of your screen. Therefore, if you change your mind after activating one of these features, just press the **F1** key.

22   WordPerfect 5.0

GUIDED ACTIVITY: EXITING WORDPERFECT 5.0

1. Press the **F7** key to Exit.

   This prompt will appear: "Save Document?(Y/N) Yes".

   You can either type "Y" or press **<ENTER>** and the document will be saved. If you type "N", the document will not be saved.

2. Type Y

   This prompt will appear: "Document to be Saved: B:\WORDWRAP".

   If you have not changed WORDWRAP since you last saved it, the message, "[Text was not modified]" will appear on the status line.

3. Press **<ENTER>**

   This prompt will appear: "Replace B:\WORDWRAP (Y/N) No".

4. Type Y

   The document WORDWRAP will be saved along with any revisions you have made. If you had typed "N", you would be prompted to enter a different filename. Your original document would still be stored in the original file, and your revised document would be stored in a new file with a new filename.

   The red light is now on in Drive B, and the message "Saving B:\WORDWRAP" appears on your screen.

   After the file is saved, you will see this prompt: "Exit WP" (Y/N) No (Cancel to return to document)". If you press the Cancel (**F1**) key you will return to the document. If you type "N" or press **<ENTER>**, a clear screen will appear. If you type "Y", WordPerfect 5.0 will be exited and a DOS prompt will appear. When you see the DOS prompt, it is safe to remove the disks and shut down the computer.

5. Type N

   A clear screen will appear.

✔ **CHECKPOINT**

   p.   Identify the key that both Saves your document and Exits WordPerfect 5.0.

   F7

q. What does the prompt "Replace B:\WORDWRAP (Y/N) No" mean?

Do you want to replace old version with the edited version

THE HELP FUNCTION

WordPerfect 5.0 allows you to access a Help screen anytime during your work on a document. Press F3 and a Help screen will appear. This screen lists, in alphabetical order, the features available in WordPerfect 5.0 along with the name of the keys that activate each feature. You can also press any function key to get information about how that key is used. After you are finished browsing through the Help information, all you need do is press <ENTER> or <SPACEBAR> to return to the document on which you were working.

GUIDED ACTIVITY: USING THE HELP SCREEN

1. Remove your WordPerfect 2 disk from Drive A and replace it with the WordPerfect 5.0 Learning disk that contains the **WPHELP.FIL** file. If you are using a hard drive, the Learning disk file **WPHELP.FIL** is recorded on the hard disk.

2. Press the **F3** (Help) key.

   The message "WPHELP.FIL not found. Insert the diskette and press drive letter:" appears.

3. Type A: to inform WordPerfect that the Learning disk is in Drive A.

4. Press <ENTER>

   A screen of instructions (figure 2-4) will appear.

5. Press the **F10** key.

   A screen of information on saving documents will appear.

6. Press <ENTER> or <SPACEBAR> to exit Help.

RETRIEVING A DOCUMENT

When you end a working session and shut down your computer, the document that you are working on does not remain in the computer's internal memory. Remember, though, that you have saved it on your data disk. When you begin a new working session, your first task will be to retrieve the document that you wish to edit.

24 WordPerfect 5.0

WP 5.0   05/05/88

Help

   Press any letter to get an alphabetical list of features.

      The list will include the features that start with that letter, along with the name of the key where the feature is found. You can then press that key to get a description of how the feature works.

   Press any function key to get information about the use of the key.

      Some keys may let you choose from a menu to get more information about various options. Press HELP again to display the template.

   Press the Enter key or Spacebar to exit Help.

FIGURE 2-4   Help Screen Instructions

GUIDED ACTIVITY: RETRIEVING A DOCUMENT

1. **Press the Shift-F10 keys.** *[handwritten: Works only if you know the name of the document.]*

   This prompt will appear in the status line: "Document to be Retrieved:".

2. Type **WORDWRAP**

   Your screen will look like figure 2-5.

Document to be Retrieved: WORDWRAP

FIGURE 2-5 Retrieving **WORDWRAP**

3. Press **<ENTER>**

   In a few seconds the document **WORDWRAP** will appear on the screen.

4. Press the **F7** key to Exit WordPerfect.

Creating Your First D...

✔CHECKPOINT

r. Identify the keys that retrieve a stored document.

Shift ~-F10

What You Have Accomplished

You have succeeded in retrieving the first document you created. The Shift-F10 keys activate the Retrieve function. When you typed **"WORDWRAP"**, you commanded your computer to look for your file, **WORDWRAP**, on the disk in Drive B.

Hint: When you Retrieve a document, it appears on the screen at the cursor location. You can Retrieve a document onto a clear screen or onto a screen that contains another document. Unless you want to combine two documents into one file, make sure you have a clear screen before retrieving a document.

REVIEW QUESTIONS

1. Why should a separate drive be designated for saving files?

2. Identify the purpose of each element of the status line. (You previously named the document.)

    a. _____

    b. _____

    c. _____

    d. _____

    e. _____

3. Which key activates the Save function?

4. Which cursor movement keys give you the fastest return to the beginning of your document?

WordPerfect 5.0

How does pressing <SPACEBAR> change the cursor position?

6. Compare the purpose of the <ENTER> key in a word-processing program with the purpose of the carriage return on a conventional typewriter.

7. Suppose that you are editing a document and wish to return to the beginning of the line you are editing. Which cursor movement key or keys should you use?

8. Which keys activate the Retrieve function?

9. Describe the procedure for saving a document.

10. Explain the importance of saving a document both during and at the end of each working session.

11. Explain the rules for naming files.

12. Suppose that you are editing a document and do not remember which keystrokes are needed to Save and Exit WordPerfect 5.0 at the same time. What is the quickest way to find the needed information?

13. Describe how the cursor is used to guide you through the creation of a document.

14. Had you typed "**WORD WRAP**" instead of "**WORDWRAP**" when you named your document, under what filename would your document have been saved?

Creating Your First Document 27

15. Which cursor movement keys provide the quickest method of movement down several pages?

16. Define the term "default."

DOCUMENTATION RESEARCH

1. Look up the description of "repeating keys" in the Getting Started section of your manual. Explain the meaning.

2. If you incorrectly type the name of a file you want to Retrieve, what message appears on the screen? Look in the Reference section of your manual.

3. WordPerfect 5.0 is **document oriented**. Explain what this means.

REVIEW EXERCISES

1. Load WordPerfect. Display and read the Help screen pertaining to the F7 key.

2. Return to a clear screen. Type any two long paragraphs from this or any other book. Observe the word-wrap feature. Insert a blank line between paragraphs.

3. Use the cursor movement keys to move around the paragraphs.

4. Add a sentence to the end of the second paragraph.

5. Insert a hard page break two blank lines below the last paragraph.

6. Retype one of the paragraphs on Pg 2 of your document.

7. Insert a hard page break two blank lines below the paragraph.

8. Delete the hard page break you inserted in step 7.

9. Save your document with the name **EXERCISE.DOC**

10. Properly Exit WordPerfect 5.0.

UNIT 3
TYPING AND PRINTING A BUSINESS LETTER

SUPPLIES NEEDED

1. WordPerfect 5.0 disks 1 and 2
2. WordPerfect Student Data disk
3. printer

OBJECTIVES

After completing this unit, you will be able to

1. correct typing errors by using specific delete keys;
2. identify and use specific toggle keys;
3. change from Insert to Typeover mode;
4. use the <TAB> key to indent;
5. insert additional text into a document;
6. print a document.

IMPORTANT KEYSTROKES

1. <TAB> key   to move cursor to the tab position
2. <BACKSPACE> key   to delete one character to the left
3. <DEL> key   to delete character the cursor is under
4. Ctrl-<BACKSPACE> keys   to delete one word
5. Ctrl-<End> keys   to delete to the end of a line (EOL)
6. Ctrl-<PgDn> keys   to delete to the end of a page (EOP)
7. <INS> key   to change from Insert to Typeover mode
8. Shift-F7   to print a document
9. F1   to restore deleted text

ASSIGNMENTS

1. Create **OLSON.LTR**
2. Edit **OLSON.LTR**
3. Print **OLSON.LTR**
4. Review Questions
5. Research Documentation
6. Review Exercises

DOCUMENT IDENTIFICATION LINE

At the bottom of each document you create or edit you should add a "document identification line." This line should include your name, the unit number, and the current date. Your instructor may require additional information (i.e., class section number). This line will assist you and your instructor in identifying particular document printouts.

GUIDED ACTIVITY: CREATING A BUSINESS LETTER

Load WordPerfect 5.0. Remember to designate Drive B as your data storage drive. A clear screen will become the typing area on which you will type your second document.

1. Press the <ENTER> key until the cursor is on the Ln that is slightly over two inches from the top of the page. The Pos will be one inch.

2. Type the current date in the format "August 20, 1989".

3. Press <ENTER> four times.

4. Type **Mr. Frank Olson**

5. Press <ENTER>

   A short line of text has been entered on the screen and the cursor is at the beginning of a new line.

6. Type **Olson Hardware Store**

7. Press **<ENTER>**

8. Type **579 Main Street**

9. Press **<ENTER>**

10. Type **Ourtown, MN 55698**

11. Press **<ENTER>**

    Four short lines of text have been entered on the screen.

12. Press **<ENTER>** to create a blank line.

13. Type **Dear Mr. Olson:**

14. Press **<ENTER>** twice.

15. Type in the text of the letter shown in figure 3-1. The lines of your document may not "wrap" at the same place as in the example. At the end of a paragraph, press **<ENTER>** twice: once to end the paragraph and begin another, and once to create a blank line between the two paragraphs.

    Pause during the course of your work to save and name your file. Name it **OLSON.LTR**

16. Press **<ENTER>** twice to insert two blank lines before the closing.

17. Type **Sincerely,**

18. Press **<ENTER>** four times.

19. Type **Marilyn Jenson**

20. Press **<ENTER>**

21. Type **Professor**

22. Press **<ENTER>** two times.

23. Type **Enclosure**

24. Press **<ENTER>** to move the cursor to the Ln slightly over eight inches from the top of the page.

25. Type **(your name) OLSON.LTR UNIT 3 (current date)**

You have added the document identification line to your document. Add to the line any additional information your instructor requires.

26. After you have finished typing your letter, press **F10** to Save it. Replace any previous version of the document.

✔ CHECKPOINT

a. Which key is used to insert blank lines between paragraphs?

---

b. When you come to the end of a letter and wish to insert six blank lines for the signature, how many times must you press **<ENTER>** to end the closing and insert the six blank lines for the signature?

EDITING A DOCUMENT

After creating a document, you need to proofread it for typing or spelling errors. You may also want to revise it by adding or deleting text. With WordPerfect 5.0, the tasks of proofreading and editing can be done right on the screen, thereby eliminating the need to retype an entire document.

GUIDED ACTIVITY: EDITING A BUSINESS LETTER

If the file OLSON.LTR is not on your screen, press **Shift-F10** to Retrieve it.

1. Move the cursor to the letter "l" in the word "Enclosure" at the end of the letter.

2. Press **<DEL>** six times.

   The letters "l", "o", "s", "u", "r", and "e" have been deleted.

3. Leave the cursor where it is and type **losure**

4. Now press **<BACKSPACE>** six times.

   The letters "losure" have again been deleted.

5. Move the cursor to the letter "c" in the word "can" in the last paragraph of the letter.

6. Press the **Ctrl-<BACKSPACE>** keys. (These are combination keys, so hold down the Ctrl key while you press **<BACKSPACE>**.)

   The word "can" has been deleted.

(current date)

Mr. Frank Olson
Olson Hardware Store
579 Main Street
Ourtown, MN 55698

Dear Mr. Olson:

Mary Schmidt was a student in five of my accounting courses in the last two years. She was an excellent student.

Ms. Schmidt demonstrated her thorough grasp of accounting concepts through her classroom contributions as well as through written assignments. Her assignments were of high quality and turned in on time.

Therefore, I can recommend Ms. Schmidt for the position of financial accounting technician in your hardware store.

Sincerely,

Marilyn Jenson
Professor

Enclosure

(your name) OLSON.LTR   UNIT 3 (current date)

FIGURE 3-1   **OLSON.LTR**

34   WordPerfect 5.0

7. Move the cursor to the "E" in the abbreviation "Enc" at the end of the letter.

8. Press the **Ctrl-<End>** keys.

   The entire line (in this case the line consists of only one word) has been deleted.

9. Save **OLSON.LTR**   Replace the previous version of the document.

✔CHECKPOINT

   c. If your cursor is positioned directly on a character that you wish to delete, which key must you press?

   _____

   d. Which keys will most quickly accomplish the task of deleting an entire line?

   _____

TOGGLE KEYS

When you press a key to turn on a specific command and then press the key again to turn the command off, you are using a **toggle key**. WordPerfect 5.0 assigns a number of commands to toggle keys. This is a convenient way to use the keyboard, for, as you become familiar with specific commands and the keyboard, toggling becomes as easy as turning a light switch on and off.

The Insert Key

If you press the **<INS>** (insert) key on your keyboard, you switch to the **Typeover mode**. In the Typeover mode the character on which the cursor is located is replaced by the character you are typing. The prompt "Typeover" appears on the status line. This is an alternative to using the delete keys to erase existing text.

Simply press **<INS>** again to toggle off the Typeover mode and return to **Insert mode**.

THE REWRITE FEATURE

You may notice that when you insert additional text in the middle of a line, the words at the right edge of the screen seem to disappear. By simply pressing any cursor movement key, you can make these words reappear in the proper format. This is WordPerfect 5.0's **Rewrite feature**; it moves existing text over to make room for the text you are adding. Whenever you edit text, either by inserting or deleting, the text on the screen is rewritten.

Typing and Printing a Business Letter   35

GUIDED ACTIVITY: USING THE <TAB> AND <INS> KEYS

The tabs in WordPerfect 5.0 have been preset to every one-half inch. Therefore, when you wish to indent a paragraph, simply press **<TAB>**.

1. Retrieve **OLSON.LTR** if necessary.

2. Move the cursor to the first letter of the first word of the first paragraph of the letter.

3. Press **<TAB>**.

   The first line of the first paragraph is now indented one-half inch. The cursor is in Pos 1.5". Move the cursor with any directional arrow key and the paragraph will be rewritten.

4. Use the <TAB> key to indent the first line of each paragraph in your letter to Mr. Olson.

5. You remember that this letter is to be a block style letter so you need to "unindent" the first line of each paragraph. Move the cursor to the first letter of the first word of any paragraph.

6. Press **Shift-<TAB>** to move one-half inch to the left.

7. Move the cursor to the first letter of the first word of another paragraph that has been indented.

8. Press the **<BACKSPACE>** key.

   You have moved the word back to the left margin by using the <BACKSPACE> key. You have deleted the hidden <TAB> code that you inserted earlier. You will learn more about hidden codes in a later unit.

9. Use the Shift-<TAB> keys or the <BACKSPACE> key to "unindent" any paragraph that is still indented.

10. Move the cursor to the space after the word "I" in the last paragraph of the letter.

11. Press the **<SPACEBAR>**

12. Type **highly**

    You have inserted a word.

13. Move the cursor to the first letter of the name "Schmidt" in the first paragraph of the letter.

36 WordPerfect 5.0

14. Press **<INS>** to toggle on the Typeover feature.

    The prompt "Typeover" will appear at the bottom of the screen.

15. Type **Schmitz**

    The name has been corrected.

16. Correct the spelling of Ms. Schmitz's name throughout the letter.

17. Press **<INS>** to toggle off the Typeover feature.

    The prompt "Typeover" has disappeared from the bottom of the screen.

18. Press the **F10** key to Save the revised letter. Replace the previous version.

✔CHECKPOINT

e. What column position will your cursor be in if you press **<TAB>** three times?

MENU

A menu is a list of choices available to the user of a software program. Menu selections are usually made with a keyboard entry. Menus simplify operations, save time, and reduce data-entry errors. You may choose an option from a menu by typing the letter or number that precedes the option or by typing the bolded letter that is part of the option name. Not all options may be chosen using this last method. Some option choices lead to more options listed on a submenu.

GUIDED ACTIVITY: PRINTING A BUSINESS LETTER

1. Retrieve **OLSON.LTR** if necessary.

2. Update the date on the Document Identification Line if necessary.

   You are ready to Print.

3. Press **Shift-F7**

   A Print menu (figure 3-2) will appear on the screen. This menu provides you with several options for printing your document. The Print menu is discussed in detail in Unit 7. For now, you will print the full text of your business letter so that you can see a **hard copy** (printed output) of **OLSON.LTR**.

Typing and Printing a Business Letter 37

```
Print

    1   - Full Document
    2   - Page
    3   - Document on Disk
    4   - Control Printer
    5   - Type Through
    6   - View Document
    7   - Initialize Printer

Options

    S   - Select Printer            Standard Printer
    B   - Binding                   0"
    N   - Number of Copies          1
    G   - Graphics Quality          Medium
    T   - Text Quality              High



Selection: 0
```

FIGURE 3-2   Print Menu

Make sure that the printer you are using is supplied with paper, and that the power, ready, and on-line lights are on. If you need guidance, check with your instructor.

4. Type **1** or **F**

   A "Please wait" prompt will appear at the bottom of your screen, and in a few seconds the printer will begin to print your document.

   You now have a copy of the business letter you typed, and it is ready to be mailed.

5. Press **F7** to Exit WordPerfect 5.0.

✓CHECKPOINT

   f. List the three steps required to print the full text of a document.

38   WordPerfect 5.0

UNDELETE

WordPerfect 5.0 saves up to three deletions. To retrieve deleted text, move the cursor to the location at which you want the text restored and press **F1**. The Undelete menu appears on the screen. The text you last deleted is highlighted at the cursor location. Select Option 1 to restore the highlighted text. Select Option 2 and use the <Up> and <Down> arrow keys to find a previous deletion; then select Option 1 to restore it.

REVIEW QUESTIONS

1. A standard business letter requires two line spaces between the salutation and the text. Which key provides these two blank lines?

2. Identify the keys that Retrieve a document.

3. If you want to print the full text of a document, which option from the Print menu should you choose?

4. You prefer typing over existing text, rather than using delete keys, to make changes. How do you switch from Insert to Typeover mode?

5. Define "toggle."

6. When you insert text within a document, existing text sometimes appears to run off the edge of the screen. Why does this occur?

7. Which key Saves a document?

8. Holding down the delete key deletes all characters from the cursor to the right margin. Which keys delete such characters more efficiently?

Typing and Printing a Business Letter 39

9. Suppose that in revising a document you discover that the information on a given page is no longer correct. How can you quickly delete the entire page?

10. List the steps required to edit the following line:

    "All the world's a staage and all the men and women players."

    a. Identify the cursor position and keystroke required to delete the extra "a" in "stage."

    b. How would you insert "merely" between the words "women" and "players"?

11. Which key would you use to indent one-half inch?

DOCUMENTATION RESEARCH

1. Describe how to delete to a Word Boundary.

2. WordPerfect 5.0 saves your last three deletions in case you decide to restore them. What message appears on the screen when the program has run out of room to store deleted text?

3. List some reasons why WordPerfect 5.0 might generate an error message.

4. Look up Cancel in the Reference section. List four uses for this key.

REVIEW EXERCISES

1. Retrieve **EXERCISE.DOC**

2. Move the cursor to the end of a sentence in the paragraph on Pg 2 of your document. Insert a sentence. Observe the rewrite feature.

3. Delete a word to the left of the cursor.

4. Delete a word to the right of the cursor.

5. Restore both words using the Undelete feature.

6. Move the cursor to the top of the document.

7. Type **This document is being used to complete the review exercises.**

8. Move the cursor to the first letter of the phrase "review exercises."

9. Toggle on the Typeover mode.

10. Type **REVIEW EXERCISES** Toggle off the Typeover mode. Delete the rest of the old heading.

11. Add a Document Identification Line at the end of your document.

12. Print all the pages of **EXERCISE.DOC.**

13. Save your document (replace the previous version) and Exit WordPerfect 5.0.

APPLICATION A

SUPPLIES NEEDED

1. WordPerfect program disks 1 and 2
2. WordPerfect Student Data disk
3. WordPerfect Learning disk
4. printer

ASSIGNMENTS

The assignments to be completed for this Application section are

1. Create **SOFTWARE.LTR**
2. Create **RESORT.LTR**
3. Create **PAPER.LTR**

APPLICATIONS

This Application section contains a number of documents that you can reproduce to apply the skills you have acquired in Units 1 through 3. Format your documents so that they look like the ones on the printed pages of this section. The lines may not wrap at the same place as the examples. Remember that right justification does not appear on the screen; it appears when a document is printed.

Use your template and the Quick Reference card to find the keystroke commands and menus you need. Remember that there is often more than one keystroke choice that can be used to create and format a document. Your primary task is to find the most efficient way to reproduce the documents.

You may also want to create your own applications - some tasks that are more meaningful to your everyday work. Your WordPerfect Student Data disk should have plenty of space available to store additional documents.

Follow the directions below to create the documents in Application A.

Document A-1

1. Name this document, **SOFTWARE.LTR**
2. Add the Document Identification Line to the bottom of the document.
3. Save the document on the Student Data disk.
4. Print the document.

Document A-2

1. Name this document, **RESORT.LTR**
2. Press the <TAB> key twice to indent each line of the prize list in the body of the letter.
3. Add the Document Identification Line to the bottom of the document.
4. Save the document on the Student Data disk.
5. Print the document.

Document A-3

1. Name this document, **PAPER.LTR**
2. Press the <TAB> key three times to indent each line of the address contained in the body of the letter.
3. Add the Document Identification Line to the bottom of the document.
4. Save the document on the Student Data disk.
5. Print the document.

3740 Johnson Drive
Denton, MN 55802
(current date)

Mr. John Holmes
Ashfield Software Company
3789 Ashfield Road
Barton, MI 55660

Dear Mr. Holmes:

Thank you for mailing the computer program you developed for auditing a general journal. We received the program this morning.

The program is not exactly like the one I saw last year when I visited your display at the software show in Minneapolis, Minnesota. This revised program will be useful to us. Therefore, we will purchase the program for use in our Accounting Department.

Thank you for submitting the program for our review.

Very truly yours,

(your name)

Document Identification Line

Document A-1   **SOFTWARE.LTR**

LONE PINE RESORT
4007 Blue Spruce Street
Barton, MI 55660
(current date)

Ms. Mary Neuman
3740 Johnson Drive
Denton, Minnesota 55802

Dear Ms. Neuman:

You have definitely won one of the prizes listed below. Just match the number on the enclosed envelope with the prize list at LONE PINE RESORT when you and Mr. Neuman visit.

       1.   Color TV
       2. $500 Cash
       3.   Patio furniture
       4.   Plastic bowl

Yes, all that you must do to receive your prize is visit LONE PINE RESORT, listen to a sales presentation and take a tour of the premises.

Come any time between 9:00 a.m. and 1:00 p.m. on Wednesday, June 10th to claim your prize. If you arrive between 9:00 a.m. and 9:15 a.m. you will receive a special gift. There is no obligation to buy, rent, or join anything when you visit.

Sincerely,

Joe Smith
Manager

Enclosure

Document Identification Line

Document A-2 **RESORT.LTR**

Ms. Jennifer Ortega
1955 201st Street
Marshall, WI 41267
(current date)

Circulation Department
Minnesota Dispatch
456 9th Street
St. Paul, MN 55104

Dear Sir:

From June 1 through August 25 of this year, I would like my newspaper mailed to the following address:

> Ms. Jennifer Ortega
> Assistant Manager
> LONE PINE RESORT
> 4007 Blue Spruce Street
> Barton, Michigan 55660

I am enclosing a check that covers the three-month subscription cost as well as the postage.

Yours truly,

Jennifer Ortega
Assistant Manager

Enclosure

Document Identification Line

Document A-3   **PAPER.LTR**

UNIT 4
SIMPLE EDITING FUNCTIONS

SUPPLIES NEEDED

1. WordPerfect 5.0 program disks
2. two WordPerfect 5.0 Student Data disks
3. printer

OBJECTIVES

After completing this unit, you will be able to

1. center text;
2. underline and boldface text;
3. revise multiple lines of text by using the Block feature;
4. insert text at the right margin;
5. copy and move a block of text;
6. convert a block of text from upper- to lowercase and from lower- to uppercase letters;
7. reveal codes.

IMPORTANT KEYSTROKES

1. F6   to boldface text
2. F8   to underline text
3. <CAPS LOCK>   to capitalize text
4. Shift-F6   to center text horizontally
5. Alt-F6   to begin a Flush Right
6. Alt-F4   to define a block of text
7. Ctrl-F4   to move or copy a block of text
8. Shift-F3   to convert a block of text from upper- to lowercase and from lower- to uppercase letters
9. Alt-F3   to reveal codes

ASSIGNMENTS

1. Revise **OLSON.LTR**
2. Print **OLSON.LTR** (Revised)
3. Create **QUOTE.TXT**
3. Review Questions
4. Research Documentation
5. Review Exercises

ENHANCEMENT FEATURES

You have discovered how easily WordPerfect 5.0 lets you manipulate text to create a simple business report or letter. WordPerfect 5.0 also provides a number of features that can enhance text to make printed copy look more attractive and professional.

The Bold Feature

Boldface text is darker than normal and is commonly used for titles and headers. A single keystroke embeds a code that instructs the printer to double-strike specified characters.

The Underline Feature

Some words and phrases, such as book and magazine titles, require underlining. You may also wish to underline portions of text for emphasis. Again, a single keystroke embeds a code that instructs the printer to underline specified characters.

Capitalization

At times you may wish to capitalize an entire string of letters. By toggling on the <CAPS LOCK> key, you can capitalize without holding down the Shift key. The <CAPS LOCK> key affects only alphabetic characters, not numbers or punctuation marks as on a conventional typewriter.

Simple Editing Functions   49

When the <CAPS LOCK> key is on, holding down the Shift key produces lowercase letters.

Centering Text

Headers and titles are often centered, either on a page or within a column. When you press the Center key, text is automatically centered around the position you select.

Hint: You can always tell when you have activated one of these enhancement features because they are revealed in the status line. When the <CAPS LOCK> key is toggled on, Pos in the status line appears in uppercase letters (POS). When either the Underline or Bold feature is toggled on, the position number in the status line and the text appear in a contrasting color or intensity. The underline does not appear on all screens, but it will appear on your printed document. If you press Center when your cursor is at the left margin, the line of text is centered on the screen.

GUIDED ACTIVITY: CREATING A LETTERHEAD

1. Use **Shift-F10** to Retrieve **OLSON.LTR**

2. Position your cursor on Ln 1", Pos 1", of the document.

3. Press the **<CAPS LOCK>** key.

4. Press the **Shift-F6** keys to activate the Center feature.

5. Press the **F6** key to activate the Bold feature.

6. Press the **F8** key to activate the Underline feature.

7. Type **woodview college of accounting**

   The typed phrase will be centered, capitalized, boldface, and underlined.

8. Press **<ENTER>**

   You have ended a short line and terminated the Center function.

9. Press the **F8** key to toggle off the Underline function.

10. Press the **<CAPS LOCK>** key to toggle back to lowercase letters.

11. Press the **Shift-F6** keys to Center.

50   WordPerfect 5.0

12. Type **415 Smith Street**

     (With the <CAPS LOCK> key off, you must again use the Shift key to capitalize letters.)

13. Press **<ENTER>**

14. Press the **Shift-F6** keys to activate the Center function.

15. Type **St. Paul, MN 55108**

16. Press **<ENTER>** four times.

17. Press the **F6** key to toggle off the Bold function.

What You Have Accomplished

You have enhanced your business letter by adding a letterhead. You have learned the keystrokes that activate commands that allow you to capitalize letters without using the Shift key, to center a line of text horizontally, to underline specific words or phrases, and to create boldface type. You have also learned that the <CAPS LOCK> key, the F6 (Bold) key, and the F8 (Underline) key are toggle keys.

✔CHECKPOINT

a. How does the status line change when you toggle on the Bold function?

_____

b. Which toggle key underlines text?

_____

c. Which toggle key creates boldface text?

_____

d. Which toggle key capitalizes alphabetic characters?

_____

e. Which keys Center text horizontally?

_____

f. How can you terminate the Center feature?

_____

Hint: You toggle a key (F6) to turn Bold on, then toggle F6 again to turn Bold off. Each time you toggle the key, a different code is embedded. Now you can insert text anywhere in the word or phrase that you have boldfaced and it will be boldface as well. This is also true of the Underline function but does not apply to <CAPS LOCK>. The Center command terminates each time you press <ENTER> and is not activated again until you press **Shift-F6**.

THE FLUSH RIGHT FEATURE

Text is usually entered from the left and aligned precisely against the left margin. There are times, however, when you might prefer to align text against the right margin. After you activate the Flush Right function, all text that you enter moves across the screen from right to left (rather than the usual left to right) and aligns flush against the right margin. This feature is often used to enter dates or business headings.

GUIDED ACTIVITY: INSERTING THE CURRENT DATE FLUSH RIGHT

Your document, **OLSON.LTR**, should be on the screen. Make sure that you are in Insert mode and that your cursor is positioned at the end of the Document Identification Line.

1. Press **Alt-F6**

   The cursor will align itself along the edge of the right margin.

2. Type the current date.

   Text will be entered from right to left.

3. Press <ENTER>

   The Flush Right feature has been terminated.

✔CHECKPOINT

g. What happened to the cursor when you pressed the **Alt-F6** keys?

THE BLOCK FEATURE

The Block feature is an efficient way to revise previously entered multiple lines of text. The Block key (Alt-F4), used in combination with other command keys, can quickly and efficiently make the changes you desire.

When you toggle on Block, a "Block on" message appears on the screen. Use the cursor movement keys to highlight the portion (block) of text you wish to revise.

GUIDED ACTIVITY: USING THE BLOCK FEATURE TO ENHANCE EXISTING TEXT

Retrieve **OLSON.LTR** if necessary.

1. Move the cursor to the first letter of the name "Mary" in the first paragraph of **OLSON.LTR**.

2. Press the **Alt-F4** keys.

   The Block feature has been turned on. A flashing message "Block on" will appear in the status line.

3. Move the cursor across the name "Mary Schmitz"

   The cursor has highlighted the block of text you wish to revise.

4. Press the **F6** key.

   The highlighted text will appear in boldface. Pressing **F6** also automatically turned off the Block and Bold functions. Notice that the boldface text on your screen contrasts with normal text.

✔ **CHECKPOINT**

   h. Which keys are used to define the area of text that is to be boldface?

---

5. Move the cursor to the first letter of the word "highly" in the last paragraph of your letter.

6. Press the **Alt-F4** keys.

   The Block feature has been turned on again.

7. Move the cursor across the word "highly" to highlight it.

8. Press the **F8** key.

   The highlighted text has been underlined. The Block and Underline features have been turned off.

9. Move the cursor to the first letter of the word "thorough" in the second paragraph.

Simple Editing Functions   53

10. Press the **Alt-F4** keys.

    The Block feature has been turned on again.

11. Highlight the words "thorough grasp"

12. Press the **F6** key.

    The highlighted text has been boldfaced. The Block and Bold features have been turned off.

13. Make sure the cursor is on the first letter of the word "thorough"

14. Press the **Alt-F4** keys.

    The Block feature has been turned on again.

15. Highlight the words "thorough grasp"

16. Press the **F8** key.

    The highlighted text is underlined. The Block and Underline features have been turned off.

17. Update the Document Identification Line. Save your document (replace the previous version).

✔CHECKPOINT

i. How does the screen display change when you press the **F6** key?

_____

j. How does pressing the **F8** key change the screen display?

_____

Hint: If you change your mind and decide not to revise text after you have blocked it, press the **Alt-F4** keys to turn off the Block feature. The Cancel key (F1) also turns off the Block feature. F1 is not a toggle key. It is a key assigned to cancel specific functions, such as turning off the Block feature.

What You Have Accomplished

You have used the Block key in combination with other function keys to revise blocks of text. You have discovered that the Block feature is an efficient way to alter the appearance of a document with a minimum number of keystrokes.

THE MOVE AND COPY FEATURES

One of the most basic editing functions is to copy and move text. When you move a block of text, you remove it from its original location and place it in a new location in your document. When you copy a block of text, you place it in an additional location in your document.

The Move and Copy features are used in combination with the Block feature. Press the **Alt-F4** keys (to turn on the Block feature); move your cursor to highlight a block of text, and press the **Ctrl-F4** keys. The Move menu (figure 4-1) will appear in the status line.

```
Move: 1 Block; 2 Tabular Column; 3 Rectangle: 0
```

FIGURE 4-1   Move Menu (Block On)

The options on this menu are defined as follows:

1 Block   Allows you to Move, Copy, delete, or append a block of text such as a sentence, paragraph, or page.

2 Tabular Column   Allows you to Move or Copy a column of text or numbers that was created with the <TAB> key or Indent feature.

3 Rectangle   Allows you to Move or Copy text that does not span the page from margin to margin. The rectangle is defined by its upper left-hand corner and its lower right-hand corners.

When you choose any one of the options on the Move menu, the Move Block submenu (figure 4-2) will appear on your screen.

```
1 Move;  2  Copy; 3  Delete   4  Append: 0
```

FIGURE 4-2   Move Block Submenu

The options on the Move Block submenu are defined as follows:

1 Move   This option is used to Move blocks of text. The highlighted (blocked) text disappears from the screen. It reappears at the cursor location when <ENTER> is pressed again.

Simple Editing Functions   55

2   Copy   This option is used to Copy blocks of text. The highlighted text does not disappear from the screen. It is copied at the cursor location when <ENTER> is pressed.

3   Delete   This option is used to delete a block of text from the document. When the <DEL> key is pressed, the highlighted text disappears from the screen. If you discover you should not have deleted the text, it may be restored to your text by using the Undelete feature.

4   Append   This option allows you to add the block of text to the end of another file that has been stored on your disk.

GUIDED ACTIVITY: COPYING A BLOCK OF TEXT

Display a clear screen.

1. Type the following quotation:

   I think one reason we admire cats, those of us who do, is their
   proficiency in one-upmanship. They always seem to come out on top, no
   matter what they are doing - or pretend they do. Rarely do you see a
   cat discomfited. They have no conscience, and they never regret.
   Maybe we secretly envy them.   Barbara Webster

2. Press <ENTER> twice.

3. Move the cursor to the first letter of the quotation.

4. Press **Alt-F4** to turn on the Block feature.

5. Highlight the entire quotation.

6. Press the **Ctrl-F4** keys.

   The Move (Block on) menu will appear.

7. Type **1**

   The Move Block submenu will appear.

8. Type **2**

   The prompt "Move cursor; press Enter to retrieve." will appear at the bottom of your screen.

9. Move the cursor two blank lines below the bottom of the first quotation.

10. Press <ENTER>

    The copy of the quotation will appear at the cursor location.

56   WordPerfect 5.0

11. Repeat steps 3 through 10 twice more. You will have a total of four quotations.

12. Save this document with the name **QUOTE.TXT**

GUIDED ACTIVITY: MOVING A BLOCK OF TEXT

Display a clear screen. Retrieve **OLSON.LTR**

1. Move the cursor to the first letter in the second sentence of the first paragraph.

2. Press the **Alt-F4** keys to turn on the Block feature.

3. Highlight the sentence.

4. Press the **Ctrl-F4** keys.

   The Move menu will appear at the bottom of the screen.

5. Type **1**

   The line of text will disappear from the screen and then the Move Block submenu appears.

6. Type **1** to choose the Move option.

   The prompt "Move cursor; press Enter to retrieve." will appear on the screen.

7. Move the cursor to the end of the second paragraph.

8. Press **<SPACEBAR>** two times.

9. Press **<ENTER>**

   The line of text will reappear at the cursor location.

10. Edit the Document Identification Line.

11. Save your document (replace the previous version).

   ✔**CHECKPOINT**

   k. List the steps needed to move a block of text.

THE BLOCK AND SWITCH FEATURES

After typing a document, you may decide to revise an entire paragraph by using all uppercase letters; or you may type a paragraph entirely in capital letters and then change your mind. The Block and Switch features let you make these changes quickly.

You can use the Block (Alt-F4) and Switch (Shift-F3) features to convert a block of text to all uppercase or all lowercase letters. First highlight the text you wish to convert, then turn on the Switch feature. The Block and Switch menu (figure 4-3) allows you to choose either upper- or lowercase letters.

```
1 Uppercase; 2 Lowercase: 0
```

FIGURE 4-3   Block and Switch Menu

GUIDED ACTIVITY: USING THE BLOCK AND SWITCH FEATURES

Retrieve **OLSON.LTR** if necessary.

1. Move the cursor to the first letter of the company name "Olson Hardware Store" in the inside address.

2. Press **Alt-F4** to turn on the Block feature.

3. Move the cursor to highlight the rest of the company name.

4. Press the **Shift-F3** keys.

   The Block and Switch menu will appear at the bottom of your screen.

5. Type **1**

   The highlighted letters will change from lower- to uppercase and the Block feature will be turned off.

6. Save your document.

✔ CHECKPOINT

1. Identify the keys that turn on the Block and Switch features.

Hint: You have noticed by now that the same editing function can sometimes be accomplished with different keystroke commands. Choosing the right alternative, can reduce the total number of keystrokes you must make. The keystrokes you choose are also determined by the task you are performing with WordPerfect 5.0. For example, the way you manipulate text in a long report or proposal differs from the way you manipulate text in a form letter.

GUIDED ACTIVITY: PRINTING A REVISED BUSINESS LETTER

Retrieve **OLSON.LTR** and update the Document Identification Line if necessary.
Your revised business letter is ready to be printed.

1. Press **Shift-F7** to access the Print menu.

2. Type **1**

    A "Please wait" message will appear in the status line, then your document will be printed.

3. Press **F7** to Exit WordPerfect 5.0.

    The revised **OLSON.LTR** should look like that in figure 4-4.

What You Have Accomplished

You have revised **OLSON.LTR**. The text of your letter is both left and right justified, which means that the first character of each line is aligned precisely against the left margin and the last character of each line is aligned precisely against the right margin. Right justification does not show on the screen but appears in the printed document.

WOODVIEW COLLEGE OF ACCOUNTING
415 Smith Street
St. Paul, MN 55108

Mr. Frank Olson
OLSON HARDWARE STORE
579 Main Street
Ourtown, MN 55698

Dear Mr. Olson:

Mary Schmitz was a student in five of my accounting courses in the last two years.

Ms. Schmitz demonstrated her **thorough grasp** of accounting concepts through her classroom contributions as well as through written assignments. Her assignments were of high quality and turned in on time. She was an excellent student.

Therefore, I <u>highly</u> recommend Ms. Schmitz for the position of financial accounting technician in your hardware store.

Sincerely,

Marilyn Jenson
Professor

(your name) OLSON.LTR (revised) UNIT 4   (current date)

FIGURE 4-4 **OLSON.LTR** (revised)

REVEAL CODES

The text on your screen appears in much the same format as your printed document. You can see boldfacing and underlining, indented paragraphs, double spacing, and so forth. However, all of the codes you have embedded are invisible.

At times it is helpful to see the codes that have been placed in your document for example to track down, the cause of a printing or print-formatting problem. The Reveal Codes feature helps you in such a situation.

When you Reveal Codes you will notice many paired codes. For example, when you toggle on the boldface feature, the code [BOLD] is inserted in your text. When boldface is toggled off, the code [bold] is inserted in the text. Notice that the on code is in uppercase while the off code is in lowercase.

When you press the **Alt-F3** keys, the screen is split in two by the Tab Ruler. The upper window displays normal text; the lower window displays the text along with the hidden codes.

A cursor appears in both the upper and lower windows. The upper-window cursor is a blinking cursor. The lower-window cursor is a rectangle that highlights the text or code it rests on. The cursor movement keys move you simultaneously through the text of each window. The Alt-F3 keys return you to the normal screen.

GUIDED ACTIVITY: REVEALING CODES

1. Retrieve **OLSON.LTR** if necessary.

2. Press **Alt-F3**

    The Tab Ruler has split the screen. Several lines of text appear above the Tab Ruler; the same text with codes embedded appears below the ruler.

    ### ✔CHECKPOINT

    m. Which keystrokes are needed to activate the Reveal Codes feature?

3. Move the cursor in the upper window until it reaches the first line of the heading.

✔CHECKPOINT

n. What two codes are embedded in front of the first line of the heading to indicate that the first line of the heading is centered and underlined?

---

4. Move the cursor in the upper window until it reaches the date line in the Document Identification Line.

✔CHECKPOINT

o. What codes in the Document Identification Line indicate that the Flush Right function was used?

---

5. Move the cursor in the upper window until it reaches the second paragraph of the body of the letter.

✔CHECKPOINT

p. What codes indicate that the words "thorough grasp" is both underlined and boldfaced?

---

6. Move the cursor through the document as you examine the codes. Notice that the settings on the Tab Ruler reflect the margin and tab settings.

MAKING BACKUP COPIES OF YOUR DOCUMENTS

You have already learned to avoid the potential loss of data by frequently using the Save function (F10). Another way to protect your data is by making backup copies. As new documents are created, copy them onto your second WordPerfect 5.0 Student Data disk. Then, if your original copy is physically damaged or the files inadvertently erased, you still have a copy of your documents.

Refer to the Copy section of Appendix A to learn how to make backup copies of your documents.

REVIEW QUESTIONS

1. The cursor movement keys are important in using the Block feature to edit text. Explain how these keys are used.

---

62   WordPerfect 5.0

2. How do you place text flush right in a document?

3. Explain how the Block feature is used.

4. Describe the process of converting an entire block of text from upper- to lower-case letters.

5. How would you go about centering text to create a letterhead for a business letter?

6. Which toggle key creates boldface type?

7. How do you turn off the Underline feature?

8. How does the screen change to let you know that the Bold function is turned on? How does it change to let you know that the Underline function is on?

9. Describe the process of Copying a Block of text.

10. Suppose that you type a business letter and then decide to place your last paragraph first. What keys are needed to rearrange your text?

11. Suppose that your document is not printing out in the format you expect. How would you investigate your printing problem?

DOCUMENTATION RESEARCH

1. You boldface text by using the F6 key. What menu may be used to boldface text?

2. List some of the features that can be used in combination with the Block key.

3. What will happen to your text if you turn on the Block feature then press the <ENTER> key?

4. Can you Block a line of text from right to left as well as from left to right?

5. The Block and Switch keys can be used together to convert text to upper- or lowercase letters. In what other way can the Switch feature be used?

6. Assume that you have finished the first chapter of your new book. You would like to set aside several paragraphs in your manuscript for use in a later chapter. Explain how this can be done.

7. What do the codes [SRt] and [HRt] mean?

8. List the codes that are embedded in your document when you issue the following commands.

    a. Center Text_____

    b. Block_____

    c. Bold_____

    d. Flush Right_____

    e. Hard Page_____

f. Soft Page _____

g. Hard Return _____

h. Soft Return _____

9. How can you differentiate an "on" code from an "off" code?

   _____

REVIEW EXERCISES

1. Retrieve **EXERCISE.DOC**

2. Move the cursor to the top of the document.

3. Type the heading **exercise**

4. Center, underline, and boldface the heading.

5. Use the Switch function to capitalize the heading.

6. Insert two blank lines under the heading.

7. Type the current date Flush Right.

8. Insert two blank lines under the date.

9. Move the cursor to the end of your document.

10. Insert a hard page break two blank lines below the end of your document.

11. Use the Block feature, then Move menu and Move Block submenu options to Copy the first page of your document to Pg 3.

12. Move the first sentence on Pg 3 to the end of the document.

13. Boldface the last sentence of your document.

14. Reveal Codes.

15. Remove the boldface code from the last sentence of the document.

16. Update the Document Identification Line, Save **EXERCISE.DOC** (replace the previous version), and Exit WordPerfect 5.0.

UNIT 5
FORMATTING TEXT FOR PRINTING

SUPPLIES NEEDED

1. WordPerfect 5.0 program disks
2. WordPerfect 5.0 Student Data disk
3. printer

OBJECTIVES

After completing this unit, you will be able to

1. use the Font menu to change the appearance of the printed page;
2. use the Format menu to set tab stops, margins, and line spacing;
3. use the Format menu to create headers and a document summary;
4. use the Format menu to change and position the page number and to center a page vertically;
5. use the Style menu to create, edit, and save a standardized document format.

IMPORTANT KEYSTROKES

1. Ctrl-F8   to format the size and appearance of text for printing
2. Shift-F8   to change the format of a line, a page, and the document for printing and to create a document summary
3. Alt-F8   to create, edit, save, and retrieve a document format
4. Shift-<TAB> to move one tab stop to the left

FORMATTING TEXT FOR PRINTING

You have discovered a number of editing functions that will make your documents attractive and your word-processing tasks easier.

Your documents must also be formatted. Whereas editing affects the appearance and content of the text, formatting affects the appearance of the document on the printed page. When you prepare a document for printing you must set margins and tabs, specify the number of spaces between lines (e.g., single, double, or triple spacing), and determine a pattern for numbering pages. With some documents you must also set headers and footers, determine column widths, or adjust the justification parameters.

Some of the formatting options WordPerfect 5.0 offers are dependent on the printer that interfaces with the computer you are using. Some printers allow you to embed a code that commands the printer to change the pitch (type size) or type style during the course of printing. There are also specialized typing functions available with WordPerfect 5.0 that can only be used with a compatible printer. These special features include overstrikes for diacritical marks in foreign words, superscripts, subscripts, and mathematical formulas.

WordPerfect 5.0 allows you to create standardized document formats with the Style key so that you can use these formats over and over. You can create a library of Styles that include format codes and text. These Styles can be inserted in any document.

In Unit 5, we focus on formatting text for printing. The unit is divided into three sections to help differentiate between each format function and to make the working sessions manageable. Unit 6 guides you through the steps required to control your printer.

FORMATTING A DOCUMENT FOR PRINTING

Ctrl-F8, Shift-F8, and Alt-F8 are the keys used to format a document. Whenever any one of these key combinations is pressed, a menu of choices is displayed. Choosing an option from a menu embeds a code in your document that the processor in turn sends to the printer.

SECTION 1

ASSIGNMENTS

1. Create **SCRIPT.TXT**
2. Review Questions
3. Documentation Research
4. Review Exercises

THE FONT MENU

When the **Ctrl-F8** keys are pressed, the Font menu appears on your screen (figure 5-1). This menu offers several options for changing the printed appearance of your text. These attributes may be chosen from the Font menu or the Size and Appearance submenus. You may select an option by typing one of the listed numbers. You must remember that the changes you make with the Font key will be printed only if your printer supports the feature. To terminate a feature, press the **<Right> arrow** key to move past the attribute code or choose the Normal option on the Font menu.

---

1 Size; 2 Appearance; 3 Normal; 4 Base Font; 5 Print Color: 0

FIGURE 5-1   Font Menu

The Font menu options are defined as follows:

- 1 Size   The size option allows you to vary the height of a character and change its position in a line. When the size option is chosen, the Size submenu (figure 5-2) is displayed on your screen.

---

1 Suprscpt; 2 Subscpt; 3 Fine; 4 Small; 5 Large; 6 Vry Large; 7 Ext Large: 0

FIGURE 5-2   Size Submenu

The Size submenu options are defined as follows:

- 1 Suprscpt   A character that is superscripted is placed one-third of a line above the other characters on the line. The superscript is not displayed on your screen but will be printed.

2 Subscpt — A character that is subscripted is placed one-third of a line below the other characters on the line. The subscript is not displayed on your screen but will be printed.

3 Fine-7 Ext Large — Options 3 through 7 change the height of a character. WordPerfect automatically adjusts line spacing, font, and other formatting features.

2 Appearance — The second Font menu option affects the style of text. When this option is chosen, the Appearance submenu (figure 5-3) is displayed on your screen. Two of the most commonly used appearance features, Bold and Undrln, have been assigned their own keys.

---

1 Bold 2 Undrln 3 Dbl Und 4 Italc 5 Outln 6 Shdw 7 Sm Cap 8 Redln 9 Stkout: 0

FIGURE 5-3   Appearance submenu

The Appearance submenu options are defined as follows:

1 Bold — The Appearance submenu allows you to boldface text. You have already used the F6 key to boldface text.

2 Undrln — The Appearance submenu allows you to underline text. You have already used the F8 key to underline text.

3 Dbl Und — This attribute underlines text with a double line.

4 Italc — This attribute prints text in italic type.

5 Outln — The printed characters will be outlined.

6 Shdw — The printed characters will have a "shadow."

7 Sm Cap — The size of the uppercase letters is reduced.

8 Redln — A vertical line is printed in the margin to designate redlined text. This feature is helpful in editing text. Before printing the final draft of the document, redline markings can be removed with an option on the Mark Text (Alt-F5) menu.

9 Stkout — A horizontal line is printed through text marked for deletion. Before printing the final draft of the document, text marked with the strikeout option can be removed from the text with an option on the Mark Text (Alt-F5) menu.

The rest of the Font menu options do not have submenus.

    3 Normal   The normal option returns you to the current font. The current font is the initial font set on the Print menu (Shift-F7).

    4 Base Font   This option is used to change the current text font. You can choose from a list of fonts that are available on your printer by highlighting the font and typing an asterisk or choosing Select.

    5 Print Color   If your printer prints in different colors, you can change the color in which text is printed.

Hint: It takes some time and patience to learn how specific print format commands affect your printed document. Do some experimenting until you find the styles that suit you and that your printer can accommodate. Always think through the commands you embed in a document, because the printer follows instructions exactly as they are given.

GUIDED ACTIVITY: USING THE SIZE AND APPEARANCE SUBMENUS

1. Type **THE FONT MENU** on a clear screen.

2. Press **<ENTER>** four times to end a short line and insert three blank lines.

3. Type **USING THE SIZE SUBMENU**

4. Press **<ENTER>** twice to end a short line and insert a blank line.

5. Type **REGULAR UPPERCASE LETTERS**

6. Press **<ENTER>** twice to end a short line and insert a blank line.

7. Press **Ctrl-F8**

    The Font menu appears on your screen.

8. Type **1** to choose Size from the Font menu.

    The Size submenu appears on your screen.

9. Type **7** to choose Extra Large from the Size submenu.

10. Type **EXTRA LARGE LETTERS**

11. Press the **<Right> arrow** key to terminate the feature.

12. Press **<ENTER>** twice.

70   WordPerfect 5.0

13. Repeat steps 7 through 12 to try options 6, 5, 4, and 3. Be sure to change what you type in step 8 to describe the option you are using.

14. Press <ENTER> twice to insert two additional blank lines.

15. Type **USING THE APPEARANCE SUBMENU**

16. Press <ENTER> twice to end a short line and insert a blank line.

17. Press **Ctrl-F8**

    The Font menu appears on your screen.

18. Type **2** to choose Appearance from the Font menu.

    The Appearance submenu appears on your screen.

19. Type **7** to choose Small Capital letters from the Size submenu.

20. Type **SMALL CAPITAL LETTERS**

21. Press the **<Right> arrow** key to terminate the feature.

22. Repeat steps 17 through 21 to try options 6, 5, 4, and 3. Be sure to change what you type in step 20 to describe the option you are using.

23. Save your document. Name it **SCRIPT.TXT**

GUIDED ACTIVITY: USING SUPERSCRIPTS

Retrieve **SCRIPT.TXT** if necessary.

1. Move the cursor to the bottom of the document.

2. Type

    The weather today is very warm. The temperature is expected to reach 98

3. Press the **Ctrl-F8** keys.

    The Font menu is displayed on your screen.

4. Type **1** to choose the Size submenu.

5. Type **1**

    You have chosen the superscript option. The Pos number will be highlighted in the status line.

Formatting Text for Printing 71

6. Type **o** (lower case letter o).

   You have typed a superscript at the cursor location. The "o" will be highlighted on your screen and superscripted when it is printed.

7. Press the **Ctrl-F8** keys.

   The Font menu appears.

8. Type **3**

   You have chosen the Normal option to terminate the superscript feature.

9. Press the **<SPACEBAR>**

10. Type **Fahrenheit**.

11. Press **<ENTER>** twice.

12. Save **SCRIPT.TXT**

    ✔**CHECKPOINT**

    a. What menu appears when the **Ctrl-F8** keys are pressed?

GUIDED ACTIVITY: USING SUBSCRIPTS

Retrieve **SCRIPT.TXT** if necessary.

1. Move the cursor to the bottom of the document.

2. Type **The chemical formula for pentane is:**

3. Press the **<SPACEBAR>** two times.

4. Type **C**

5. Press the **Ctrl-F8** keys.

   The Font menu will appear on the screen.

6. Type **1**

   The Size submenu will appear on the screen.

7. Type **2**

72 WordPerfect 5.0

You have chosen Subscript from the menu. The Pos number will be highlighted in the status line.

8. Type **5**

The "5" will be highlighted on your screen.

9. Press the **<Right> arrow** key once.

You have turned off the Subscript feature.

10. Type **H**

11. Press the **Ctrl-F8** keys.

The Font menu will appear on your screen.

12. Type **1**

The Size submenu will appear on the screen.

13. Type **2**

You have chosen Subscript from the menu.

14. Type **12**

15. Press the **<Right> arrow** key once.

You have turned off the Subscript feature.

16. Type the Document Identification Line.

17. Save **SCRIPT.TXT**

18. Print **SCRIPT.TXT**

✔**CHECKPOINT**

b. Which keystrokes activate the Subscript feature?

What You Have Accomplished

The **SCRIPT.TXT** document that you have just created illustrates the options on the Size and Appearance submenus of the Font menus. Your printed document will illustrate how your printer handles the options on the Size and Appearance submenus. If your printer cannot print certain options it will substitute another feature. For example, one printer I use cannot print in italics so the text was underlined. Often a printer that uses continuous-feed paper cannot adjust well enough to print superscripts or subscripts. You can print **SCRIPT.TXT** on any different printer available to you to see how these options are handled on it.

✔ CHECKPOINT

    c.   What two methods can be used to turn a Size or Appearance submenu option off?

REVIEW QUESTIONS

1. On what submenu would you find the Double Underline feature?

2. How will characters be printed when you use the Superscript option on the Size submenu?

3. The Font menu lists five options. Describe them.

4. How do you change the base font for your printer?

DOCUMENTATION RESEARCH

1. Refer to the user's manual to determine how you can discover which attributes listed on the Font menu and its submenus are available on your printer.

2. What WordPerfect 5.0 feature determines how font attributes are displayed on your screen?

REVIEW EXERCISES

1. Display a clear screen.

2. Use the subscript option to create the following formula for sulfuric acid:

    H_2SO_4

3. Use the superscript and subscript features to reproduce the following text:

    Jack and Jill went ^{up} the hill to fetch a pail of water.
    Jack fell $_{down}$ and broke his crown and Jill came tumbling after.

4. Create your own personal letterhead using various Size and Appearance options.

5. Save your document. Name it **FONT.TXT**

6. Print **FONT.TXT**

SECTION 2

ASSIGNMENTS
1. Edit **QUOTE.TXT**
2. Create **SCHEDULE**
3. Edit **HUMAN.REL**
4. Edit **WORDWRAP**
5. Review Questions
6. Documentation Research
7. Review Exercises

THE FORMAT MENU

When the **Shift-F8** keys are pressed, the Format menu (figure 5-4) appears on your screen. This menu is divided into four submenus and offers numerous options for changing the default format. Some of these options will show on your screen as well as when your document is printed. When you insert a format change code in your document, the new format is in effect from that point on.

```
Format

    1 -     Line
                    Hyphenation              Line Spacing
                    Justification            Margins Left/Right
                    Line Height              Tab Set
                    Line Numbering           Widow/Orphan Protection

    2 -     Page
                    Center Page (top to bottom)   New Page Number
                    Force Odd/Even Page           Page Numbering
                    Headers and Footers           Paper Size/Type
                    Margins Top/Bottom            Suppress

    3 -     Document
                    Display Pitch            Redline Method
                    Initial Codes/Font       Summary

    4 -     Other
                    Advance                  Overstrike
                    Conditional End of Page  Printer Functions
                    Decimal Characters       Underline Spaces/Tabs
                    Language

Selection: 0
```

FIGURE 5-4 Format Menu

76   WordPerfect 5.0

The Format menu options are defined as follows:

> 1 - Line.   The Line submenu allows you to format characteristics of the lines of your document. The Format Line submenu (figure 5-5) shows the current option settings.

```
Format: Line

   1 - Hyphenation                          Off

   2 - Hyphenation Zone -      Left         10%
                               Right        4%

   3 - Justification                        Yes

   4 - Line Height                          Auto

   5 - Line Numbering                       No

   6 - Line Spacing                         1

   7 - Margins     -  Left                  1"
                      Right                 1"

   8 - Tab Set                              0", every 0.5"

   9 - Widow/Orphan Protection              No

Selection:  0
```

FIGURE 5-5   Format Line Submenu

> Hyphenation   Hyphenation is used to improve the appearance of a document by keeping spaces between words more regular; ragged right margins become less ragged, and right-justified margins have less prominent spaces between words.
>
> When you begin hyphenation, WordPerfect guides you through your text, pausing at the end of each line that contains a word that can be hyphenated. WordPerfect indicates a suggested location for placement of a hyphen, then allows you to decide if the division is acceptable.
>
> Hyphenation Zone   The hyphenation zone determines if a word will be wrapped to the next line or hyphenated when the Hyphenation feature has been activated. The zone is set by indicating a percentage of the line length as the left and right hyphenation zone. The

smaller the hyphenation zone the more hyphenation will be required.

You can increase or decrease the hyphenation zone by accessing the Format Line submenu and selecting the Hyphenation Zone option.

Justification   This submenu options allow you to turn justification on or off. The default setting is justification on. When justification is on, the right margin will be even when your document is printed. This feature does not appear on your screen. If justification is off, the right margin will be uneven as it appears on your screen.

Line Height   WordPerfect automatically assigns a line height to each different font or font attribute. You can set even line height regardless of the font or attribute you are using.

Line Numbering   You can number the lines of a document with this option. The numbering can be continuous throughout the document or can be stopped and restarted. You can number every line, every second line, or every third line. You can select the starting number. You can automatically restart numbering with each new page and determine where in the left margin you want the line number printed.

Line Spacing   This option changes the space between lines of text. You can use this option to double or triple space a document or part of a document.

Margins Left/Right   The default setting for the left and right margins is one inch, which allows sixty-five characters per line in pica type on standard 8-1/2" x 11" paper. You can change the margin settings for part of or an entire document.

Tab Set   When this option is chosen, the current tab settings are displayed on your screen (figure 5-6). You can set several types of tabs in your document. Tabs are preset every one-half inch.

```
L.....L.....L.....L.....L.....L.....L.....L.....L.....L.....L.....L.....L.....L
!     ^     !     ^     !     ^     !     ^     !     ^     !     ^     !     ^
1"          2"          3"          4"          5"          6"          7"
Delete EOL (clear tabs); Enter Number (set tab); Del (clear tab);
Left; Center; Right; Decimal; .= Dot Leader
```

FIGURE 5-6   Tab Set Submenu

The Tabs Setting submenu:

To clear all previous tab settings, move the cursor to the first tab and press the **Ctrl-<End>** keys.

To delete one tab, move the cursor to the tab set on the ruler and press **<DEL>**

There are four tab styles. Each style aligns text differently when you move the cursor to the tab setting and type. The Left style is the default. When you press tab and type text, the text moves to the right. The Center style centers text at the tab setting. The Right style moves text to the left as you type. The Decimal style lines up text on a decimal point (default) or some other character.

To set new evenly spaced tab stops, move the cursor to the starting point, type "L", "C", "R", or "D" for the style, then type "0" (zero), "," (comma), then the interval number.

Hint: When you are setting new evenly spaced tabs, you do not have to type the L for Left-style tab settings as left-style is the default setting.

To set a single tab, move the cursor to the desired position on the Tab Set submenu and type "L", "C", "R" or "D" to indicate the tab style.

To set a dot leader, move the cursor to the tab and type a "." (period). When you press the **<TAB>** key while typing, a dot leader is inserted.

To exit the Tabs Setting submenu and return to your document, press F7 twice.

Widow/Orphan Protection   This option allows you to prevent a single line of a paragraph from being stranded on a page. WordPerfect defines a **widow line** as the first line of a paragraph left alone at the bottom of one page while the rest of the paragraph is on the following page. An **orphan line** is defined as the last line of a paragraph left alone at the top of one page while the rest of the paragraph is located on the preceding page. The default setting is "No." The setting can be changed to "Yes" to turn on Widow/Orphan protection anywhere in a document.

GUIDED ACTIVITY: USING THE FORMAT LINE SUBMENU

1. Retrieve **QUOTE.TXT**

2. Move the cursor to the blank line below the first quotation.

3. Press **<ENTER>** to insert another blank line.

4. Type **The above quotation has the default settings of one-inch left and right margins, single line spacing, and right justification is on.**

5. Press **<ENTER>** twice to end the line and insert a blank line.

GUIDED ACTIVITY: CHANGING THE MARGINS

1. Retrieve **QUOTE.TXT** if necessary.

2. Move the cursor to the first letter of the second copy of the quotation.

3. Press the **Shift-F8** keys to access the Format menu.

4. Type **1** to choose Line from the Format menu.

   The Format Line submenu appears on the screen.

5. Type **7** to choose Margins.

   The cursor will move to the left-margin setting.

6. Type **2.5** to reset the left margin to two and one-half inches.

7. Press **<ENTER>** to enter the left-margin setting and move the cursor to the right-margin setting. Notice that WordPerfect automatically set the measurement to inches.

8. Type **2.5** to set the right margin to two and one-half inches.

9. Press **<ENTER>** to enter the right margin setting.

10. Press **F7** to return to your document.

    Notice that the second, third, and fourth copies of the quotation have two and one-half inch margins.

11. Move the cursor to the blank line below the second quotation.

12. Press **<ENTER>** to insert a blank line.

13. Type **The above quotation has two and one-half inch margins.**

14. Press **<ENTER>** to insert a blank line.

15. Save your document.

✔CHECKPOINT

   d. What keystrokes are used to access the Format Line submenu?

MARGIN RELEASE

To type text within the left margin, press the **Shift-<TAB>** keys. Each time you press these keys, the cursor jumps one tab stop to the left, even into the left margin.

    e.   When you change margin settings, how is that change displayed on the screen?

GUIDED ACTIVITY: RIGHT JUSTIFICATION

1. Retrieve **QUOTE.TXT** if necessary.

2. Move the cursor to the first letter of the third copy of the quotation.

3. Press the **Shift-F8** keys to access the Format menu.

4. Type **1** to access the Format Line submenu.

5. Type **3** to choose the Justification option.

6. Type **N** to turn the right-justification option off.

7. Press **F7** to return to your document.

    The third copy of the quotation will be printed with an even left margin and an uneven right margin.

8. Move the cursor to the blank line following the third quotation.

9. Press **<ENTER>** to insert a blank line.

10. Type **The above quotation is left justified only.**

11. Press **<ENTER>** to insert a blank line.

12. Move the cursor to the first letter of the fourth quotation.

13. Press the **Shift-F8** keys to access the Format menu.

14. Type **1** to choose Line from the Format menu.

    The Format Line submenu appears on the screen.

15. Type **7** to choose Margins.

    The cursor will move to the left-margin setting.

16. Type **1** to reset the left margin to one inch.

17. Press **<ENTER>** to enter the left-margin setting and move the cursor to the right-margin setting.

18. Type **1** to set the right margin to one inch.

19. Press **<ENTER>** to enter the right margin setting.

20. Press **F7** to return to your document.

21. Move the cursor to the first letter of the fourth copy of the quotation.

22. Press the **Shift-F8** keys to access the Format menu.

23. Type **1** to access the Format Line submenu.

24. Type **3** to choose the Justification option.

25. Type **Yes** to turn on the right-justification option.

26. Press **F7** to return to your document.

27. Save your document.

GUIDED ACTIVITY: LINE SPACING

1. Move the cursor to the first word of the fourth copy of the quotation.

2. Press the **Shift-F8** keys to access the Format menu.

3. Type **1** to access the Format Line submenu.

4. Type **6** to choose the Line Spacing option.

5. Type **2** to set double line spacing.

6. Press **<ENTER>** to reset the line spacing.

7. Press **F7** to return to the document.

8. Move the cursor to the line below the fourth quotation.

9. Type **The above quotation has double-spaced lines.**

10. Save **and Print QUOTE.TXT**

82   WordPerfect 5.0

✔ CHECKPOINT

f. How does the screen display change to reflect a line-spacing setting of double-spaced lines?

What You Have Accomplished

You have used the Format Line submenu to change margins and line spacing. You have also formatted a section of your document to have a ragged-right margin, that is, right justification is turned off. These options can be reset any time during the course of typing a document.

GUIDED ACTIVITY: CHANGING TAB SETTINGS

1. Display a clear screen.

2. Press the **Shift-F8** keys.

    The Format menu will appear.

3. Type **1** (or **L**)

    The Format Line submenu will appear.

4. Type **8**

    The Tabs Setting submenu will appear.

5. Press the **Ctrl-<End>** keys.

    All of the tabs from the cursor forward have been deleted.

6. Type **5**

7. Press **<ENTER>**

    Your first tab stop is set at Pos 5.0".

8. Type **7**

9. Press **<ENTER>**

    A tab stop will be set at Pos 7.0".

10. Press **F7** to Exit the Tabs Setting submenu.

11. Press **0** to Exit the Format Line submenu.

12. Press **0** to Exit the Format menu and return to a clear screen.

13. Save the tab settings in a file named **SCHEDULE**

✔ CHECKPOINT

g. What keystrokes are required to access the Tabs Setting submenu?

_____

h. Describe the steps required to remove all existing tabs.

_____

i. Identify the keystrokes that allow you to return to the text from the Tabs Setting submenu.

_____

Hint: The process of using submenus can at first be confusing, especially when a program is designed with multiple layers of submenus. Just remember that each menu choice follows a predesigned path, and that your computer will do nothing that you do not command it to do. In addition, WordPerfect 5.0 is designed to lead you through each submenu by providing prompts on the submenu screens. There is always a way back from a submenu to the main menu.

FALL QUARTER SCHEDULE		
CLASS	TIME	ROOM
Accounting 130	8-9 a.m. MWF	1210
Accounting 131	10-11 a.m. MWF	1530
Accounting 161	10-11:40 a.m. TTH	2320
Accounting 264	11-12 a.m. MWF	1210
Accounting 141	6-9 p.m. W	2320

FIGURE 5-7 SCHEDULE

GUIDED ACTIVITY: USING TAB SETTINGS

Retrieve **SCHEDULE** if necessary.

84 WordPerfect 5.0

1. Type the text in figure 5-7, using the <TAB> key to move the cursor horizontally across the line to each tab stop. Press **<ENTER>** at the end of each line.

2. Add the Document Identification Line.

3. Save and print **SCHEDULE**

> 2 - Page   When you choose this option on the Format menu (figure 5-4) the Format Page submenu (figure 5-8) appears. The options on this submenu affect the size of the printed page. With this menu you can set top and bottom margins, assign a page number position, and include headers and footers. This menu can be used to format the pages in an entire document or to format pages individually. None of the options from the Format Page submenu affect your document's appearance on the screen, but they will be included in your final printed document. Figure 5-8 shows the option default settings.

```
Format: Page

    1 - Center Page (top to bottom)          No

    2 - Force Odd/Even Page

    3 - Headers

    4 - Footers

    5 - Margins -Top                         1"
                Bottom                       1"

    6 - New Page Number                      1
        (example: 3 or iii)

    7 - Page Numbering                       No page numbering

    8 - Paper Size                           8.5" x 11"
                                             Standard

    9 - Suppress (this page only)

Selection: 0
```

FIGURE 5-8 Format Page Submenu

The options on the Format Page submenu are defined as follows:

Center Page (top to bottom)	This option allows you to center text vertically, that is, to format a page so that your printed document has equal top and bottom margins.
Force Odd/Even Page.	This option forces the current page to have either an odd or even page number. For example, you have chosen Odd. If the page number would normally be odd, that number is retained. If the page would normally be even, the page will be numbered with the next odd page number.
Headers and Footers	You can print the same text at the top or bottom of each page, odd pages, or even pages. A **header** is information placed at the top of the page. A **footer** is information placed at the bottom. Neither headers nor footers are part of the regular text. WordPerfect allows you to format two headers and two footers per page, but they must be placed in different locations (e.g., one header at the left margin and one at the right). You may also alternate the position of the headers and footers on odd- and even-numbered pages.
Margins Top/Bottom	You can reset the default one-inch top and bottom margins. These margins are measured from the top or bottom edge of the paper.
New Page Number	This option renumbers pages by inserting a new page numbering code. It allows you to choose between arabic and roman styles.
Page Numbering	This option allows you to choose the position of page numbers. When this option is chosen, a diagram of possible page number positions appears on your screen. Each position is designated by a number. The code Ctrl-B (this code appears in your document as ^B) allows you to insert the page number anywhere in your document.
Paper Size/Type	The Paper Size/Type is set for standard 8.5" x 11" paper. If your printer is capable of printing different size forms, you can reset this option.

86   WordPerfect 5.0

    Suppress   When this option is chosen, a list of page format options appears on your screen. You type the number of the feature you want to turn off for the current page, then type **n** for No.

GUIDED ACTIVITY: CREATING HEADERS

1. Retrieve the file **HUMAN.REL** from the WordPerfect 5.0 Student Data disk.

2. Move the cursor to the top of the first page of **HUMAN.REL**.

3. Press the **Shift-F8** keys.

    The Format menu will appear on your screen.

4. Type **2** to display the Format Page submenu.

5. Type **3**

    The Headers submenu will appear at the bottom of your screen.

6. Type **1** to select Header A.

7. Type **3**

    You have chosen to place Header A on odd-numbered pages. A blank screen will appear.

8. Type **Printer Formatting**

    This is the header that will be printed on odd-numbered pages.

9. Press the **F7** key.

    The Page Format menu will reappear on your screen. Header A has been saved.

10. Type **3**

    The Header submenu will reappear on your screen.

11. Type **2** to select Header B.

    You have chosen a second header.

12. Type **4**

    You have chosen to place Header B on even-numbered pages. A blank screen will appear.

Formatting Text for Printing 87

13. Type **WordPerfect 5.0**

    This is the header that will appear on even-numbered pages.

14. Press the **F7** key.

    The Page Format menu will reappear. Header B has been saved.

15. Press **0** twice.

    Your text will reappear on the screen. The headers you chose will not be visible on the screen, but they will be included on the printed document.

16. Save **HUMAN.REL**

What You Have Accomplished

You have used the Page Format menu to include two different headers on your document. One of the headers will be printed on even-numbered pages and one will be printed on odd-numbered pages. You have also learned that the F7 key saves the headers you have chosen.

✔CHECKPOINT

   j. Identify the keystrokes that access the Page Format Menu.

   _____

   k. Describe how the Headers submenu is used to place headers on even-numbered pages.

   _____

Hint: When you are creating headers or footers, you may also make use of other WordPerfect 5.0 features such as boldfacing, underlining, centering, or placing text flush right. Press the appropriate keys before you enter the header or footer text on the Headers or Footer submenu.

GUIDED ACTIVITY: CHANGING THE PAGE NUMBER

Retrieve **HUMAN.REL** if necessary.

1. Press the **Shift-F8** keys.

   The Format menu will appear on your screen.

88   WordPerfect 5.0

2. Type **2**

    The Format Page submenu will appear on your screen.

3. Type **6**

    The cursor will move to the New Page Number option.

4. Type **vi** to choose the new page number, roman numeral six.

5. Press **<ENTER>**

6. Press **0** (zero) twice.

    Your document will reappear on the screen. The new page number will appear in the status line. If you Reveal Codes by pressing the Alt-F3 keys, you will see the embedded code for the new page number in roman numerals.

GUIDED ACTIVITY: INSERTING A PAGE NUMBER AT THE BOTTOM CENTER OF EACH PAGE

Retrieve **HUMAN.REL** from your Student Data disk if necessary.

1. Press the **Shift-F8** keys.

    The Format menu will appear on your screen.

2. Type **2**

    The Format Page submenu will appear on your screen.

3. Type **7**

    The Format Page Numbering screen will appear on your screen.

4. Type **6**

    You have chosen to place a page number at the bottom center of every page of the document.

5. Press **0** (zero) twice.

    Your document will reappear on the screen. The page numbers will not be visible on the screen, but they will be included in the printed document.

6. Save and Print **HUMAN.REL**

    Examine your printed document to see if each header and the page numbering are correct.

✔CHECKPOINT

1. Which keystrokes are required to select a format for numbering pages?

GUIDED ACTIVITY: CENTERING A PAGE VERTICALLY

1. Retrieve **WORDWRAP** from your Student Data disk.

2. Move the cursor to the top of the document.

3. Press the **Shift-F8** keys to access the Format menu.

4. Type **2**

   The Format Page submenu will appear on your screen.

5. Type **1**

   You have chosen to center **WORDWRAP** on the printed page.

6. Press **0** (zero) twice.

   WORDWRAP will reappear. It will not appear centered on the screen, but it will be centered vertically when it is printed.

7. Save and Print **WORDWRAP**

✔CHECKPOINT

m. What keystrokes did you need to center the page vertically?

---

3 - Document.   When you choose the third option on the Format menu (figure 5-4), the Format Document submenu appears. This submenu allows you to format characteristics of the entire document. The Format Document submenu (figure 5-9) shows the option default settings.

```
Format: Document

    1 - Display Pitch -      Automatic               Yes
                             Width                   0.1"

    2 - Initial Codes

    3 - Initial Font                                 Normal

    4 - Redline Method                               Printer Dependent

    5 - Summary


    Selection: 0
```

FIGURE 5-9   Format Document Default Screen

The options on the Format Line submenu are defined as follows:

  Display Pitch   This option determines the width of a character displayed on the screen (not when printed). WordPerfect automatically adjusts the character display if text would overlap on the screen.

  Initial Codes/Font   This option allows you to reset WordPerfect code and font defaults for the current document.

  Redline Method   The method of indicating redlined text is set to use whatever method your printer has defined. If your printer supports it, you can set the redline method to "left" to print a horizontal line in the left margin or "alternating" to print the horizontal bar in the left margin on even-numbered pages and in the right margin on odd-numbered pages.

  Summary   This option allows you to create a summary of information about your document. This summary is not printed but can help you find a file. The document summary lists the filename and creation date. You can include the subject, typist, author, a descriptive filename, and comments. If you do not choose to enter comments, WordPerfect automatically displays the first 400 characters of the document.

GUIDED ACTIVITY: CREATING A DOCUMENT SUMMARY

1. Retrieve **HUMAN.REL**

2. Press the **Shift-F8** keys.

   The Format menu appears.

3. Press **3**

   The Format Document submenu appears.

4. Press **5**

   The Document Summary screen appears. Notice the first 400 characters of the document displayed in the comment box.

5. Press **2** to move the cursor to the Subject/Account area.

6. Type **Human Relations**

7. Press **<ENTER>** to enter the subject.

8. Type **3** to move the cursor to the Author area.

9. Type **Ms. M. Simonson**

10. Press **<ENTER>** to enter the author's name.

11. Type **4** to move the cursor to the Typist area.

12. Type your name as typist.

13. Press **<ENTER>** to enter the typist's name.

14. Type **5** to move the cursor to the Comment box.

15. Type the following comment:

    This article outlines how important good human relations are in the workplace.

16. Press **<ENTER>** two times to insert a blank line in the comment box.

17. Press **F7** to Save the Document Summary and Exit the Document Summary screen.

18. Save **HUMAN.REL**

92 WordPerfect 5.0

✔ CHECKPOINT

n. Which keystrokes are required to access the Document Summary Screen.

GUIDED ACTIVITY: DISPLAYING A DOCUMENT SUMMARY

1. Retrieve **HUMAN.REL**

2. Press the **Shift-F8** keys to access the Format menu.

3. Press **3** to access the Format Document submenu.

4. Press **5** to access the Document Summary screen you previously created.

5. Press **0** to return to your document.

6. Exit WordPerfect 5.0.

   4 - Other.   When you choose the fourth option on the Format menu (Figure 5-4), the Format Other submenu appears. The Format Other submenu allows you to format miscellaneous document characteristics. The Format Other submenu (figure 5-10) shows the option default settings.

```
Format: Other

    1 -     Advance

    2 -     Conditional End of Page

    3 -     Decimal/Align Character           .
            Thousands' Separator              ,

    4 -     Language                          EN

    5 -     Overstrike

    6 -     Printer Functions

    7 -     Underline -   Spaces              Yes
                          Tabs                No


Selection: 0
```

FIGURE 5-10   Format Other Submenu

The options on the Format Other submenu are defined as follows:

Advance
: This option allows you to instruct your printer to print text a specified distance up, down, left, or right from the current printing position. You can also instruct the printer to print at a specified position.

Conditional End of Page
: This option allows you to keep a designated number of lines of text together on the same page. For example, if a page end occurs in the middle of a body of text such as a quotation that should appear on one page, you can command WordPerfect to move the entire quotation to the next page. This feature is useful in avoiding problems during major revisions.

Decimal Characters
: You can assign a character on which to line up text vertically when using the <TAB> key. The default setting is a "." (a period or decimal point).

Language
: If you have purchased additional Speller, Thesaurus, and Hyphenation disks in a language other than English, this option allows you to edit multilingual documents.

Overstrike
: Overstrike allows you to print more than one character in the same position. Overstrike is useful for creating scientific symbols and foreign characters not available with your printer.

Printer Functions
: This options allows you to control your printer in special printing situations. The Kerning option on the Printer Functions option screen allows you to reduce white space between specific pairs of letters. The Printer Command option allows you to enter special printer codes. The Word and Letter Spacing option adjusts the space between adjacent words and letters. The default setting is "Optimal". Word Spacing Justification Limits adjusts space between words in justified text.

Underline Spaces/Tabs
: WordPerfect is preset to underline spaces but not tabs. You can reset either of these settings using this option on the Format Other submenu.

What You Have Accomplished

In following this section's Guided Activites, you have created two headers and inserted page numbers at the bottom center of each page of **HUMAN.REL**. You have also centered **WORDWRAP** vertically on a page. You printed **HUMAN.REL** and **WORDWRAP** to see the results of your page-formatting commands and you experimented with your printer to find out which WordPerfect 5.0 features it can accommodate. You also created a document summary to save with **HUMAN.REL**.

REVIEW QUESTIONS

1. Identify the keystrokes required to access the Format menu.

2. There are nine options on the Format Line submenu. Identify the option you would choose to avoid printing the first or last line of a paragraph alone on a page.

3. What are headers? Where are they located on a printed document?

4. Suppose that you are creating a document that must be printed on legal size rather than standard size paper. How would you go about formatting a page to include additional lines of text?

5. What option on the Format Other submenu would you choose to keep together the text lines of a quotation that you do not want printed on separate pages?

6. Suppose that you are creating a document with headers but do not want to include the headers on your title page. How would you go about suppressing those headers for that page alone?

7. WordPerfect 5.0 provides a number of options for positioning page numbers on a page. What procedure is required to position numbers at the bottom center of every page?

8. Suppose that you are typing a rather short letter and would like the text of the letter centered on a page. How do you use the Format Page submenu to accomplish this task?

Formatting Text for Printing   95

DOCUMENTATION RESEARCH

1. What WordPerfect features can be used when creating a header or footer?

2. If you are editing a document, how can you keep a header code from moving?

3. How do you insert a page number in headers and footers?

REVIEW EXERCISES

1. Retrieve **EXERCISE.DOC**

2. Move the cursor to the top of the document.

3. Set the page number to arabic 101. Reveal Codes to see the New Page Number setting.

4. Set the margins to Left = 1.5" and Right = 1.5"

5. Clear all the Tab settings. Set a tab at Pos 2.5".

6. Indent the first line of each paragraph on the first page (now page 101) of your document.

7. Enter the code to number this page at the bottom center.

8. Enter the code to the the following header flush right on odd-numbered pages:

EXERCISE.DOC
Page ^B

(The Ctrl-B code inserts the page number.)

9. Enter the code to put the following header flush left on even-numbered pages:

Unit 5
Page ^B

10. Move the cursor to the top of the second page of your document. (Be sure the cursor is on Ln 1".)

11. Cancel the instruction to number the document pages at the bottom center.

12. Change the margins back to the default setting of Left = 1" and Right = ~~7.53"~~. 1"

13. Delete all tab settings. Set tabs every one-half inch.

14. Use the Tab key to indent the paragraphs on this page two tab stops.

15. Move the cursor to the top of the third page.

16. Enter the code to double space this page.

17. Save (replace previous version) and Print **EXERCISE.DOC**. Were all the formatting codes entered correctly? If not, correct your errors and reprint only the incorrectly formatted pages. Do not waste printer paper. (Move the cursor to the page you want to reprint, press the **Shift-F7** keys, then choose "2 - Page" to print the page where the cursor is resting.) When you are done, Save again and Exit WordPerfect.

SECTION 3

ASSIGNMENTS
1. Create **DOCID**
2. Review Questions
3. Documentation Research
4. Review Exercises

THE STYLES MENU

When the **Alt-F8** keys are pressed, the Styles menu (figure 5-11) appears on your screen. The options on this menu allow you to create, edit, save, and retrieve a style. Styles that have been created are listed on this menu. A style can include formatting codes and text. If the same formatting codes and text are used often, this is an efficient way to standardize the appearance of text. A Style is saved with your document. Styles that will be used with several files can be saved in a Style library.

```
┌─────────────────────────────────────────────────────────────────────┐
│                                                                     │
│    Styles                                                           │
│                                                                     │
│    Name           Type         Description                          │
│                                                                     │
│                                                                     │
│                                                                     │
│                                                                     │
│  1 On; 2 Off; 3 Create; 4 Edit; 5 Delete; 6 Save; 7 Retrieve; 8 Update:  0 │
└─────────────────────────────────────────────────────────────────────┘
```
FIGURE 5-11   Styles Menu

The options on the Style menu are defined as follows:

Name	The names of Styles you have already created are listed.
Type	The type of a Style you have already created is listed. There are two types of styles. The open style sets a format for an entire document. It cannot be turned off. The paired style can be turned on and off within a document.
Description	The Style description lists your description of what the style does. You can use a description of up to 54 characters.
On	This option inserts a Style at the cursor position.
Off	This choice terminates a Style.
Create	You must create a Style before you can use it. The Create option allows you to create a Style. When you choose Create, the Styles Edit screen (figure 5-12) appears. You enter the Style name, type, description, codes to be included in the Style, and the function of the <ENTER> key in a paired style. In a paired Style, the <ENTER> key can perform its normal function, can turn the Style off, or can turn the Style off and on.

```
Styles:  Edit

  1 - Name

  2 - Type           Paired

  3 - Description

  4 - Codes

  5 - Enter          HRt

Selection:  0
```

FIGURE 5-12   Styles Edit Screen

4 Edit	This option on the Styles menu allows you to edit a style.
5 Delete	Delete will erase a Style highlighted in the Style list.
6 Save	A Style is always saved with the current document. To save a Style in a Style library for use with other documents, choose this option. You will be asked to name the file that will contain the library of Styles. The Styles library file must be created with the Setup key.
7 Retrieve	If a Styles library has been created, you can retrieve the library into the current document. WordPerfect automatically retrieves the Style library file if no Styles have been defined for the current document.
8 Update	Use this option to edit the Style library.

GUIDED ACTIVITY: CREATING A STYLE

1. Retrieve **WORDWRAP**

2. Press the **Alt-F8** keys.

   The Styles menu appears.

3. Type **3** to Create a Style.

   The Styles Edit screen appears.

4. Type **1** to move the cursor to the Name area.

Formatting Text for Printing 99

5. Type **DOCID**

6. Press **<ENTER>** to enter the Style name.

7. Type **3** to move the cursor to the Description area.

8. Type the following Style Description:

   Document Identification Line.

9. Press **<ENTER>**

   You have entered the Style Description. The Style Description may be up to 54 characters long.

10. Type **4** to choose the Codes option.

    The Reveal Codes screen will appear. This screen includes a comment box. The cursor will be above the comment box.

11. Press the **<CAPS LOCK>** key.

    While nothing appears on your screen (except "Pos" in the status line has changed to uppercase), you have entered the code to turn on the <CAPS LOCK> feature.

12. Type the following:

    (YOUR NAME), UNIT 5, DOCID

    Your name, the word "unit", and the document name DOCID have been entered in uppercase both above the comment box and below the Tab Ruler.

13. Press **Alt-F6** to enter the Flush Right code.

14. Press **Shift-F5** to access the Date/Outline menu.

15. Type **2** to enter the Date Code.

    The current date (the date you entered when loading WordPerfect) will appear on the screen Flush Right. When you use this Style again, the current date will be displayed.

16. Press the **<CAPS LOCK>** key to turn off the <CAPS LOCK> feature.

17. Press **F7** to Save the Style with **WORDWRAP**.

18. Type **0** (zero) to return to the Styles menu.

19. Type **6** to Save.

    The prompt "Filename:" will appear on your screen.

20. Type **STYLELIB**

21. Press **<ENTER>**

    The Style has been saved in a separate file named **STYLELIB**.

22. Type **0** (zero) to return to your document.

23. Save **WORDWRAP** (replace previous version).

    ✔**CHECKPOINT**

    o. Identify the keystrokes which access the Styles menu.

GUIDED ACTIVITY: USING A STYLE

Retrieve **WORDWRAP** and move the cursor below the end of the text.

1. Press the **Alt-F8** key to access the Styles menu. The **DOCID** Style is highlighted.

2. Type **1** to turn the Style On.

    The Document Identification Line is inserted in the document.

3. Print the page.

4. Save the document. Name it **DOCID**.

Hint: To Edit a Style press **Alt-F8**, **4** to Edit, then **4** for Codes. Make the desired changes, then press **F7** to Exit, **0** (zero) to return to the Styles menu, then **6** to Save. Enter a new filename, press **<ENTER>**, then **0** (zero) to return to your document. The Style will reflect your changes. You could use this method to edit DOCID for various documents.

GUIDED ACTIVITY: USING STYLELIB

1. Display a clear screen.

2. Press the **Alt-F8** key to access the Styles menu.

3. Type **7** to Retrieve.

   The prompt "Filename:" will appear on your screen.

4. Type **STYLELIB** then press **<ENTER>**

   The Styles menu is displayed with **DOCID** highlighted.

5. Type **1** to Retrieve the highlighted Style. The Document Identification Line is shown on your screen and inserted in you document.

6. Save this document with the name **SAMPLE**.

What You Have Accomplished

In this section you created and used a Style. You saved the Style **DOCID** with a document and in a Styles library. You used the Style you created to add the Document Identification Line to a document.

REVIEW QUESTIONS

1. Which keys access the Style menu?

   _____

2. Describe how to edit a Style.

   _____

3. How would you save a Style in a Style library?

   _____

4. Describe the procedure for activating a Style within a document.

   _____

5. Describe how you will use **STYLELIB** to add the Document Identification Line to documents you create in the future.

   _____

DOCUMENTATION RESEARCH

1. How could the Styles feature be used to format a book?

   _____

2. How can you use the Block feature to create a Style?

   _____

3. Describe the procedure for using a Style in existing text.

   _____

REVIEW EXERCISES

1. Create a Style to set margins to Left = 2.0" Right = 2.0".

2. Name this Style **MARGINS** Save **MARGINS**.

3. Retrieve **EXERCISE.DOC**

4. Move the cursor to the top of the third page.

5. Use the Style **MARGINS** to reset the margins on the third page. Notice that the text on the third page has been rewritten to fit the new margin setting.

6. Save **EXERCISE.DOC** and Exit WordPerfect 5.0.

UNIT 6
CONTROLLING THE PRINTER

SUPPLIES NEEDED

1. WordPerfect 5.0 program disks 1 and 2
2. WordPerfect 5.0 Student Data disk
3. printer

OBJECTIVES

After completing this unit, you will be able to

1. print multiple copies of a document;
2. print a block of text;
3. use the Printer Control menu to stop, resume, and cancel print jobs;
4. print a document stored on a data disk;
5. use the View Document feature to view the format of a document before printing.

IMPORTANT KEYSTROKES

Shift-F7   to use the Print menu

ASSIGNMENTS

1. Print **WORDPERF.TXT**
2. Print **OLSON.LTR**
3. Print **WORDWRAP**
4. Cancel a print job
5. View **HUMAN.REL**
6. Review Questions
7. Documentation Research
8. Review Exercises

PRINTING

In Unit 5 you made some decisions about how you wanted the text of your document arranged on the printed page. You learned that some formatting decisions relate to the type of printer you use. In Unit 6 you will discover how to control the printer so that it prints your documents the way you want.

Units 5 and 6 should be used in close association with one another. Learning more about your printer will help you to use the formatting options that WordPerfect 5.0 provides. Learning more about formatting options will help you to make full use of your printer's capabilities.

Printing can be the most frustrating part of learning to use a word-processing program. Keep in mind, though, that the troubles you encounter usually have simple solutions. The most common printing problems are the result of incorrect commands sent from the computer to the printer. Therefore it is important that you think through each command that you embed in the document you are creating or editing.

Sometimes printing problems are the result of a damaged disk; this is why you should always have backup copies of both program disks and data storage disks.

Occasionally a printing problem is caused by the printer itself. Check the obvious. Is the printer plugged in and set up properly? Is it supplied with paper?

THE PRINT MENU

When you press the **Shift-F7** keys, the Print menu (figure 6-1) appears on your screen. The Print menu allows you to control the actions of your printer. You can print one or more than one copy, or select the printer you want to perform your printing tasks. You can also queue print jobs to print in an assigned order while you edit another document.

You may select a print option by typing one of the listed numbers.

```
    Print

        1 - Full Document
        2 - Page
        3 - Document on Disk
        4 - Control Printer
        5 - Type Through
        6 - View Document
        7 - Initialize Printer

    Options

        S - Select Printer          HP LaserJet Series II
        B - Binding                 0"
        N - Number of Copies        1
        G - Graphics Quality        Medium
        T - Text Quality            High




        Selection: 0
```

FIGURE 6-1   Print Menu

The Print menu options are defined as follows:

1 Document   A "Please wait" prompt appears in place of the Print menu and the entire document, that is, all pages, are printed.

2 Page   A "Please wait" prompt appears in place of the Print menu and the current page of text (the one shown in the status line) is printed.

3 Document on Disk   This option allows you to print a page or an entire file stored on disk.

4 Control Printer   The Control Printer Submenu (figure 6-2) appears on the screen. This submenu advises you of the current status of the printer and lists the jobs you have sent to it. You can select an option by typing one of the listed numbers or letters.

106   WordPerfect

```
Print: Control Printer

Current Job

Job Number:  None                        Page Number:  None
Status:      No print jobs               Current Copy: None
Message:     None
Paper:       None
Location:    None
Action:      None


Job List

Job  Document                Destination         Print Options




Additional Jobs Not Shown: 0




1 Cancel Job(s); 2 Rush Job; 3 Display Jobs; 4 Go (start printer); 5 Stop: 0
```

FIGURE 6-2   Printer Control Submenu

The Control Printer submenu options are defined as follows:

1 Cancel Job(s)	One or all print jobs can be canceled.
2 Rush Job	The priority of a document waiting on the Job List can be changed so that it is printed immediately.
3 Display Jobs	The complete Job queue, that is, all jobs waiting to be sent to the printer, is displayed.
4 Go (start printer)	If the printer has been stopped (option 5), this command will direct it to start printing again. Printing restarts at the beginning of a document.
5 Stop	The printer stops printing but print jobs are not canceled. This command is useful when the printer paper runs out or jams, or when a ribbon needs replacing. Select option 4 to restart the printer.

Controlling the Printer

5 Type Through — Option 5 on the Print menu allows you to use the printer like a typewriter. It can print either a character or a line at a time as they are being typed at the microcomputer keyboard.

6 View Document — This option on the Print menu allows you to view the format of an entire document before it is printed. Margins, headers, footers, footnotes, and page numbers are included. You can scroll through the document to view it at 100% (actual size) or 200% (twice actual size). You can also select Full Page to view an entire page or choose to see facing pages. You can not edit the document when you are in View Document.

7 Initialize Printer — This option is used to download soft fonts if they are available for your printer.

S Select Printer — This menu option allows you to define printers and select a printer for a document. The current printer selection is shown to the right of this option and is saved with the document.

B Binding — This option lets you allow for binding by selecting the amount of space to shift text to the right on odd-numbered pages and to the left on even-numbered pages.

N Number of Copies — This option allows you to choose how many copies of a page or entire document you want printed.

G Graphics Quality and T Text Quality — This option allows you to choose the print-quality level of a document. Generally, lower print qualities require less time to print.

GUIDED ACTIVITY: PRINTING TWO COPIES OF A SINGLE PAGE

1. Retrieve **WORDPERF.TXT**

2. Press the **Shift-F7** keys.

    The Print menu will appear on your screen.

3. Type N to move the cursor to the Number of Copies option.

4. Type **2**

    The printer will be commanded to print two copies of your document.

5. Press **<ENTER>**

108   WordPerfect

The cursor will return to its original location next to the word "Selection."

6. Make sure your printer is turned on and set up properly.

7. Type **2** to choose the Page option on the Print menu.

    A "Please wait" prompt will appear at the bottom of your screen. In a few seconds the printer will begin to print the page on which your cursor was resting. When one copy is finished, the printer will automatically feed the paper up to the top of the next page and print another copy.

8. Follow steps 2 and 3 to change the Number of Copies back to one.

What You Have Accomplished

You have learned that the Shift-F7 keys allow you to access the Print menu from which you can control the actions of your printer. You have also learned that the Print menu lets you designate the number of copies to be printed. You directed your printer to print two copies of a single page.

✔**CHECKPOINT**

a. Which keystrokes are needed to access the Print menu?

b. Describe how to command your printer to print two copies of a document.

c. What is the procedure for printing a single page of a document?

GUIDED ACTIVITY: PRINTING A BLOCK OF TEXT

1. Move the cursor to the beginning of the second paragraph in **WORDPERF.TXT**.

2. Press the **Alt-F4** keys.

    The Block function has been turned on.

3. Move the cursor to the bottom line of the second paragraph.

    The second paragraph is now highlighted.

4. Press the **Shift-F7** keys.

    The prompt "Print Block (Y/N) No" will appear at the bottom of your screen.

5. Type **Y**

   The highlighted text will be printed.

6. Press the **Alt-F4** keys to toggle off Block.

7. Display a clear screen or continue on to the next Guided Activity.

✔ CHECKPOINT

   d. Which keys are used to highlight a block of text for printing?

   ---

   e. What is the default value for the Number of Copies option on the Print menu?

GUIDED ACTIVITY: STOPPING AND RESTARTING A PRINT JOB

Display a clear screen.

1. Retrieve **OLSON.LTR**

2. Press the **Shift-F7** keys.

   The Print menu will appear on your screen.

3. Type **2**

   The page on which the cursor was resting will be printed. After a few lines have been printed, stop the print job.

4. Press the **Shift-F7** keys to display the Print menu.

5. Type **4** to display the Control Printer submenu.

6. Type **5**

   A warning message and the prompt "Are you sure? (Y?N) No" will appear at the bottom of your screen.

7. Type **Y**

   The printer will stop printing. Advance the printer paper to the top of the next page before continuing.

110 WordPerfect

8. Type **4** to choose the "Go (start printer)" option.

   The printer will resume printing from the beginning of the page on a new sheet of paper.

9. Press <ENTER> twice.

   Your document will reappear on the screen.

✔ CHECKPOINT

f. What keystrokes are needed to command the printer to stop printing a document?

---

g. How can you restart the printer after you have stopped it?

GUIDED ACTIVITY: PRINTING A DOCUMENT STORED ON A DATA DISK

Display a clear screen.

1. Press the **Shift-F7** keys to display the Print menu.

2. Type **3**

   The prompt "Document name:" appears at the bottom of your screen.

3. Type **WORDWRAP**

4. Press <ENTER>

   The prompt "Page(s): (All)" will appear on your screen.

5. Press <ENTER>

   You have accepted the default of "all" pages. All pages of the document will be printed. Since **WORDWRAP** is only one page long, the entire document will be printed.

6. Clear the screen.

Controlling the Printer   111

✔ CHECKPOINT

h. What keystrokes are required to print a document directly from its storage location on a data disk?

---

i. How does the Print menu allow you to print a partial document?

GUIDED ACTIVITY: CANCELING A PRINT JOB

1. Press the **Shift-F7** keys to access the Print menu.

2. Type **3** to select the Document on Disk option.

   The prompt "Document name:" will appear.

3. Type **HUMAN.REL**

4. Press **<ENTER>**

   The prompt "Page(s): (All)" will appear.

5. Press **<ENTER>**

   You have accepted the "all" default. All pages of the document will be printed.

6. Press **<ENTER>**

   HUMAN.REL has been placed in the Job List and will be printed.

   After a few lines have printed, cancel the print job.

7. Type **4** to access the Control Printer submenu.

8. Type **1**

   The prompt "Cancel all print jobs? (Y/N) No" will appear on the Control Printer submenu screen.

9. Type **Y**

   All print jobs listed will be canceled.

   The print jobs have been erased from the job list. Print instructions have also been cancelled and must be reentered in order to print the document.

Therefore, typing "G" after commanding the printer to Cancel will not restart your printer.

What You Have Accomplished

You have used the Print menu to print a file directly from your data disk. You have learned that you can direct your printer to start and stop printing on any page. You have also learned how to stop, restart, and cancel a print job.

✔CHECKPOINT

j. How do you cancel a print job?

Hint: Stop printing when you need to fix a problem with the printer itself (e.g., to change the ribbon or realign the paper).

Cancel printing when a document is not being printed in the format you expect. It will probably be necessary to start over with new printing instructions. When you cancel a print job, it is best to turn off the power on your printer and then turn it on again. The printer's memory needs to be cleared so that signals will not be distorted when new commands are given. Remember to set the printer to top-of-form before turning it back on again.

VIEW DOCUMENT FEATURE

As you know, many formatting features do not show on the monitor. The View Document feature allows you to view the format of a document before you print it. The formatting features such as margins, headers, footers, footnotes, endnotes, subscripts, superscripts, page numbers, graphics, and right justification are shown in as close to the printed version as possible. You can scroll through the document with the cursor movement keys but you cannot edit the document until you Exit the View Document screen.

You can use the View Document feature to see an entire page (default) to get an overview of the page layout. You can enlarge the page to actual size by choosing 100% from the View Document submenu, or you can enlarge the page to twice actual size by choosing 200% from the submenu.

You can also choose to see facing pages of a multiple page document by choosing Facing Page from the View Document submenu. WordPerfect will show the odd-numbered page on the right and the preceding even-numbered page on the left. Use the Exit (F7) key to Exit the View Document screen and return to the document.

GUIDED ACTIVITY: VIEWING A DOCUMENT

Retrieve **HUMAN.REL**

1. Move the cursor to the second page of the document.

2. Press **Shift-F7**

    The Print menu appears on the screen.

3. Type **6** to select View Document.

    The prompt "Please wait" will appear. In a few seconds the current full page will appear on your screen.

4. Type **1**

    A portion of the current page is shown at actual size (100%). Notice that also displayed are the headings that you added to the document in Unit 5.

5. Type **2**

    A portion of the current page is shown at twice its actual size (200%).

6. Type **4**

    Facing pages are shown. The even-numbered page is to the left and the odd-numbered page is to the right. If you choose option 4 (Facing Pages) when the current page is page 1, only page 1 will appear on the screen.

7. Press **F7** to Exit View Document.

8. Exit WordPerfect 5.0

REVIEW QUESTIONS

1. What happens to a print job after you have issued the Cancel command?

2. How does the printer respond when you choose Page option (2) on the Print menu?

3. Suppose that you need six copies of a document for a meeting. How do you use the Print menu to obtain these copies?

4. It is possible to control the printer to print only one paragraph on a page. Explain how this can be done.

5. Which keystrokes are needed to access the Print menu?

6. How can you terminate a print job after printing has begun?

7. The Control Printer submenu contains a Job List. Explain what a Job List is.

8. Explain the difference between the Stop command and the Cancel command on the Control Printer submenu.

9. What keystrokes are needed to View a document?

DOCUMENTATION RESEARCH

1. Describe the procedure for printing only a few pages of a long document directly from your data disk.

2. What does the printer do with a currently printing document when a Rush Print Job command is given?

3. You have sent six print jobs to the printer. How can you see a list of all of these jobs?

4. Information about the status of the current print job is displayed on the Control Printer submenu. Examine this menu to find out what information is contained under the Current Job heading.

REVIEW EXERCISES

1. Retrieve **EXERCISE.DOC**

2. Print two copies of the second page of your document.

3. View your document. Notice that you can see the headings and the page numbers.
4. Block and print one paragraph from the first page of the document.

5. Enter the commands to print the full document, then access the Control Printer submenu. Stop printing. Resume printing. Cancel the print job.

6. Exit WordPerfect 5.0.

APPLICATION B

SUPPLIES NEEDED

1. WordPerfect program disks 1 and 2
2. WordPerfect Learning disk
3. WordPerfect Student Data disk
4. printer

ASSIGNMENTS

The assignments to be completed for this Application section are

1. Create **INVITE.TXT**
2. Create **TABS**
3. Create **INTER.LET**
4. Create **SUM.TXT**

APPLICATIONS

This Application section contains a number of documents that can be reproduced to apply the skills you have acquired in Units 4 and 5. Format your documents so that they look like the ones on the printed pages of this section. Remember that right justification and other formatting features do not appear on the screen, they appear when a document is printed.

118 WordPerfect 5.0

Use your template and the Quick Reference card to find the keystroke commands and menus you need. Remember that there is often more than one keystroke choice that can be used to create and format a document. Your primary task is to find the most efficient way to reproduce the documents.

You may also want to create your own applications - some tasks that are more meaningful to your everyday work. Your WordPerfect Student Data disk should have plenty of space available to store additional documents.

Follow the directions below to create the documents in Application B.

Document B-1

1. Name this document **INVITE.TXT**
2. Center, boldface, and underline the lines as shown.
3. Center the text vertically on the page.
4. Double space the text.
5. Add the Document Identification Line at the bottom of the document.
6. Save and Print the document.

Document B-2

1. Name this document **TABS**
2. Create a Style to set a tab stop at Pos 1.75".
3. Save the Style in your Style library, **STYLELIB.**

Document B-3

1. Name this document **INTER.LET**
2. The letter is from your instructor to you.
3. Create a heading that contains your name, the page number and the date for the second page of the letter. This header should be followed by two blank lines.
4. Use the Style **TABS** created in Document B-2 to set a tab stop at Pos 1.75".
5. Indent the numbered items to Pos 1.75".
6. Use the Style **DOCID** to add the Document Identification Line at the bottom of the document.
7. Save and Print your document.

Document B-4

1. Name this document **SUM.TXT**
2. Create the Document B-4 text.
3. Add the Document Identification Line at the bottom of the document.
4. Save and Print **SUM.TXT**

You are cordially invited

TO A SURPRISE BIRTHDAY PARTY

for

<u>**JAYNEE HODGES**</u>

Friday, August 28, 1990

Beginning at 8 p.m.

3327 Croft Avenue, St. Paul

Gag gifts only for **Jaynee's** <u>**40th**</u> birthday.

<u>**RSVP**</u> Marney Upjohn, 798-7675

Document B-1 **INVITE.TXT**

(your name)
(your street address)
(your city, state, and ZIP code)
(current date)

Dear (your first name):

Now that you have gained skills for employment, your next task is to get that first job.

Landing a job is not easy, but with proper preparation, you can present the best _you_ for the job. The first step is to prepare a resume that will show a prospective employer that you are ideally suited to perform the job. Information regarding preparation of the resume is available in textbooks found in the library.

After you have completed your resume, remember its purpose: to get you in the door. Your performance during the interview will determine whether or not you are offered the job.

A job interview is a process designed to achieve particular objectives, not only for the employer but also for you.

Following are some ways you can prepare yourself for the interview:

1. Find out everything you can about the company - what it does, how long it has been in existence, where it is located, name of president, vice president, etc. -Start with the library.

2. Get a small notebook and pen to use during the interview. Have ready a list of questions to ask the interviewer.

3. Take extra copies of your resume with you to use in completing the application form or to leave with other prople in other departments of the company.

4. Select an "interview" suit in a basic color - navy, grey, taupe. Choose accessories carefully, maintaining a professional image.

5. Select a professional haircut and use makeup carefully. Be fresh and clean from head to toe to fingertip.

(your name)
Page 2
(current date)

6. Be prepared to explain your background - educationally and professionally.

7. Be prepared for some of the questions routinely asked in interviews:

   What are your career goals - long term? short term?

   What are you doing to achieve these goals?

   Other examples of potential questions may be found in interviewing technique books in the library.

8. Anticipate the opportunity to question the interviewer. Following are some of the questions you might ask.

   Could you explain in more detail what my actual responsibilities and duties would be?

   How would my performance be evaluated?

   How would I be supervised?

   What are my opportunities for advancement with your firm?

   Is there a probationary period?

   Save questions regarding salary, vacations, sick leave, etc., until another time.

Learning good interviewing habits now will benefit you for the rest of your life. As opportunities arise, you will be able to take advantage of them by selling yourself and your abilities.

Good luck to you.

Sincerely yours,

(your instructor's name)

Document B-3   **INTER.LET**

The summation of several numbers could be indicated by the formula:

$A_1 + A_2 + A_3 \ldots A_n$

Two squared equals four.

$2^2 = 4$

The chemical formula for sulfric acid is

H_2SO_4

The temperature today is -2° Fahrenheit.

Document B-4 SUM.TXT

PART 2
INTERMEDIATE EDITING FEATURES

Part 2 teaches you to modify and enhance documents. You learn to locate and replace text, create footnotes and endnotes, and use the window feature to divide the screen and edit two documents at once.

Part 2 also teaches you to manage files (documents): to delete, rename, and search files, or block a part of a file for storage in a separate file.

After completing Part 2, you will be able to use WordPerfect 5.0 to create and edit both single and multi-page documents. Application C follows Unit 9. Each application section includes exercises to practice the skills you acquired in previous units.

UNIT 7
DISCOVERING MORE WORDPERFECT FUNCTIONS

SUPPLIES NEEDED

1. WordPerfect program disks 1 and 2
2. WordPerfect Student Data disk
3. printer

OBJECTIVES

After completing this unit, you will be able to

1. insert the current date anywhere in a document;
2. indent a paragraph from either margin;
3. use the <ESC> (Escape) key to repeat a character;
4. use the Search feature to find specific words;
5. use the Replace feature to find and replace specific words;
6. use the Footnote/Endnote feature to format footnotes;
7. use the Window feature to divide the screen and edit two documents at once.

IMPORTANT KEYSTROKES

1. Shift-F5   to insert the current date
2. F4   to indent text from the left margin
3. Shift-F4   to indent text from both the left and right margins
4. <ESC> key   to repeat a character or feature a specified number of times
5. F2   to search for text
6. Alt-F2   to replace text with other text
7. Ctrl-F7   to format footnotes or endnotes
8. Ctrl-F3   to display the Tab Ruler
9. Ctrl-F3   to divide the screen
10. Ctrl-F9   to sort a list

ASSIGNMENTS

1. Create **GLENN.TXT**
2. Edit **GLENN.TXT**
3. Edit **WORDPERF.TXT**
4. Edit **OLSON.LTR**
5. Edit **HUMAN.REL**
6. Review Questions
7. Documentation Research
6. Review Exercises

THE DATE AND TIME FEATURE

WordPerfect provides a Date and Time feature that automatically inserts the current date and/or time. When you activate the Date and Time feature, a Date menu appears on your screen. From this menu, you can choose the location and format of the date and time. Option 3 allows you to embed a function code that automatically updates your document each time it is retrieved or printed.

If you fail to enter the date and time when you load the program, January 1, 1980, and the time transpired since boot-up, are inserted into the text.

The Date Menu

When you press **Shift-F5**, the Date menu (figure 7-1) appears. You can select an option by typing one of the listed numbers.

---

1 Date Text; 2 Date Code; 3 Date Format; 4 Outline; 5 Para Num; 6 Define: 0

FIGURE 7-1   Date Menu

Discovering More WordPerfect Functions   127

The first three options on this menu are defined as follows:

- 1 Date Text   The date you entered when you loaded WordPerfect is inserted wherever the cursor is positioned. This date will remain the same even when the document is Retrieved at a later date.

- 2 Date Code   A code is inserted to automatically to change to and display the current date each time you retrieve or print the document.

- 3 Date Format   A Format submenu (figure 7-2) appears. This submenu displays the various formats that you can select and combine into a pattern for displaying the date and/or time. When you do not make a choice, the program chooses the default pattern, which is the name of the month, the date, and the year; for example, "December 31, 1986".

```
Date Format

     Character     Meaning
         1         Day of the Month
         2         Month (number)
         3         Month (word)
         4         Year (all four digits)
         5         Year (last two digits)
         6         Day of the Week (word)
         7         Hour (24-hour clock)
         8         Hour (12-hour clock)
         9         Minute
         0         am / pm
         %         Used before a number, will:
                       Pad numbers less than 10 with a leading zero
                       Output only 3 letters for the month or day of the week

     Examples:  3 1, 4         = December 25, 1984
                %6 %3 1, 4     = Tue Dec 25, 1984
                %2/%1/5 (6)    = 01/01/85 (Tuesday)
                8:90           = 10:55am

Date format: 3 1, 4
```

FIGURE 7-2   Format Submenu

GUIDED ACTIVITY: INSERTING THE DATE AUTOMATICALLY

1. Display a clear screen.

2. Press <ENTER> five times.

   Several blank lines have been inserted at the top of the page.

3. Press the **Alt-F6** keys.

    The cursor will align itself along the edge of the right margin.

4. Press the **Shift-F5** keys.

    The Date menu will appear on the screen.

5. Type **2**

    The current date, entered flush against the right margin, is now on your screen.

    You have inserted a code in the document you will create. Now each time you retrieve this document, the current date (the one you enter when loading WordPerfect) will be displayed on the screen flush right.

    Name this document "**GLENN.TXT**" when you save it.

What You Have Accomplished

You have embedded a code into **GLENN.TXT** that displays and prints the current date each time this document is retrieved. You have commanded the computer to place the date flush right. It will be displayed in the default format. This is a convenient way to handle form letters, because the date that is now on your screen will automatically be updated every time you retrieve or print this document.

✔CHECKPOINT

a. Which keys access the Date menu?

    _____

b. What is the default pattern for displaying the current date?

    _____

INDENTING

As you create and edit your documents, you may want to set off a block of text by indenting it. A paragraph can be indented from the left margin only or double indented from both the left and right margins. In addition, a **hanging paragraph** can be created by starting the first line of the paragraph at the left margin and then indenting all of the remaining lines.

The Indent key (F4) lets you indent automatically without having to press the <TAB> key at the beginning of each line. The Shift-F4 (Double Indent) keys let you indent from both margins automatically. By pressing **Shift-<TAB>** after turning on the Indent, you can create a hanging paragraph. Pressing **<ENTER>** terminates the Indent feature.

GUIDED ACTIVITY: TYPING A PARAGRAPH

1. Retrieve **GLENN.TXT** if necessary.

2. Press **<ENTER>** twice.

3. Type the paragraph in figure 7-3.

4. Save **GLENN.TXT**

People are afraid of the future, of the unknown. If a man faces up to it, and takes the dare of the future, he can have some control over his destiny. That's an exciting idea to me, better than waiting with everybody else to see what's going to happen.
　　　　　　　　　　　　　　　　　　　　　John H. Glenn, Jr.

FIGURE 7-3 **GLENN.TXT**

GUIDED ACTIVITY: INDENTING TEXT FROM THE LEFT MARGIN

1. Press **<ENTER>** three times.

2. Press the **F4** key.

   The Indent feature has been turned on.

3. Type the paragraph in figure 7-3 again.

4. Press **<ENTER>**

   The Indent feature has been turned off.

   ✔**CHECKPOINT**

   c. Which key controls the Indent feature?

GUIDED ACTIVITY: INDENTING TEXT FROM THE RIGHT AND LEFT MARGINS

1. Press **<ENTER>** twice.

2. Press the **Shift-F4** keys twice.

   Double Indent has been turned on, and your cursor has moved to the second tab stop.

3. Type the paragraph in figure 7-3 again.

4. Press **<ENTER>**

   Double Indent has been turned off.

   ✔**CHECKPOINT**

   d. How is the text on the screen formatted when the **Shift-F4** keys are pressed?

GUIDED ACTIVITY: CREATING A HANGING PARAGRAPH

1. Press **<ENTER>** twice.

2. Press **F4**

   Indent has been turned on.

3. Press **Shift-<TAB>** to move the first line of text one tab stop to the left.

4. Type the paragraph in figure 7-3 again.

   The first line of the paragraph will be flush against the left margin. The remaining lines will be indented from the left margin.

5. Press **<ENTER>** five times.

   Indent has been turned off, and several blank lines have been inserted at the bottom of the document.

   ✔**CHECKPOINT**

   e. What two keystrokes are required to create a hanging paragraph?

What You Have Accomplished

You have learned how to indent a paragraph from the left margin and how to double indent a paragraph. You have also learned the procedure for creating a "hanging" paragraph. Indented paragraphs are used for long quotes or to emphasize particular elements within a long document. The choice of one of the three styles is a matter of personal preference.

REPEATING A CHARACTER OR FEATURE

Sometimes it is necessary to repeat a character several times when typing a document. By using the <ESC> (Escape) key, you can command the computer to repeat a specific alphabetic character, numeric character, or punctuation mark a specified number of times. The following list includes the features that can be repeated by using the <ESC> key. The default number for the Repeat feature is eight. Therefore, unless you command the computer to do otherwise, a character or feature will automatically be repeated eight times.

Features That May Be Repeated:

1. Arrow keys   The cursor moves a specified number of lines.

2. Delete word   A specified number of consecutive words are deleted.

3. Delete character   A specified number of characters are deleted.

4. Macro   A macro is repeated a specified number of times. Macros will be discussed in Unit 11.

5. Page Up/Down   The cursor scrolls up or down a specified number of pages.

6. Screen Up/Down   The cursor scrolls up or down a specified number of screens.

7. Word Left/Right   The cursor moves a specified number of words either to the right or to the left.

GUIDED ACTIVITY: USING THE REPEAT FEATURE

1. Move the cursor to Ln 1", Pos 1", of **GLENN.TXT**.

2. Press the **<ESC>** key.

    The Repeat feature has been turned on. The prompt "Repeat Value = 8" will appear in the status line.

3. Type **65**

The feature or character you type next will be repeated sixty-five times.

4. Type * (asterisk).

Sixty-five asterisks will appear on Ln 1" of your document.

5. Press <ESC> to turn on Repeat again.

The prompt "Repeat Value = 8" will appear.

6. Type **50**

The next feature or character you type will be repeated fifty times.

7. Press the **<Down> arrow** key.

The cursor will move four lines past the last typed line of your document. It will not move down fifty lines because fifty lines have not been keyed in.

8. Press **Shift-F6** to Center.

9. Press **<ESC>** to Repeat.

10. Type **30** after the prompt.

11. Type * (asterisk).

Thirty asterisks will be centered on the last line of the document.

12. Add the Document Identification Line to **GLENN.TXT**. Save and Print **GLENN.TXT**. Your printed document will look like that in figure 7-4.

✔ CHECKPOINT

f. Which key do you press to activate Repeat?

___

g. Identify the keystrokes required to repeat a character.

___

What You Have Accomplished

You have used WordPerfect's Repeat feature to add asterisks across the top and bottom of your document **GLENN.TXT**. You have also learned that the cursor will not move beyond the end of a document (the area you have typed in).

SEARCH AND REPLACE

Someday, after spending many hours creating a document, you may discover that you have repeatedly misspelled a word. Or you may decide that another word would better communicate your meaning. Maybe you would like to examine the document to verify that you did use a particular word correctly or that you did not neglect to mention someone's name. Instead of reading the document word by word, you can use WordPerfect's Search and Replace features to find and replace words automatically.

Search

You can search for both text and codes from any location within your document. A forward search will find any word or code you specify from the cursor forward through your document. A reverse search will find any word or code you specify from the cursor backward through your document. It is important to type the exact string of characters for which you are searching.

When you press **F2**, you will see the prompt "Srch:". Type the exact string of characters you want to find, then press **F2** again. A forward search will begin. The cursor stops as soon as it finds the character string that you are seeking and waits for your decision. Each time you press **F2**, WordPerfect continues its search.

If you would rather search backward, press the **Shift-F2** keys for the same response in the reverse direction.

Replace

A word can be replaced automatically if you use the Search key in combination with the Replace key. You can either replace words automatically or approve each replacement individually. The Alt-F2 keys turn on the Replace feature. Type "Y" for automatic replacement or "N" for individual replacement. Press the **<Up>** arrow key to Search and Replace backwards from the cursor. Press the **<Down>** arrow key to Search and Replace forward from the cursor. Then type the exact string of characters or code that you wish to replace and press **F2**. You will see the prompt "Replace with:". Type the new string of characters or codes, press **F2**, and begin searching and replacing.

Using both the Search and Replace features simultaneously to automatically replace words is referred to as a Global Search and Replace.

Hint: To find and replace whole words rather than character strings that may be a part of another word (e.g., "his" in "history"), enter spaces before and after the word to be replaced.

****

(today's date)

People are afraid of the future, of the unknown. If a man faces up to it, and takes the dare of the future, he can have some control over his destiny. That's an exciting idea to me, better than waiting with everybody else to see what's going to happen. John H. Glenn, Jr.

> People are afraid of the future, of the unknown. If a man faces up to it, and takes the dare of the future, he can have some control over his destiny. That's an exciting idea to me, better than waiting with everybody else to see what's going to happen. John H. Glenn, Jr.

>> People are afraid of the future, of the unknown. If a man faces up to it, and takes the dare of the future, he can have some control over his destiny. That's an exciting idea to me, better than waiting with everybody else to see what's going to happen. John H. Glenn, Jr.

People are afraid of the future, of the unknown. If a man faces up to it, and takes the dare of the future, he can have some control over his destiny. That's an exciting idea to me, better than waiting with everybody else to see what's going to happen. John H. Glenn, Jr.

****

FIGURE 7-4 **GLENN.TXT** (Revised)

GUIDED ACTIVITY: SEARCHING UP AND DOWN

1. Retrieve the file **WORDPERF.TXT** from your WordPerfect Student Data disk.

2. Move the cursor to the first letter of the first word in **WORDPERF.TXT** to begin a forward search.

3. Press the **F2** key.

    The prompt "Srch:" will appear in the status line.

4. Type **WP** (Do **not** press <ENTER>).

    You have identified a character string for WordPerfect to find.

5. Press the **F2** key.

    The Search has begun. The cursor will stop at the first occurrence of "WP".

6. Press the **F2** key to continue the search.

    "Srch: WP" will appear on the screen.

7. Press the **F2** key again. The cursor will stop at the next occurrence of "WP".

8. Continue searching for "WP" by pressing the **F2** key.

    When the Search has been completed, a "Not found" message will appear briefly in the status line.

9. Move the cursor to the last letter of the last word in your document to begin a reverse search.

10. Press the **Shift-F2** keys.

    The prompt "Srch:" will appear in the status line.

11. Type **PC** over "WP".

    You have identified a character string for WordPerfect to find.

12. Press the **Shift-F2** keys.

    The search has begun. The cursor will stop at the first occurrence of "PC".

13. Press the **Shift-F2** keys to continue the Search.

    When the Search has been completed, a "Not found" message will appear briefly in the status line.

136 WordPerfect 5.0

✔ CHECKPOINT

h. Which keystroke is needed to search for a character string from the beginning to the end of a document?

---

i. How will you know if the character string you are searching for does not occur in the part of the document that has been searched?

---

j. Which keystrokes are needed to search in reverse?

Hint: You can cancel the Search anytime by pressing the Cancel key (**F1**).

GUIDED ACTIVITY: AUTOMATIC SEARCH AND REPLACE

Retrieve **WORDPERF.TXT** if necessary.

1. Move the cursor to the first letter of the title of **WORDPERF.TXT**

2. Press the **Alt-F2** keys.

   The prompt "w/Confirm? (Y/N) No" will appear in the status line. If you type "Y", the cursor will stop at each occurrence of the designated character string and let you confirm its replacement. If you type "N" (the default), all designated character strings will automatically be replaced.

3. Type N or press **<ENTER>**

   You have commanded the program to replace the designated character string automatically. The prompt "Srch:" will appear in the status line.

4. Press the **<Down> arrow** key to indicate a forward Search.

5. Type **WP**

   You have identified a character string for which WordPerfect will search.

6. Press the **F2** key.

   The prompt "Replace with:" will appear in the status line.

7. Type **WordPerfect**

   You have identified a character string that will replace the character string "WP".

8. Press the **F2** key.

   Search and Replace has begun. "WP" will automatically be replaced with "WordPerfect".

9. Save and Print **WORDPERF.TXT.**

   The printed document will look like that in figure 7-5.

✔ CHECKPOINT

   k. What keystrokes are required to automatically replace a character string?

FOOTNOTES AND ENDNOTES

Footnotes and endnotes are notes of reference, explanation or comment placed outside regular text on a printed page. Footnotes are placed at the bottom of a referenced page. Endnotes are compiled and placed at the end of a document.

WordPerfect 5.0 automatically numbers footnotes and endnotes and arranges them on a printed page. The text of a footnote or endnote can be edited just like normal text. The Endnote Placement option on the Footnote/Endnote menu lets you change the placement of the footnote.

The Footnote/Endnote Menu

When you press **Ctrl-F7**, the Footnote/Endnote menu (figure 7-6) appears. You can select an option by typing one of the listed numbers.

WordPerfect CORPORATION

Business Acquisition.

In business, the smart money is spent in areas that improve the bottom line. Areas like productivity and efficiency. That's why a lot of companies today are investing their money in WordPerfect 5.0 for powerful business word processing.

Substantial dividends.

With unsurpassed business features for the IBM PC and compatibles, WordPerfect 5.0 pays for itself again and again with professional documents turned out in record time. Features include an elegant thesaurus, 115,000-word spelling dictionary, columns displayed side-by-side on screen, math capabilities, split screen, and line drawing.

In addition, WordPerfect Corporation offers an excellent site licensing program so major customers can receive the software and support they need for a pre-determined, discounted fee.

The top seller.

With so much to offer, WordPerfect 5.0 has now become the best-selling word processor for the IBM PC, according to market research firm Info-Corp. And customers like Merrill Lynch, Upjohn and General Dynamics are leading the way.

Maximize your investment.

Get the word processor designed to improve your company's bottom line. WordPerfect 5.0. It's the perfect corporate investment. For more information, call or write WordPerfect Corp., 288 West Center St., Orem, Utah 84057, (801) 227-4000.

FIGURE 7-5　　WORDPERF.TXT

```
1 Footnote;  2 Endnote;  3 Endnote Placement:  0
```

FIGURE 7-6   Footnote/Endnote Menu

The options on this menu are defined as follows:

    1 Footnote   Select this option to create a footnote. The Footnote submenu (figure 7-7) appears on your screen.

```
Footnote:  1 Create;  2 Edit;  3 New Number;  4 Options:  0
```

FIGURE 7-7   Footnote Submenu

The options on this submenu are defined as follows:

        1 Create   A blank screen appears along with the number of the current footnote. The status line on this screen displays the current position and line number of the cursor.

        2 Edit   Select this option to edit a footnote. The prompt "Footnote number?" appears on your screen. Type the number of the footnote you wish to edit.

        3 New Number   The prompt "Footnote number?" appears on your screen. Use this option when you want footnote numbering to start at a particular number. For example, you might want to start footnote numbering over again at the beginning of each chapter in a book.

    2 Endnote   Select this option from the Footnote/Endnote menu to create an endnote. The Endnote submenu (figure 7-8) appears on the screen.

```
Endnote:  1. Create;  2 Edit;  3 New Number;  4 Options:  0
```

FIGURE 7-8   Endnote Submenu

The first three options on this submenu have the same definitions as on the Footnote submenu. The Options selection on this submenu allows you to change the formatting of the endnote.

3 Endnote Placement   When the third option on the Footnote/Endnote menu is chosen, an Endnote Placement code is placed in your document. The message "Endnote Placement. It is not known how much space endnotes will occupy here. Generate to determine." Press the **Alt-F5** keys, then select Generate so that WordPerfect can determine the space needed for the Endnotes you have created. The endnotes will be printed at the Endnote Placement code.

GUIDED ACTIVITY: CREATING FOOTNOTES

1. Retrieve **HUMAN.REL** from your WordPerfect Student Data disk.

2. Move the cursor to the second page of the document, under the heading "Human Relations Competencies" and after the words "individual benefits" at the end of the first paragraph.

3. Press the **Ctrl-F7** keys.

   The Footnote/Endnote menu appears on your screen.

4. Type **1**

   The Footnote submenu appears.

5. Type **1** to choose the Create option.

   A blank screen will appear. The status line on this screen will display the current Pos and Ln number of the cursor.

6. Type the following text:

   Ralph Johnson, <u>Personnel Management for Today</u>, Smith and Westin, New Haven, 1983, pp. 7-8.

   Your first footnote has been created. WordPerfect will save enough lines at the bottom of the page of text so that the footnote can be printed.

7. Press the **F7** key.

   HUMAN.REL will reappear on your screen.

8. Move the cursor to the end of the next paragraph. The paragraph ends with the words "work together."

9. Press the **Ctrl-F7** keys.

10. Type **1** to access the Footnote submenu.

11. Type **1** to create a second footnote.

12. Type the following text on the editing screen:

    Ibid, p. 17.

13. Press the **F7** key.

    HUMAN.REL will reappear on your screen.

14. Move the cursor to the third page of the document and to the end of the second paragraph under the heading "Handling Frustrations." This sentence ends with the words "inner aggressions."

15. Press the **Ctrl-F7** keys.

16. Type **1** to access the Footnote submenu.

17. Type **1** to create a third footnote.

18. Type the following text on the editing screen:

    Ibid, p. 22-23.

19. Press the **F7** key.

    HUMAN.REL will reappear on your screen.

20. Move the cursor to the fourth page of the document and to the end of the second sentence of the first paragraph under the heading "Renewing Your Attitude". This sentence ends with the words "improve your attitude."

21. Press the **Ctrl-F7** keys.

22. Type **1** to access the Footnote submenu.

23. Type **1** to create a fourth footnote.

24. Type the following text on the editing screen.

    Marilyn Jones, <u>Positive Attitudes</u>, Macintosh and Macintosh, New York, 1980, p. 52.

25. Press the **F7** key to return to the document.

26. Save and Print **HUMAN.REL**

27. Exit WordPerfect 5.0.

THE TAB RULER

The Tab Ruler displays the tab and margin settings that are being used in the document you are currently editing. Each triangle in the Tab Ruler indicates a tab setting. Each bracket indicates a margin setting. A brace is used to indicate that a tab and margin setting are in the same position. If the document you are editing contains a number of different tab or margin settings, the Tab Ruler changes to reflect the settings at the cursor location.

A Tab Ruler is usually used to split a screen into two windows so that you can edit two documents at the same time. However, you may also display the Tab Ruler to edit a single document.

The <Up> and <Down> cursor movement keys are used to adjust the position of the Tab Ruler. <ENTER> is used to anchor the Tab Ruler in place.

When you press the **Ctrl-F3** keys, the Screen menu (figure 7-9) appears. Select option 1 to access the Tab Ruler or to split the screen into two windows.

---

0 Rewrite; 1 Window; 2 Line Draw: 0

FIGURE 7-9 Screen Menu

The Window option is defined as follows:

1 Window   This option is used to split your screen so that you can edit two documents at the same time. The prompt "Number of Lines in this Window:" appears. If you plan to split screens, respond to the prompt by typing the number of lines you need to display your current document or use the <Up> or <Down> arrow key to place the Tab Ruler then press <ENTER> to anchor it. The remaining lines are used to display the second document you will edit.

If you want the Tab Ruler to appear but do not want to split screens, answer the prompt "Number of Lines in this Window:" by using the <Down> arrow key to move the Tab Ruler to the bottom of your screen. Then press <ENTER> to anchor it in place.

When you want to delete the Tab Ruler, press **Ctrl-F3**, select the Window option and enter 0 (zero) in response to the prompt. You can also remove the Tab Ruler by pressing **Ctrl-F3**, typing **1**, then typing any mumber equal to or greater than twenty-four (the number of lines on a screen).

GUIDED ACTIVITY: DISPLAYING THE TAB RULER

1. Retrieve **OLSON.LTR** **Move the cursor to the body of the letter.**

2. Press the **Ctrl-F3** keys.

   The Screen menu will appear on your screen.

3. Type **1**

   The prompt "Number of Lines in this Window:" will appear.

4. Type **8**

5. Press **<ENTER>**

   The Tab Ruler will be anchored on the ninth line of your screen.

6. Press **Shift-F8** to access the Format menu.

7. Type **1** to access the Format Line submenu.

   Delete the tab settings. Notice that the Tab setting indicators on the Tab Ruler have changed to reflect the lack of tab settings.

8. Use the cursor-movement keys to scroll back the lines of your document. Watch the Tab Ruler change to reflect the tab settings at the cursor position.

9. Press the **Ctrl-F3** keys.

   The Screen menu will appear on your screen.

10. Type **1**

    The prompt "Number of Lines in this Window:" will appear.

11. Type **30**

    Any number of lines greater than the number of lines on a screen (i.e., 24) will remove the Tab Ruler.

12. Press **<ENTER>**

    The window is closed.

13. Exit WordPerfect **without** Saving the document, as we do not want to save the new tab settings.

✔ CHECKPOINT

l. Which keystrokes are needed to display the Tab Ruler?

---

m. How is the Tab Ruler removed from the screen?

SPLIT SCREEN

When you split the screen to create two windows, you can edit two documents at the same time. Each document appears with its own status line in a separate window. The Tab Ruler is used to separate the two windows. When your cursor is positioned in the upper window, the triangles on the Tab Ruler point up. When the cursor is in the lower window, the triangles point down.

Select the window option on the Screen menu to split your screen. Answer the prompt by typing the number of lines you need to display your first document in the upper window. The default setting is 24, which is the total number of lines on the screen. Therefore, if you select 24, you will not really have a split screen because you will not be able to see two documents at the same time. Since a window must contain at least two lines, type "22" or less after the prompt for a true split screen.

Press the Switch key (**Shift-F3**) to move the cursor between windows. Each window is controlled separately, so any functions you activate affect only the document in which your cursor is located. Be sure that you Exit both documents before you Exit WordPerfect 5.0.

REVIEW QUESTIONS

1. Suppose that your company repeatedly sends a form letter during the course of the month. How would you format that letter to avoid changing the date each time you send it?

---

2. Suppose the form letter you send out requires that you to the current date within the body of the text. How would you go about accomplishing this task?

---

3. Which keys would you use to insert a string of twenty asterisks on a page of a document?

Discovering More WordPerfect Functions   145

4. You have come upon a rather long quote from a renowned scientist and decide that it is just what you need to make a point in the proposal you are writing. Which keystrokes will most quickly and efficiently set the paragraph in one tab stop from the right and left margins?

5. Which keystrokes must you use to create a hanging paragraph?

6. Identify the keys that access the Date menu.

7. What is the default number for the Repeat feature?

8. How can you use the Repeat feature to scroll a document up eight pages? up ten pages?

9. Which keys are needed to delete eight consecutive words?

10. Suppose that you have just finished typing a long document and it occurs to you that you should have typed "chairperson" instead of "chairman." How can you quickly replace each incorrect word with the correct one?

11. Which keys are needed to Split the Screen.

12. You have just finished writing a proposal and have a nagging suspicion that you have overused the word "collaborate." How can you quickly examine your document and selectively replace the word?

13. Explain how to anchor the Tab Ruler at the bottom of your screen when you wish to use it to edit a single document.

DOCUMENTATION RESEARCH

1. Suppose that you wish to use the Indent feature to indent a paragraph twelve spaces. How do you change the indent value of the indent key?

2. Using the Date and Time feature, select a format for displaying the date and time. What is the maximum number of characters that can be used in a format pattern?

3. How is the Replace feature used to find whole words (e.g., **not**, instead of can**not** or a**not**her)?

4. If you type all upper case letters to search for a specific word, how will the WordPerfect program respond?

5. List the WordPerfect features that can be used in a replace string.

6. How can you return the cursor to its original position after completing a Search and Replace?

7. How can you delete text or a code when using the Search and Replace features?

8. How can you place Endnotes on a separate page?

REVIEW EXERCISES

1. Retrieve **EXERCISE.DOC**

2. Create at least three (use your imagination) Endnotes for this document.

3. Enter a Endnote Placement code at the end of your document. Generate the Endnotes. Update the Document Identification Line. Print **EXERCISE.DOC**

4. With **EXERCISE.DOC** still on your screen, Split the screen in half.

5. Retrieve **WORDWRAP** into the lower window.

6. Move the cursor back and forth between the windows.

7. Add the current date code to both documents. Use a date format other than the default.

8. Save both documents and Exit WordPerfect 5.0.

UNIT 8

FILE MANAGEMENT

SUPPLIES NEEDED

1. WordPerfect program disks 1 and 2
2. WordPerfect Student Data disks

OBJECTIVES

After completing this unit, you will be able to use the list files to

1. list all files in a directory;
2. retrieve a file;
3. delete a file;
4. rename a file;
5. print a file;
6. copy a file.

IMPORTANT KEYSTROKES

1. F5   to list files
2. Ctrl-F5   to lock a document

ASSIGNMENTS

1. Retrieve **WORDWRAP**
2. Print **WORDWRAP**
3. Rename **DUMMY**
4. Delete **SMART**
5. Review Questions
6. Documentation Research
7. Review Exercises

FILE MANAGEMENT

You have by now created a number of documents and stored them as specific files on your WordPerfect Student Data disk. You gave each of your files a meaningful name to make it easier to remember which document you stored in a specific file. As your store of documents increases, it becomes less practical for you to remember all of the documents you have created. This is when WordPerfect's List Files feature (F5) is valuable. It helps you organize your files so that they can be easily retrieved, printed, copied, renamed, or even erased.

Your data storage disk is much like the filing cabinet in a traditional office. Both are used to store units of information on "files." When information is needed, the file is opened, read, revised, and then closed.

The operating system (DOS) maintains a directory of the files you have stored. When you press **F5** (List Files), the name of the default drive and/or directory appears on the status line. If you press <ENTER>, the directory, a list of files in alphabetical order, appears on the screen along with the List Files menu (figure 8-1). To see the files in another directory on another disk, change the drive designation (e.g., A: or B:).

A sample directory is included in figure 8-1. The header displays the directory name, the current date, and the time of day. It also informs you how much storage space (in bytes) is left on your data disk and how much storage space the document you are working on takes up (in bytes). Each filename listing includes file size (in bytes) and the date and time it was last edited and saved.

Select a file you wish to open by highlighting it with the cursor-movement keys. Then select an option from the List Files menu by typing one of the displayed numbers.

```
12/30/88  22:02            Directory B:\*.*
Document size:      790   Free:  338944   Used:    17703       Files:    9

. <CURRENT>     <DIR>              .. <PARENT>    <DIR>
DUMMY    .          853  12/21/88 08:21   ECON    .DOC     414  10/19/88 06:42
FRANKLIN.           470  10/20/88 01:47   HUMAN   .REL    6174  12/21/88 08:43
NEIL     .DOC       399  10/19/88 06:44   PARKS   .       5418  08/02/88 08:13
WILLIAM  .          152  10/20/88 01:48   WORDPERZ.DOC    1683  10/20/88 04:22
WORDPERF.TXT       2140  12/29/88 16:57




     1 Retrieve; 2 Delete; 3 Move/Rename; 4 Print; 5 Text In;
     6 Look; 7 Other Directory; 8 Copy; 9 Word Search; N Name Search: 6
```

FIGURE 8-1   List Files Menu and Sample Directory

The options on the List Files menu are defined as follows:

    1 Retrieve   A copy of the file highlighted by the cursor is retrieved and placed on the screen. If you are editing another document when you press **F5**, the retrieved document is inserted where the cursor was resting. Text below the cursor is pushed down to make room for the retrieved document. Make sure you clear your screen before retrieving a document unless you intend to append a file. Use this option when you do not remember the name of the file you wish to retrieve or when you need information from a file that you are not currently working on.

    2 Delete   The prompt "Delete filename? (Y/N) No" appears on the screen. Type "Y" to erase (delete) the file. Press any other key if you change your mind and decide to keep the file after all. Be careful. Once a file is erased it cannot be restored.

    3 Move/Rename   The prompt "New name:" appears at the bottom of your screen. Choose this option and give your file a new name. Renaming files may be necessary as your store increases and you need to reorganize.

    4 Print   The highlighted file is sent directly to the printer. This saves time when you want to print a document that does not need editing.

152 WordPerfect 5.0

5 Text In
: A copy of a file created with a program other than WordPerfect and stored on your data disk can be retrieved and placed on the screen. An ASCII format file must be created to translate the file. Refer to your WordPerfect manual for an explanation of this procedure.

6 Look
: This option lets you examine, but not edit, the contents of a file. It also lets you view the filenames in another directory.

7 Other Directory
: The prompt "New directory = 'current directory'" appears on the screen. Type the name of the new directory you wish to create. The prompt "Create 'new directory' Y/N No" will appear. Type "Y" and a new directory is created.

8 Copy
: A copy of the highlighted file can be placed in another file, in another directory, or on another disk.

9 Word Search
: The prompt "Word Pattern:" appears on the screen. With this option, you can search the first page of files, entire files, and Document Summaries for a particular word, phrase, or word pattern. Use the ? to denote a missing character and use * to denote more than one missing character in a word pattern. Enclose all words and word patterns in double quotation marks. For example, "letter" will select all files that contain the word "letter". "l?ne" will select all the files that contain words that match this word pattern (e.g., "line", "lone", "lane"). The word pattern, "student*disk" will select all the files that contain a phrase startinh with the word "student" and ending with the word "disk" (e.g. "student data disk").

N Name Search
: Use this option when you are searching for a particular file in a long list of files. Choose the option by typing "N", then start typing the filename. The cursor will move to the first filename that matches the letters you have typed. As you continue typing the filename the cursor will move to the file that matches. You may have to type only a few letters of the filename you want to match.

GUIDED ACTIVITY: USING LIST FILES TO RETRIEVE A DOCUMENT

1. Display a clear screen and be sure your "WordPerfect 5.0 Student Data" disk is in Drive B.

2. Press the **F5** key to activate the List Files function.

   A message showing the default directory will appear on the screen. If the default directory is not "B," change the directory to "B" by typing **=B**

File Management   153

3. Press **<ENTER>**

   The directory of your WordPerfect Student Data disk will appear on the screen.

4. Highlight the file **WORDWRAP**

5. Type **1** to Retrieve the file.

   WORDWRAP will appear on the screen.

GUIDED ACTIVITY: USING LIST FILES TO PRINT A DOCUMENT

1. Display a clear screen.

2. Press the **F5** key, then **<ENTER>**, for List Files.

   The directory of your WordPerfect Student Data disk will appear on the screen.

3. Highlight the file **WORDWRAP**

4. Type **4**, then press **<ENTER>** to Print all the pages of the file.

   WORDWRAP will be printed without being retrieved, and the List Files menu will reappear.

GUIDED ACTIVITY: USING LIST FILES TO LOOK AT A FILE

1. Highlight the file **DUMMY**

2. Type **6** to activate the Look option.

   The file **DUMMY** will appear on the screen.

3. Press **Exit (F7)** or any other key to return to the list of files.

GUIDED ACTIVITY: USING LIST FILES TO RENAME A FILE

1. Highlight the file **DUMMY**

2. Type **3** to Rename the file.

   The prompt "New Name:" will appear at the bottom of your screen.

3. Type **SMART**

4. Press <ENTER>

   The file **DUMMY** has been renamed **SMART**.

GUIDED ACTIVITY: USING LIST FILES TO DELETE A FILE

1. Highlight the file **SMART**

2. Type **2** to Delete the file.

   The prompt "Delete B:\SMART?(Y/N) No" will appear at the bottom of your screen.

3. Type **Y**

   The file **SMART** will be erased and will no longer be listed.

4. Press **F1** to return to a clear screen.

LOCKED DOCUMENTS

If you need to protect or "lock" a document, you can do so by inserting a secret password. This password must then be entered before a document can be retrieved or printed.

This feature may be convenient for those documents that require top security but do not use it indiscriminately. Once you lock a document, you cannot retrieve it except with your password-and secret passwords are easy to forget.

To lock a document, press the **Ctrl-F5** keys to access the Text In/Out menu. Select option 2, then option 1, and then type your secret password. You will be prompted to enter the password again. This is the program's way of guarding against typing errors. The password will not appear on the screen.

After entering your secret password, you will be prompted to enter the name of the file you are locking.

To retrieve a locked document, press **Shift-F10** to Retrieve or **F5** for the list of files. You will be prompted to enter your secret password.

If you lock a document and then decide that the document is more secure unlocked, press **Ctrl-F5** and select option 2, then option 2 again. You will first be prompted to enter the name of your document, and then to enter your secret password. If you enter the password incorrectly, the message "File is Locked" appears on your screen. If you cannot recall your secret password, you will never see your document again!

REVIEW QUESTIONS

1. What is the purpose of a directory?

2. Identify each of the components contained in the header of a directory.

3. The List Files menu contains ten options. Which option lets you retrieve a file to edit?

4. How is a file selected from a directory on the List Files screen?

5. Suppose that you want to retrieve a particular file in a large directory but cannot remember the exact filename. How can you most efficiently examine the contents of a file without first retrieving it?

6. Suppose that you would like to erase some outdated files from your data storage disk. How would you do so?

7. Suppose that you are writing a novel. You store each chapter in a separate file, named by chapter (e.g., **CHAP1.NOV**). By the time you get to your tenth chapter, you have already made extensive revisions and even inserted new chapters. You realize that your system of naming files is no longer practical. How will you reorganize?

8. Why should the Locked Document feature be used with caution?

DOCUMENTATION RESEARCH

1. What cursor-movement keys can be used to move through a long list of files?

156   WordPerfect 5.0

2. How can you mark a group of files for printing, deletion, or copying?

---

3. Suppose that your default drive is A. You would like to see the directory of files stored on the disk in Drive B. Describe how this can be done.

---

4. The directory lists each file by its filename and its size in bytes. Use the Glossary to find the meaning of "byte."

---

5. Suppose that when you attempt to Print a file, the message "Document not formatted for current printer. Continue? (Y/N) No" appears on the screen. Can you print the document? How?

REVIEW EXERCISES

1. Type the following text on a clear screen: **There is nothing wrong with making mistakes. Just don't respond with encores. Anon.**

2. Add the Document Identification Line. Save this file. Name it **LOCK.EX**

3. Retrieve **LOCK.EX** if necessary.

4. Lock **LOCK.EX** (using the password, "lock") Save the document.

5. List Files and Retrieve **LOCK.EX** Print the document.

6. Unlock **LOCK.EX** Save the document.

7. Use the Rename option on the List Files menu to change the filename **EXERCISE.DOC** to **EXER.WP**

8. Change the filename **EXER.WP** back to **EXERCISE.DOC**

9. Use the Print option on the List Files menu to print **LOCK.EX**

10. Use the Name Search option on the List Files menu to highlight the filename **HUMAN.REL**

11. Use the Word Search option on the List Files menu to search all your documents for the word **afraid** In which document(s) does the word appear?

12. Exit WordPerfect 5.0.

UNIT 9

SPELLER AND THESAURUS

SUPPLIES NEEDED

1. WordPerfect 5.0 program disks 1 and 2
2. WordPerfect 5.0 Speller disk
3. WordPerfect 5.0 Thesaurus disk
4. WordPerfect 5.0 Student Data disk
5. printer

OBJECTIVES

After completing this unit, you will be able to

1. correct spelling errors with the WordPerfect 5.0 Speller;
2. add and delete words from the dictionary;
3. count the number of words on a page;
4. select synonyms with the WordPerfect 5.0 Thesaurus.

IMPORTANT KEYSTROKES

1. Ctrl-F2   to use the Speller
2. Alt-F1   to use the Thesaurus

158   WordPerfect 5.0

ASSIGNMENTS

1. Edit **ECON.DOC**
2. Edit **NEIL.DOC**
3. Review Questions
4. Documentation Research
5. Review Exercises

THE SPELLER

Proofreading is a critical part of editing a document. It is up to you to check your document for meaning and word usage. However, the WordPerfect 5.0 Speller can save you proofreading time by checking for spelling errors.

The WordPerfect 5.0 Speller contains a dictionary of over 120,000 words. It is made up of a main word list and a common word list. You may also maintain a supplementary dictionary file of words that are not included in the main dictionary.

The WordPerfect 5.0 Speller program compares the words in a document to the list of correctly spelled words in the dictionary. With the Speller, you can check an entire document, a single page, or an individual word. You can also check words phonetically or according to a pattern. Therefore, even when you can only get close to the spelling of a word, the WordPerfect 5.0 Speller can find the correct spelling.

The WordPerfect 5.0 Speller program is stored on a separate disk. Therefore the document you wish to spell-check must first be retrieved; then your Student Data disk must be removed from Drive B and replaced with the Speller disk. If you are using a hard disk system, first retrieve the document you wish to check, then start the Speller.

Hint: Always make certain that your document has been saved on your data storage disk before loading the WordPerfect 5.0 Speller.

THE CHECK MENU

When you press **Ctrl-F2**, the Speller is started and the Check menu (figure 9-1) appears on the screen. You can select an option from this menu by typing one of the listed numbers.

Check: 1 Word; 2 Page; 3 Document; 4 New Sup. Dictionary; 5 Look Up; 6 Count: 0

FIGURE 9-1 Check Menu

Speller and Thesaurus 159

The Check menu options are defined as follows:

1 Word   The word on which your cursor is located is checked for spelling errors. If the word is spelled correctly, the cursor jumps to the next word. If the word is not spelled correctly (that is, not found in the dictionary), it is highlighted and a Not Found submenu appears along with a list of possible replacement words. You can either choose the word with the correct spelling or choose one of the submenu options.

2 Page   The page on which your cursor is located is checked for spelling errors. The Speller starts its spell-check at the beginning of the page. Each word not spelled correctly (that is, not found in the dictionary) is highlighted and the Not Found submenu appears on the screen along with a list of possible replacement words. You can either choose the word with the correct spelling or select a submenu option.

3 Document   The entire document is spell-checked from beginning to end. A "Please wait" message appears at the bottom of the screen until the Speller finds a misspelling.

When the Speller is finished, the total number of words checked appears at the bottom of the screen.

Anytime you wish to stop a spell-check, press the Cancel key (**F1**).

4 New Sup. Dictionary   When you choose this option, you can switch from the main dictionary to a supplementary or user-created dictionary. The Speller Utility program on the Speller disk can help you to create a new dictionary when the vocabulary you use is specialized (for example, legal or medical terms).

5 Look Up.   A "Word Pattern" prompt appears on your screen. A word pattern can be created using a ? for each letter questioned or an * for successive missing letters. The Speller matches the pattern to words contained in the dictionary and displays a list of possible replacement words. For example, you can find the correct spelling for the word "aristocratic" by typing aris*rat*, and for "blatant" by typing "blat?nt".

6 Count   The words in your document are counted, and the word count is displayed at the bottom of your screen.

THE NOT FOUND SUBMENU

Each time the WordPerfect 5.0 Speller finds a misspelled word in the document you are spell-checking, the word is highlighted and the Not Found submenu (figure 9-2) appears on your screen. From this submenu, you can either select a replacement word or choose a submenu option. You may select an option by typing one of the listed numbers.

160   WordPerfect 5.0

Not Found: 1 Skip Once; 2 Skip; 3 Add Word; 4 Edit; 5 Look Up: 0

FIGURE 9-2   Not Found Submenu

The options on the Not Found submenu are defined as follows:

1 Skip Once   If you choose this option, the highlighted word is skipped over and the spell-check continues. The next time the skipped word appears in your document, it is again highlighted.

2 Skip   If you choose this option, the highlighted word is skipped over and the spell-check continues. If the skipped word appears again in your document, it is ignored.

3 Add Word   The highlighted word is added to the supplementary dictionary and the spell-check continues. You can add the supplementary dictionary to the main dictionary by using the Speller Utility program on the Speller disk.

4 Edit   When you choose this option, the cursor jumps to the highlighted word and you can make a correction yourself. Then press **<ENTER>** and the spell-check continues.

5 Look Up   A "Word Pattern" prompt is displayed on your screen. You can create a pattern using ? or * for missing characters. This option is also available on the Check menu.

THE DOUBLE WORD SUBMENU

If the Speller finds a duplicate word (the same word typed twice in succession), the Double Word submenu (figure 9-3) appears on your screen.

Double Word: 1 2 Skip; 3 Delete 2nd; 4 Edit; 5 Disable double word checking

---

FIGURE 9-3   Double Word Submenu

This submenu contains five options, defined as follows:

1 2 Skip   By pressing either **1** or **2** the highlighted double words are are skipped over and the spell-check will continues.

3 Delete 2nd   The second occurrence of the word is deleted.

4. Edit The cursor jumps to the highlighted words; you edit these as desired.

5. Disable double word checking If you prefer not to check double word occurrences, use this option to disable the feature.

GUIDED ACTIVITY: SPELL-CHECKING

Always make certain that your document has been saved on your data storage disk before loading the WordPerfect 5.0 Speller.

1. Retrieve **ECON.DOC** from your Wordperfect Student Data disk. Remove this disk from Drive B.

2. Insert the WordPerfect 5.0 Speller disk into Drive B.

3. Move the cursor to the beginning of the **ECON.DOC** document.

4. Press the **Ctrl-F2** keys.

    The Check menu will appear on the screen.

5. Type **2** to spell-check the page.

    The first misspelled word will be highlighted and a list of replacement words will appear.

6. Type the letter in front of the correct spelling. The highlighted word will be replaced and the spell-check will continue.

7. The first set of double words will be highlighted.

8. Type **3** to delete the second occurrence.

9. The spell-check will continue. Continue to spell-check the page. After the spell-check has been completed, the number of words checked will appear at the bottom of your screen.

✓CHECKPOINT

   a. How many words were spell-checked?

---

10. Remove the Speller disk and replace it with your WordPerfect 5.0 Student Data disk.

11. Add the Document Identification Line. Print and Save **ECON.DOC**

162   WordPerfect

What You Have Accomplished

You have loaded the Speller program and used it to spell-check a short document. The Speller found misspelled words as well as double word occurrences. You have now proofread your document for spelling errors.

THE THESAURUS

The WordPerfect 5.0 Thesaurus helps you choose exactly the right words as you create your documents. It displays a list of nouns, verbs, and adjectives that are similar in meaning to a word you might want to revise. You can either direct the Thesaurus to automatically replace a word or to keep the word you originally typed.

Like the WordPerfect 5.0 Speller, the WordPerfect 5.0 Thesaurus is stored on a separate disk. To use the Thesaurus, remove your data disk from Drive B and insert the Thesaurus disk. When you are finished with the Thesaurus, return your data disk to Drive B so that you can save your files.

When you want to use the Thesaurus, move the cursor to the word you would like to revise and press the Alt-F1 keys. The Thesaurus menu and a sample screen (figure 9-4) will appear on your screen. The upper part of your screen displays four lines of your document. The lower part of your screen is divided into three columns, each containing subgroups of reference words. Use the arrow keys to move through the columns.

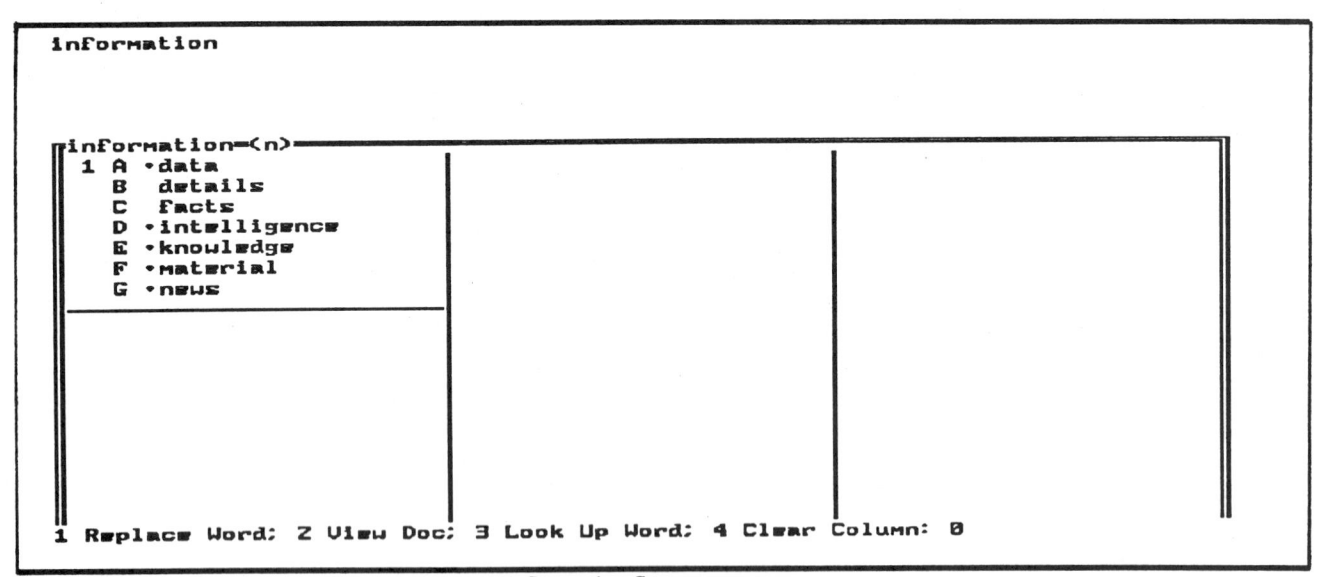

```
information


┌information-(n)──────────┐
 1 A •data
   B  details
   C  facts
   D •intelligence
   E •knowledge
   F •material
   G •news









1 Replace Word; 2 View Doc; 3 Look Up Word; 4 Clear Column: 0
```

FIGURE 9-4   Thesaurus Menu and Sample Screen

The Thesaurus menu contains four options that allow you to look up words in four different ways. The options are defined as follows:

    1 Replace Word   The prompt "Press letter for word" appears. You may select a word from the displayed list of replacement choices by typing the letter printed in front of the word.

Speller and Thesaurus 163

2 View Doc — Use this option to place your cursor back into the document. Press the Exit key to return to the Thesaurus. This option may also be used when you wish to see more text before choosing a replacement word.

3 Look Up Word — The prompt "Word" appears. With this option you can look up a word that does not appear in the document. Type the word you want to look up, and a list of words with similar meanings appears on the screen.

4 Clear Column — The list of replacement words can be cleared one column at a time to make room for additional words you need to look up.

To exit the Thesaurus, press **<ENTER>**, **<SPACEBAR>**, or **F7**.

The WordPerfect 5.0 Thesaurus makes use of three special terms to guide you in your quest for the perfect word. These terms are defined as follows:

Headword — A headword is a word that can be looked up in the Thesaurus. If you see the message "Not a Headword," it means that the word you want to look up is not listed.

Reference — A reference word is a word that is similar in meaning to the headword. Reference words are displayed in columns under the headword. References that are preceded by bullets (.) are also headwords and can be looked up separately.

Subgroups — Subgroups are groups of reference words with the same connotation. They are arranged in numbered groups under the headword.

GUIDED ACTIVITY: USING THE THESAURUS

In this activity you use the WordPerfect 5.0 Thesaurus to restore a famous quotation.

1. Retrieve **NEIL.DOC** and move the cursor to the beginning of the document.

2. Replace your WordPerfect 5.0 Student Data disk with the Thesaurus disk.

3. Place the cursor on the first incorrect word in **NEIL.DOC**.

4. Press the **Alt-F1** keys.

    A list of words and the Thesaurus menu will appear on the screen.

5. Type **1** to choose the Replace Word option from the Thesaurus menu.

    The prompt "Press letter for word" will appear on your screen.

6. Type the letter in front of the correct word. The highlighted word will be replaced.

164 WordPerfect

7. Find the next incorrect word in **NEIL.DOC**.

8. Continue using the Thesaurus to replace words in this document until you have restored the quotation to its authentic version.

9. Remove the Thesaurus disk and replace it with your WordPerfect 5.0 Student Data disk.

10. Add the Document Identification Line. Print and Save **NEIL.DOC**

✓**CHECKPOINT**

b. Which option do you choose from the Thesaurus menu to replace a word in a document?

What You Have Accomplished

You have loaded the Thesaurus program and used it to replace words in your document. An electronic thesaurus is very easy and convenient to use. Choosing appropriate antonyms and synonyms will improve your writing.

REVIEW QUESTIONS

1. Assume that you have typed a document and are ready to spell-check it. Which option from the Check menu do you choose?

2. Explain what happens when the WordPerfect 5.0 Speller finds a misspelled word.

3. Suppose that you work for a pharmaceutical firm that makes frequent use of medical terms. How can you set up the WordPerfect 5.0 Speller so that these specialized terms can be looked up?

4. Imagine that you are a highly skilled project manager but a terrible speller. Because of this limitation, the reports you write take a great deal of time and effort. How can you use the WordPerfect 5.0 Speller to correctly spell the words you are only capable of guessing at?

Speller and Thesaurus   165

5. Imagine that you are a freelance writer and are paid by the word. How can you use the WordPerfect 5.0 Speller to determine quickly how many words are contained in your manuscript?

6. How can you cancel a spell-check?

7. Explain what happens when the Speller checks the following sentence:

   At times you you will make a typing error.

   How can you delete one of the "you"s?

8. Suppose that as the Speller checks your document, it highlights many specialized words that are correctly spelled but are not found in the main dictionary. How can you add these words to the dictionary so that the next time you want to spell-check your documents these specialized words will be found?

9. Both the WordPerfect 5.0 Speller and the WordPerfect 5.0 Thesaurus are stored on separate disks. Explain how to load each of these programs on a dual-drive computer system.

10. What does the term "headword" mean in the Thesaurus program?

11. The meaning of a word depends on the context in which it is used. How does the Thesaurus allow you to consider context before making word-replacement decisions?

12. Suppose that you place your cursor on a word and access the Thesaurus to look up its meaning. You then decide that the word does not communicate what you mean. How can you use the Thesaurus to investigate the meaning of another word you are considering?

DOCUMENTATION RESEARCH

1. How does the Speller program handle the words you have instructed it to skip during a spell-check?

2. What is the Speller Utility program on the Speller disk used for?

3. How does the WordPerfect 5.0 Speller react when it finds a word with a number in it?

4. How do you use the cursor-movement keys to move through the columns of a Thesaurus screen?

5. Name the three ways words can be looked up in WordPerfect 5.0's Thesaurus.

REVIEW EXERCISES

1. Retrieve **EXERCISE.DOC**

2. Spell-check your document. Correct any typing or spelling errors. How many words does **EXERCISE.DOC** contain?

3. Use the Thesaurus to find both a synonym and an antonym for a word of your choice.

4. Replace one occurrence of the word with a synonym and one occurrence with an antonym.

5. Update the Document Identification Line. Save **EXERCISE.DOC**

APPLICATION C

SUPPLIES NEEDED

1. WordPerfect 5.0 program disks 1 and 2
2. WordPerfect 5.0 Speller disk
3. WordPerfect 5.0 Thesaurus disk
4. WordPerfect 5.0 Learning disk
5. WordPerfect 5.0 Student Data disk
6. printer

ASSIGNMENTS

The assignments to be completed for this Application section are

1. Create **LAKEWOOD.DOC**
2. Create **REPLACE.TXT**
3. Create **BUSINESS.TXT**
4. Create **MICRO.TXT**
5. Create **FRANKLIN**
6. Create **WILLIAM**

APPLICATIONS

This Application section contains a number of documents that can be reproduced to practice the skills you have acquired in Units 1 through 9. Some instructions are listed below to guide you in creating the Application C documents.

Use your template and the Quick Reference card to find the keystroke commands and menus you need. Remember that there is often more than one keystroke choice that can be used to create and format a document. Your primary task is to find the most efficient way to reproduce the documents.

You may also wish to experiment with naming and renaming files, or with copying and deleting files. The more adept you become at managing your files, the easier and more productive your word-processing tasks will become.

You may also want to create your own applications - some tasks that are more meaningful to your everyday work. Your WordPerfect Student Data disk should have plenty of space available (use List Files to find out how much) to store additional documents.

Follow the directions below to create the documents in Application C.

Document C-1
1. Name this document **LAKEWOOD.DOC**
2. Use the Date and Flush Right features to insert the current date.
3. Double Indent the paragraphs two tab stops as shown.
4. Underline and boldface the text as shown.
5. Add the Document Identification Line at the bottom of the document.
6. Save and Print the document.

Document C-2
1. Name this document **REPLACE.TXT**
2. Type the sentence as shown.
3. Use the Search and Replace features to replace "x" with the word **so**
4. Add the Document Identification Line to the bottom of the document.
5. Save and Print the document.

Document C-3
1. Name this document **BUSINESS.TXT**
2. Type this quote as shown.
3. Use the Search and Replace features to replace the "b" with the word **business**
4. Add the Document Identification Line to the bottom of the document.
5. Save and Print the document.

Document C-4
1. Name this document **MICRO.TXT**
2. Type the sentence as shown.
3. Use the Search and Replace features to replace:
    "IBM" with **International Business Machines**
    "PC" and "PC's" with **Personal Computers**
    "C" with **Compaq**
    "micros" with **microcomputers**
    "z" with **Zenith**
4. Add the Document Identification Line to the bottom of the document.
5. Save and Print two copies of the document.

Document C-5
1. Retrieve **FRANKLIN** from your WordPerfect 5.0 Student Data disk.
2. Use the WordPerfect 5.0 Speller disk to correct typographical and spelling errors.
3. Add the Document Identification Line to the bottom of the document.
4. Save and Print the document.

Document C-6
1. Retrieve **WILLIAM** from your WordPerfect 5.0 Student Data disk.
2. Use the WordPerfect 5.0 Theasaurus disk to return the document to its original form.
3. Add the Document Identification Line to the bottom of the document.
4. Save and Print the document.

(current date)

LAKEWOOD SCHOOL
LAND DEVELOPMENT COMMITTEE

Dear Members of the Land Development Committee:

We need your help as we continue our work on our nature trail and camping area in the wooded lots at our school.

SATURDAY, APRIL 20 AT 8:30 A.M.

On this day, we will finish clearing the nature trail and camping area and we will chip the cut-down tree branches and spread the chips on the nature trail and camping area. (We have rented a mechanical chipper.)

Bring: Chain saws, wheelbarrows, sprayers, rakes, and gloves.

SATURDAY, APRIL 27 AT 8:30 A.M.

On this day we will plant the trees (seedlings) that we have obtained.

Bring: Planting bars, shovels, wheelbarrows, buckets, and gloves.

We need lots of manpower and womanpower for this work. Recruit and bring a friend if you can.

Enthusiasm on this committee is running very high. Let's keep up the momentum. This project will provide a wonderful nature appreciation and camping experience for our youth -- and it will beautify our school property! This is one of our Top Priority projects.

Jim Johnson, Principal

Document C-1 **LAKEWOOD.DOC**

Never in the field of human conflict was x much owed by x many to x few.
    WINSTON CHURCHILL

Document C-2 **REPLACE.TXT**

Call on a b man at b times only, and on b, transact your b and go about your b, in order to give him time to finish his b.   WELLINGTON

Document C-3 **BUSINESS.TXT**

Some computer labs use IBM PC's while others use Z or C PC equipment. There are many other brands of micros that are also IBM compatible.

Document C-4 **MICRO.TXT**

PART 3
SPECIAL FEATURES

Part 3 teaches you to use the Select, Sort, Merge, and Macro functions to accomplish repetitive word-processing tasks more efficiently. Part also teaches you to arrrange text in columns and to create a table of contents. In Unit 14, you learn how to use the Math function. In Unit 15 you will learn how to add graphic images to your documents. Part 3 also reinforces some of the skills you acquired in Parts 1 and 2.

Part 3 contains Applications D and E. It contains exercises to apply the skills you acquired in Parts 1, 2, and 3. The documents you create in unit exercises and the application section are stored on the Student Data disk.

UNIT 10
SELECTING, SORTING AND MERGING

SUPPLIES NEEDED

1. WordPerfect 5.0 program disks 1 and 2
2. WordPerfect 5.0 Student Data disk
3. printer

OBJECTIVES

After completing this unit, you will be able to

1. sort a list;
2. select and sort a specific list of records;
3. define the terms "record," "field," "line," and word;
4. define the terms "primary file" and "secondary file";
5. merge information from primary and secondary files to form one document;
6. use a secondary file to create a new document;

IMPORTANT KEYSTROKES

1. Ctrl-F9   to display the Merge/Sort menu
2. F9   to insert a code that identifies the end of a field or to continue a merge after pausing
3. Shift-F9   to insert a code that identifies the end of a record

176   WordPerfect 5.0

4. Merge codes:

^C	to stop a merge temporarily so that additional information can be entered from the keyboard
^D	to insert the current date automatically during a merge
^E	to mark the end of a record in a secondary file
^F	to merge a numbered field into a document
^O	to display a message on the status line
^Q	to stop the merge
^R	to mark the end of a field in a secondary file
^S	to link secondary files
^P	to link primary files
^T	to send merged text directly to the printer
^N	to signal the program to look for the next record in the secondary file

ASSIGNMENTS

1. Sort **PARKS**
2. Create **PARKLIST.SF**
3. Create **PARKLIST.PF**
4. Create **PARK.LTR**
5. Sort **PARKLIST.SF**
6. Create **UTAH.SF**
7. Create **UTAH.ENV**
8. Review Questions
9. Documentation Research
10. Review Exercises

RECORDS, FIELDS, LINES, WORDS, AND KEYS

WordPerfect 5.0 defines records, fields, words, and keys as follows:

Records   **Records** are units of a file that can be sorted. In WordPerfect, a record can be a line, a paragraph, or a merge record. You will learn more about merging lines and records later in this unit.

Fields   Records can be divided into **fields**. Each field in a group of records must contain the same type of data (e.g., the third field of each record might be the street address). You can create a sublist of records that contain a specific field (e.g., all customers that live in Minnesota). WordPerfect 5.0 counts fields in a record from top to bottom. By entering a minus sign (dash) in a sort Key, WordPerfect 5.0 will count fields from bottom to top.

Lines   A **line** is made up of words and ends with either a soft or hard carriage return. When doing a Line Sort, each line is a record. WordPerfect 5.0 5.0 counts lines in a multiple-line field from top to bottom. By entering

Selecting, Sorting and Merging 177

a minus sign (hyphen) in a sort key, WordPerfect 5.0 will count lines from bottom to top.

Words   **Words** are separated by a space in a line, field or record. WordPerfect 5.0 counts words in a line from left to right. By entering a minus sign (dash) in a sort key, WordPerfect 5.0 will count words from right to left.

Keys   **Keys** are words within a record on which the record is sorted. You can specify up to nine fields. Key 1 has priority. If the key is the same for more than one record, Key 2 will be used to subsort. For example, if Key 1 is Smith in two records, but Key 2 is Albert in one record and Zelda in the second record, then the records would be sorted based on Key 2.

There are two types of keys. A **numeric** key is made up of numbers and can contain commas, dollar signs, and periods (e.g., $1,567.98). Numeric keys may be of unequal length.

An **alphanumeric** key contains either letters or numbers. Each alphanumeric key that contains numbers (e.g., telephone numbers, ZIP codes, or social security numbers) must be of the same length.

SORTING AND SELECTING

The Sort feature is found on the Merge/Sort menu (figure 10-1). Press **Ctrl-F9** to access this menu, then select Sort and enter your Sort criteria on the Sort menu (figure 10-2). You may Sort lines, paragraphs, or records in a secondary merge file. The Sorted text can be displayed on your screen or stored on disk. If you Save your document before you Sort, the Sort criteria are Saved with the document. You can Sort a Block of text.

---

1 Merge; 2 Sort; 3 Sort Order: 0

FIGURE 10-1   Merge/Sort Menu

You can Select and Sort specific records. For example, you can create an alphabetical list of all inventory items that cost more than $5.00. Cost would be Key 1 and item name would be Key 2. To select records, access the Merge/Sort menu by pressing **Ctrl-F9**, then press **4** for Select.

178 WordPerfect 5.0

```
                                                      Doc 2 Pg 1 Ln 1" Pos 1"
  C     ▲    ▲    ▲    ▲    ▲            ▲    ▲    ▲    ▲    ▲            )
  -------------------------------- Sort by Line --------------------------------

  Key Typ Field Word         Key Typ Field Word         Key Typ Field Word
   1   a   1     1            2                          3
   4                          5                          6
   7                          8                          9
  Select


  Action                     Order                      Type
  Sort                       Ascending                  Line sort

  1 Perform Action; 2 View; 3 Keys; 4 Select; 5 Action; 6 Order; 7 Type: 0
```

FIGURE 10-2 Sort menu

The Sort menu options are defined as follows:

1 Perform Action		This option begins the Sort. The sorted document will either appear on your screen or can be saved in a file on a disk.
2 View		This option allows you to scroll through the text on the upper half of your screen. When you are done, press F7 to return to the Sort menu.
3 Keys		Use this option to define the numeric or alphanumeric keys (fields) on which to sort lines, paragraphs and lists of merge records. You can choose up to nine keys on which to sort. Key 1 has priority. If two fields are the same, then WordPerfect 5.0 uses Key 2, etc., to subsort.
4 Select		This option allows you to enter the criteria to select specific records for sorting.
5 Action		Choose this option after you have entered Select criteria.
6 Order		You may Sort in ascending or descending order. In ascending order, letters are sorted from A to Z and numbers from 0 to 9. In descending order, the letters and numbers are sorted in reverse order.
7 Type		This option allows you to choose the type of sort. You can choose "line", "paragraph", or "merge for merge records".

GUIDED ACTIVITY: SORTING A LIST

1. Retrieve **PARKS** from your Student Data disk.

2. Move the cursor to the "A" in Acadia, the first park name in the list.

3. Block (Alt-F4) the whole list of National Parks.

4. Press **Ctrl-F9** to access the Sort menu.

5. Press **1** to select Perform Action.

    After a few seconds the Sort menu will disappear and the alphabetized list will appear on the screen.

6. Add the Document Identification Line to the bottom of the document. Save and Print **PARKS**

MERGING

Merging tasks with a word-processing package means combining data from two or more files to create a new document. Every merging operation requires a **primary file** that contains the text and codes that direct the merge operation. A primary file is merged with variable information from either a secondary file, other user files, or the keyboard.

A **secondary file** is composed of a group of related records (a data base). A **record** is defined as a collection of data items or fields that relate to a single unit. A **field** is defined as a meaningful item of data such as a social security number. The secondary files (your data base) you will generally use for your merge tasks are composed of a group of records (one for each individual) divided into fields of meaningful data (e.g., name, address, age, telephone number).

Merge operations primarily used by businesses and organizations that frequently mail form letters or organizational notices. A basic letter is created and stored in the primary file. A record of information on each customer or client is created and stored in the secondary file. Then the two files are merged and a personalized letter is created for each record in the secondary file. It is important to keep the records on the secondary file up to date and complete so that your merging operations are truly efficient.

THE SECONDARY FILE

It is important to create a comprehensive secondary file that contains all the information you need for a merging operation. Each record should contain the same number of fields; each field should have the same type of information. A field can contain any type or length of information. When you have finished entering a field, press **F9** (Merge R); the code ^R will be inserted to signify the end of a field. When you have completed a record, press **Shift-F9** (Merge E), then press E; the code ^E and a hard page break will be inserted to indicate the end of a record.

GUIDED ACTIVITY: CREATING A SECONDARY FILE

1. Load WordPerfect 5.0, taking care to insert the current date.

2. Display a clear screen.

3. Type **Superintendent**

4. Press the **F9** key.

    You have signified the end of the name field. The ^R will appear on your screen immediately after "Superintendent," and the cursor will jump to the next line.

5. Type **Bryce National Park**

6. Press the **F9** key.

    You have signified the end of the park-name field. The ^R will appear on your screen, and the cursor will jump to the next line.

7. Type **Bryce Canyon, Utah 84717**

8. Press the **F9** key to insert the ^R code and signal the end of the city-state-ZIP code field.

9. Press the **Shift-F9** key. Type **E**

    You have signified the end of a record and inserted the ^E and Hard Page Break codes. The cursor will jump to the next line. Do not insert <ENTER> after the ^E.

10. Create another record by repeating the previous steps; use the following information:

    Superintendent^R
    Canyonlands National Park^R
    Moab, Utah 84532^R
    ^E

    Both records contain the same number of fields with the same type of information.

Selecting, Sorting and Merging   181

11. Create another record using the following information:

   Superintendent^R
   Grand Teton National Park^R
   Moose, Wyoming^R
   ^E

12. Press **F7**

   Save your records. Name the document **PARKLIST.SF** You have created a secondary file that will be used for future merge operations.

13. Clear the screen.

   ✔**CHECKPOINT**

   a. Which key inserts a code at the end of a field?

   _____

   b. Which key inserts a code at the end of a record?

   _____

What You Have Accomplished

You have created a secondary file, that contains the records of three individuals. Each record consists of three fields. Each field contains the same type of information. You have stored your secondary file on your Student Data disk under the filename **PARKLIST.SF**. This file will later be merged with another document in a primary file.

Hint: When you are creating your data base (secondary file), never insert a space between the last character in a field and a merge code. Also, be careful **not** to separate fields by pressing the **<ENTER>** key.

THE PRIMARY FILE

The primary file usually contains a basic letter with embedded codes to symbolize the placement of variable information from a secondary file. When the **Shift-F9** keys are pressed, the Merge Codes menu (figure 10-3) appears on your screen. From this menu, you may choose a code to insert in your basic letter. You can select a code just by typing the individual letter; the carat (^) is displayed automatically.

182   WordPerfect 5.0

---

^C; ^D; ^E; ^F; ^G; ^N; ^O; ^P; ^Q; ^S; ^T; ^U; ^V:

FIGURE 10-3   Merge Codes Menu

GUIDED ACTIVITY: CREATING A PRIMARY FILE

1. Start with a clear screen. Press **Shift-F9**

   The Merge Codes menu will appear on your screen.

2. Type **D**

   "^D" will appear on your screen. You have embedded a code that automatically inserts the current date each time this file is retrieved.

3. Press **<ENTER>** six times to create blank lines.

4. Press **Shift-F9**

   The Merge Codes menu will appear on your screen.

5. Type **F**

   The prompt "Field:" will appear at the bottom of your screen.

6. Type **1**

7. Press **<ENTER>**

   Your screen will look like this: "^F1^". You have embedded a code that will retrieve information from field one (the name field) on your secondary file.

8. Press **<ENTER>**

9. Press **Shift-F9** to access the Merge Codes menu.

10. Type **F**

    The prompt "Field:" will appear at the bottom of your screen.

11. Type **2**

12. Press **<ENTER>**

    Your screen will look like this: "^F2^". You have embedded a code that will retrieve information from field two (the park-name field) on your secondary file.

13. Press <ENTER>

14. Press **Shift-F9** to access the Merge Codes menu.

15. Type **F**

16. Type **3** after the prompt.

17. Press <ENTER>

    Your screen will look like this: "^F3^". You have embedded a code that will retrieve information from field three (the city-state-ZIP-code field) on your secondary file.

18. Press <ENTER> three times to insert two blank lines between the address and the salutation.

19. Type **Dear**

20. Press <SPACEBAR> once.

21. Press **Shift-F9** to display the Merge Codes menu.

22. Type F, then 1

23. Press <ENTER>

    Your screen will look like this: "^F1^". You have embedded a code that will retrieve information from field one (the name field).

24. Type : (colon).

25. Press <ENTER> three times to create two blank lines.

26. Type the following text and codes into the body of your letter (use the default margin settings of 1", 1"). Use the Shift-F9 keys to access the Merge Codes menu. The ^C temporarily stops the merge so that you can enter information from the keyboard. The ^O embeds a code that directs the program to display your typed message during a merge operation.

184 WordPerfect 5.0

> Please ^F2 ^F1, send me any information you have available about camping at ^F2. I will be taking my vacation next summer during the month of ^O type vacation month ^O^C. My address is as follows:
>
> (your name)
> (your street address)
> (your city, state, ZIP)
>
> Thank you in advance ^F2 ^F1 for the information. I am anxious to start planning my vacation.
>
> Sincerely,
>
>
> (your name)
> (Document Identification Line)

27.   Press **F7** to Save your file and clear the screen. Name your file **PARKLIST.PF**

✓ CHECKPOINT

> c. Which keys access the Merge Codes menu?

What You Have Accomplished

You have typed a basic form letter that contains all the codes required to merge with the records in a secondary file. You saved this letter in a primary file named **PARKLIST.PF**. Now, each time you wish to mail this letter, you can merge it with your secondary file to create a personalized letter.

MERGING AND PRINTING

When both a primary and a secondary file have been created, merge operations can begin. Each time WordPerfect 5.0 encounters an ^F, information from a specific field in a record is automatically inserted into your basic letter. Each time WordPerfect 5.0 encounters a ^C, merge operations are suspended until you insert information from the keyboard and press **F9** to continue. Each time WordPerfect 5.0 encounters an ^E, it directs the printer to end one letter and begin another until all records on the secondary file are used. You may save copies of your completed letters under a new filename.

When you are ready to begin merging, press **Ctrl-F9**. The Merge/Sort menu (figure 10-1) will appear. Option 1 on this menu is used for merging.

GUIDED ACTIVITY: MERGING AND PRINTING A PERSONALIZED LETTER

1. At a clear screen, press the **Ctrl-F9** keys.

    The Merge/Sort menu will appear on the screen.

2. Type **1**

    The prompt "Primary file:" will appear in the status line.

3. Type **PARK.LIST.PF**

    You have entered the name of your primary file.

4. Press **<ENTER>**

    The prompt "Secondary file:" will appear in the status line.

5. Type **PARKLIST.SF**

    You have entered the name of your secondary file.

6. Press **<ENTER>**

    Your first merged document has appeared on the screen. Your message "type vacation month" is displayed in the status line. The cursor is positioned after the word "of."

7. Type **August** (in response to your message).

8. Press the **F9** key to continue the merge operation.

    A hard page break has been inserted and your second merged document has appeared on the screen.

9. Type **August** in response to your message.

10. Complete the third merged document.

11. Press **F7** to Save, and clear your screen. Store your three letters in a file **PARK.LTR**

12. Print **PARK.LTR**

    Notice that the letters are merged and printed in the same order as the records were entered in the secondary file.

186　WordPerfect 5.0

✔CHECKPOINT

d. Which keys access the Merge/Sort menu?

---

e. What happens when the printer encounters an ^O code?

---

f. What happens when the printer encounters a ^C code?

What You Have Accomplished

You have merged a primary and a secondary file to create three personalized letters. You stored all three letters in a third file **PARK.LTR**. You Printed the three letters.

ENVELOPES

Now that you have Merged and Printed your letters, you will want to address envelopes for mailing the letters. You can automate this task with the WordPerfect 5.0 Merge feature. If you wish to print the letters or envelopes in a specific order (for instance, by ZIP code to take advantage of bulk postage rates), you can use the Sort feature. Specific merge records can be Selected as well as Sorted.

GUIDED ACTIVITY: SORTING MERGE RECORDS

1. Retrieve **PARKLIST.SF** to a clear screen.

2. Press **Ctrl-F9** to access the Merge/Sort menu.

3. Type **2** to select Sort.

    The message "Input file to sort: (Screen)" appears on your screen. If you had not already Retrieved the file you want to sort, you could enter a filename on your disk.

4. Press **<ENTER>** to sort the file on your screen.

    The message "Output file for sort: (Screen)" appears on your screen. If you type a filename, the sorted records will be saved on disk with that name.

5. Press **<ENTER>** to display the sorted records on your screen.

    Your screen is now divided with a few records on the top half, and the Sort submenu on the bottom half. Notice that the Sort submenu is headed "Sort by Line".

Selecting, Sorting and Merging   187

6. Type **7** to select Type from the Sort submenu.

   The Type submenu appears.

7. Type **1** to sort merge records.

   Notice the Sort submenu is now headed "Sort Secondary Merge File".

8. Type **3** to select Keys from the Sort submenu.

   The Keys submenu appears at the bottom of your screen. You are going to create a Merge Key that specifies criteria for sorting the merge records in **PARKLIST.SF**. The cursor is at the "a" in Key 1.

9. Press the **<Right> arrow** key to move the cursor to the Field number and accept a Type "a", alphanumeric, sort.

10. Type **3**

    The "3" indicates that the ZIP code is in the third field from the top of each record in **PARKLIST.SF**.

11. Press the **<Right> arrow** key twice to move the cursor to the Word number.

    The third field in your merge record has only one line so you accepted the default "1" as the Line number.

12. Type **-1** (minus one).

    Because words in a field are counted from left to right and because the cities in the merge records are sometimes more than one word, you used "-1" to indicate that the words in the field should be counted from right to left. The ZIP code is always the last (rightmost) word in the third field.

13. Press **F7** to Save the key with **PARKLIST.SF**

    The Sort submenu appears on your screen.

14. Type **1** to select "Perform Action".

    In a few seconds the sorted merge records appear on your screen. The records are in ascending (the default) ZIP code order. If a record has a blank ZIP code field, that record(s) would be displayed at the top of the sorted records so you know that the sort key information is missing.

15. Save and Replace **PARKLIST.SF**

    If you were to merge **PARKLIST.SF** with a primary file, the documents would be created in ascending order by ZIP code.

188   WordPerfect 5.0

> **Hint:** If you decide to send letters to only the national park superintendents located in Utah, you can select those records and sort them in descending ZIP code order.

GUIDED ACTIVITY: SELECTING AND SORTING RECORDS

1. Retrieve **PARKLIST.SF** if necessary.

2. Press **Ctrl-F9** to access the Merge/Sort menu.

3. Type **2** to Sort the records.

4. Press **<ENTER>** twice to sort the file on your screen and to display the selected and sorted records on your screen.

   The Sort submenu appears at the bottom of your screen and is headed "Sort Secondary Merge File".

5. Type **6** to select Order from the Sort submenu.

   The Order submenu appears on your screen.

6. Type **2** to select Descending from the Order submenu.

   The Sort submenu appears on your screen.

7. Type **3** to select Keys from the Sort submenu.

   The cursor moves to "Type a" for Key 1 and the Keys submenu appears at the bottom of your screen.

8. Press the **<Right> arrow** key three times.

   You have accepted Type a (alphanumeric) Field and Line numbers and moved the cursor to the Word number.

9. Type **-2** (minus two).

   You have indicated that the state name is the second word from the right end of the third field.

10. Press **F7** to Save Key 1.

    The Sort submenu appears on your screen.

11. Press **4** to choose "Select" from the Sort submenu.

    The cursor moves to the "Select" criteria area and select symbols appear at the bottom of the screen.

12. Type **Key1=Utah**

13. Press **<ENTER>**

    The Sort submenu appears at the bottom of your screen.

14. Type **1** to select "Perform Action" from the Sort submenu.

    In a few seconds the selected and sorted records (two) will appear on your screen in descending ZIP-code order.

15. Save the selected and sorted records with the filename **UTAH.SF**

What You Have Accomplished

You defined a "key" and sorted an entire file in ascending order based on the ZIP code. You created another "key" and specified criteria for selecting specific records and sorted those selected records in descending order. You saved the file with the name **UTAH.SF.** You can merge **UTAH.SF** with **PARKLIST.PF** to print letters only to national parks in Utah.

GUIDED ACTIVITY: ADDRESSING ENVELOPES

1. Clear the screen.

2. Press **Shift-F8** to access the Format menu.

3. Type **2** to access the Page submenu.

4. Type **8** to choose "Paper Size and Type."

    The Paper Size submenu appears on your screen.

5. Type **5** to choose the standard 9.5" x 4" business envelope size.

    The Paper Type submenu appears on your screen.

6. Type **5** to select Envelope size paper from the Paper Type submenu.

    The Format Page submenu appears on your screen. Notice the message "(*requested form is unavailable)" in the lower right-hand corner of the screen. The message means that no special instructions for the envelope form have been defined, but WordPerfect 5.0 will still print the address.

7. Type **5** to choose Margins from the Page submenu.

8. Type **2.5"** for the Top margin for a business envelope.

190   WordPerfect 5.0

9. Press **<ENTER>** to enter the top margin and move the cursor to the bottom margin setting.

10. Type **0** (zero) to set the bottom margin to zero.

11. Press **<ENTER>** to enter the bottom margin.

12. Press **F7** to return to the clear screen

13. Press **Shift-F8** to access the Format menu.

14. Type **1** to access the Line submenu.

15. Type **7** to choose Margins from the Line submenu.

    The cursor moves to the left margin setting.

16. Type **4.5"** to set the left margin.

17. Press **<ENTER>** to enter the left margin and move the cursor to the right-margin setting.

18. Type **0"** (zero inches) to set the right margin.

19. Press **<ENTER>**

    The right margin is set at .25", the minimum setting.

20. Press **F7** to return to the document (clear screen).

    Your cursor is at Ln 2.5" and Pos 4.5".

21. Press **Shift-F9** to access the Merge Codes menu.

22. Type **F**

    The "Field:" prompt appears on your screen.

23. Type **1**

24. Press **<ENTER>** twice.

    The code, ^F1^ , is embedded in your primary file. This code will retrieve information from field one of your **UTAH.SF** or **PARKLIST.SF** secondary file.

25. Follow steps 21 through 24 to add the ^F2^ and ^F3^ codes to the primary file.

26. Save this document as **ENVELOPE.PF**

27. Merge the secondary file, **UTAH.SF**, and the primary file, **ENVELOPE.PF**. Name the merged file **UTAH.ENV**

GUIDED ACTIVITY: PRINTING ENVELOPES

1. Retrieve **UTAH.ENV**

2. Press **Shift-F7** to print **UTAH.ENV**

   Rather than using envelopes, you might cut 9.5" x 4" rectangles. If you use sheet-fed or continuous-feed printer paper loaded in your printer in the usual way, each envelope will be printed on a separate sheet of paper.

   WordPerfect will "beep" at you and display a message on the Control Printer submenu telling you to "Insert paper" and "Press 'G' to continue".

3. Press **1** to print the full document.

4. Press **4** to access the Control Printer submenu. Notice the message next to the "Action:" heading.

5. If you are using your printer's regular paper, go on to the next step. If you are using envelopes or cut rectangles, load one in the printer.

6. Type **G** to indicate that printing should continue.

   The first envelope will be printed. The computer will again "beep" and the same message will appear on the Control Printer submenu.

7. Follow the previous two steps to print the rest of the envelopes. If you are using continuous-feed paper, you will have to type G twice: once to advance the paper and once to print.

8. Return to your document and Exit WordPerfect 5.0.

MAILING LABELS

A merge operation can also be used to produce mailing labels. The addresses you need are already stored in your data base in **UTAH.SF** or **PARKLIST.SF**. Another primary file must be created, however, for the mailing labels. Use the same procedure you used to create the primary file for envelopes.

FORMATTING MAILING LABELS

Before merging files to print labels, you must select a label format. Assume that your labels are 1-7/16" x 4" and single width. (This means that the labels are arranged one after another on 4-inch-wide continuous-feed paper.)

192 WordPerfect 5.0

Setting the Left, Right, Top, and Bottom Margins

Set the left margin at .5" and the right margin at 0" to format a page with a 1/2-inch-wide left margin.

Set the top margin at .25" and the bottom margin at 0".

Creating the Page Format

Access the Format menu (Shift-F8), then the Page submenu, and then the Paper size submenu. Select "Other" from the Paper size submenu and enter 4" for the page width and 1.44" (the decimal equivalent of 1-7/16") for the page height.
Creating a Mailing Label Primary File

Create the mailing label file using the same procedure used for the envelope primary file.

✔CHECKPOINT

g. Which menus are needed to set the page format for a mailing label or an envelope?

_____

h. Which menu is needed to set the right and left margins?

_____

MORE ON MERGING

Merging is a timesaving feature that allows you to print hundreds of form letters while you are using your computer for other purposes. You can merge text from several primary files to assemble one comprehensive document. The code for linking primary files is: ^P(filename)^P. You can also link secondary files to one another. For example, you may create a number of secondary files that fulfil specific mailing requirements, then combine the data from several secondary files for a larger mailing. The code for linking secondary files is ^S(filename)^S.

The automatic printing code (^T) allows you to embed a merge code that sends each merged letter directly to the printer. This code eliminates waiting for the merging operation to be completed before printing the merged letters. A Next code (^N) tells the program to look for the next record in the secondary file and repeat the automatic printing process until all the records in the secondary file have been merged with the primary file. The automatic printing code is efficient except for merge operations that do not require keyboard entries.

You can stop a merge operation in progress by inserting the Quit command (^Q). Place a ^Q anywhere in either a secondary or primary file and the merging operation will end.

REVIEW QUESTIONS

1. Explain the meaning of "secondary file" as it is used in merging operations.

2. Define "record" as it is used to create a data base.

3. Define "field" as it is used to create a data base.

4. Which code is used to indicate the end of a field?

5. Which code is used to indicate the end of a record?

6. Which code should you choose from the Merge Codes menu to indicate that you have inserted a message in your primary document?

7. If you would like to enter text from your keyboard, which code should you embed in your primary document?

8. Explain the meaning of "primary file" as it is used in merging operations.

9. What is the most prevalent use for a merge operation?

DOCUMENTATION RESEARCH

1. A secondary file is often referred to as an "address file." How much information can be placed in a secondary file?

2. The fields contained in each record within a secondary file can vary in size. Explain how to enter two address lines in a single field.

---

3. Suppose that field seven on a secondary file you are creating contains a social security number. Some of your clients, however, do not have social security numbers. How would you handle field seven when creating a record for these individuals?

---

4. If you are working with a very large secondary file, it is possible that the internal memory capacity of the computer you are using will not be large enough to handle the merge operation. Suggest several ways to solve this problem.

REVIEW EXERCISES

1. Create a Page Format for 1-7/16" x 4" mailing labels.

2. Create a primary file for the mailing labels. Name the file **LABELS.PF**

3. Merge **UTAH.SF** with **LABELS.PF** Name this file **LABELS.EX** Save **LABELS.EX**

4. Retrieve and Print **LABELS.EX** on whatever paper your printer normally uses.

5. Draw a rectangle 1-7/16 x 4 inches around each address to see if the formatting was done correctly.

6. Enter a list of five book titles on a clear screen.

7. Sort the list so that the titles are in alphabetical order.

8. Add a Document Identification Line to the bottom of the document.

9. Name the document **TITLES.DOC**

10. Print and Save the document. Exit WordPerfect 5.0.

UNIT 11
MACROS

SUPPLIES NEEDED

1. WordPerfect 1 and 2 disks
2. WordPerfect Student Data disk
3. printer

OBJECTIVES

After completing this unit, you will be able to

1. create and use macros.

IMPORTANT KEYSTROKES

1. Ctrl-F10   to define a macro
2. Alt-F10   to start a macro

ASSIGNMENTS

1. Edit **WORDWRAP** using a Macro
2. Retrieve and Print **WORDWRAP** with a Macro
3. Review Questions
4. Documentation Research
5. Review Exercises

MACROS

When you create a **macro**, you program WordPerfect to do with one keystroke what is normally done with several keystrokes. The macros you create are stored in a file and retrieved whenever they are needed. A macro can consist of commands or commands and text.

A macro is useful for any word-processing task that requires repetitive keystokes. For example, if you type many letters with the same closing, you can store that closing in a macro file; then with a single keystroke you can insert the closing into your document.

A macro can also be used to store a series of commands. For example, you may use the same series of Print Format instructions to prepare your form letters for printing. By placing these instructions in a macro file, you can enter the necessary commands with just one keystroke.

Macros can be chained together in such a way that several sets (files) of text or commands are executed one after another. A macro can be repeated a specific number of times by using the <ESC> key. A macro can be nested (embedded) within another macro. The nested macro will be executed at the point where it is embedded.

The first step in creating a macro is to name it. You can name a permanent macro in two ways: either type a name using two to eight characters or hold down <Alt> while typing a single letter from A to Z. WordPerfect automatically adds the extension ".WPM" to identify the macro file. After you name the macro you can enter a macro description of up to 39 characters.

To start the execution of a macro, press **Alt-F10**, then type the name of the macro. The text or commands stored in the macro file are automatically inserted into the document you are creating. To start execution of a macro named with the <Alt> key, hold down Alt then type the letter you used to name the macro.

GUIDED ACTIVITY: CREATING A PERMANENT MACRO TO PRINT A DOCUMENT

Turn your printer off while creating this macro.

1. Press the **Ctrl-F10** keys.

   The prompt "Define macro:" will appear in the status line.

2. Type **Print**

   You have named this macro file "Print."

3. Press <ENTER>

   The message "Description:" appears on the screen.

Macros   197

4. Type **This macro will print a document.**

5. Press **<ENTER>**

   The message "Macro Def" will appear. Each keystroke made from now until the macro has been defined will be stored in this macro file.

6. Press the **Shift-F7** keys.

   The Print command has been entered into the macro definition. This is the first instruction that will be executed when this macro is retrieved. The Print menu will also appear on the screen.

7. Type **1**

   The full-text option (option 1 on the Print submenu) has been entered into the macro definition.

8. Press **Ctrl-F10** again.

   You have completed the task of defining a macro. The "Macro Def" message has disappeared from the status line.

9. Exit and clear the screen.

What You Have Accomplished

You have defined a macro that will print the full text of a document. The macro has been stored in a file named **PRINT.WPM**. Each time you retrieve this file, the full text of the document you are working on will be printed.

✔**CHECKPOINT**

   a. Which keys are used to define a macro?

   _____

   b. How is a macro definition ended?

   _____

GUIDED ACTIVITY: CREATING A MACRO TO STORE MARGIN SETTINGS

1. Begin with a clear screen.

2. Press the **Ctrl-F10** keys to define a macro.

   The prompt "Define macro:" will appear at the bottom of the screen.

3. Type **Margins**

   You have named a macro file.

4. Press <ENTER>

   The message "Description:" will appear on the screen.

5. Type **This macro will set 2" side margins.**

6. Press <ENTER>

   The flashing message "Macro Def" will appear in the status line. Each keystroke made from now until the macro has been defined will be stored in this macro file.

7. Press the **Shift-F8** keys.

   The Format menu will appear on the screen.

8. Type **1**

   The Line Format submenu will appear on the screen.

9. Type **7** to choose Margins.

10. Type **2**

11. Press <ENTER>

    Notice that WordPerfect automatically entered the inch symbol (") for you. The left margin has been reset to 2".

12. Type **2**

13. Press <ENTER>

    The right margin has been set to 2".

14. Type 0 (zero) twice to return to your document.

    The new margin settings have been stored in the macro file named **MARGINS.WPM.**

15. Press the **Ctrl-F10** keys.

    You have completed the macro definition.

✔ CHECKPOINT

    c. When do you begin defining a macro?

GUIDED ACTIVITY: CREATING A MACRO THAT CONTAINS TEXT

This macro creates a centered heading in a document. The macro is named with the Alt key.

1. Begin with a clear screen.

2. Press the **Ctrl-F10** keys to define a macro.

3. Press the **Alt-H** keys.

    This macro will be named **ALTH.WPM** and the message "Description:" will appear on the screen.

4. Press **<ENTER>** five times to bypass the "Description" and insert four blank lines at the top of your document.

5. Press the **<Home>,<Home>,<Up>** arrow keys to move the cursor to the beginning of the document.

6. Press the **Shift-F6** keys to turn on Center.

7. Type your name.

    Your name will be centered on the first line of a document when this macro is retrieved.

8. Press **<ENTER>** to start a new line.

9. Press the **Shift-F6** keys to activate the Center feature.

10. Type **Unit 11 Macros**

    This title will be centered on the second line of your document when this macro is retrieved.

11. Press **<ENTER>** to terminate the Center feature.

12. Press the **Ctrl-F10** keys.

    You have completed this macro definition. The macro has been saved with the name **ALTH.WPM**.

✔**CHECKPOINT**

    d. How do you name a macro using the Alt key?

GUIDED ACTIVITY: RETRIEVING A MACRO

Turn your printer on.

1. Clear the screen.

2. Retrieve **WORDWRAP**

3. Press the **Alt-H** keys.

    You have retrieved the macro named **ALTH.WPM**. Two lines of a centered heading will automatically be inserted into your document.

4. Press the **Alt-F10** keys.

    The prompt "Macro:" will appear on the screen.

5. Type **Margins**

    You have identified the filename of the macro you wish to retrieve.

6. Press **<ENTER>**

    The margins you specified will be set automatically.

7. Press the **Alt-F10** keys to start a macro.

8. Type **Print**

    You have identified the filename of the macro you wish to retrieve.

9. Press **<ENTER>**

    The document **WORDWRAP** will be printed.

10. Press **F7** to Exit and Save. Name your document **WRDWRP2**

✔**CHECKPOINT**

    e. How do you retrieve a macro?

f. How do you retrieve a macro that was named by using the Alt keys?

What You Have Accomplished

You have retrieved three macros that were stored in separate files on your data storage disk. The text stored in the **ALTH.WPM** file was automatically inserted into your document. The commands stored in your other two files were automatically executed when the macro was retrieved.

The document **WORDWRAP** was automatically printed with a centered header and adjusted line margins.

Hint: Each macro file you create is listed in the directory. You can identify them by looking for the ".WPM" extension. A macro can be retrieved only with the Macro keys. If you attempt to retrieve it with the Retrieve (Shift-F10) or List Files (F5) command, you could damage the macro files.

GUIDED ACTIVITY: CREATING A MACRO CHAIN

This macro will retrieve a file, insert a heading, change the margin settings, and print a document.

1. Begin with a clear screen.

2. Press the **Ctrl-F10** keys to define a macro.

    The prompt "Define macro:" will appear in the status line.

3. Type **Chain** to name this macro.

4. Press **<ENTER>**

    The message "Description:" appears on the screen.

5. Type **This macro chains four macros.**

6. Press **<ENTER>**

    The prompt "Macro Def" will appear in the status line.

7. Press the **Shift-F10** keys to Retrieve.

    The prompt "Document to be retrieved:" will appear in the status line.

8. Type **WORDWRAP**

WordPerfect 5.0

9. Press <ENTER>

   The document **WORDWRAP** will appear on the screen.

10. Press the **Alt-F10** keys to start the second macro in the chain.

    The prompt "Macro" will appear in the status line.

11. Press the **Alt-H** keys to start the second macro in your chain.

12. Press the **Alt-F10** keys to start the third macro in the chain.

    The prompt "Macro" will appear in the status line.

13. Type **Margins** to start the third macro in the chain. Press <ENTER>

14. Press the **Alt-F10** keys to start the fourth macro in the chain.

    The prompt "Macro" will appear in the status line.

15. Type **Print** to name the macro you are starting.

16. Press <ENTER>

    The prompt "Macro Def" will appear in the status line.

17. Press the **Ctrl-F10** keys.

    You have completed the task of defining a macro chain. WordPerfect will save this macro chain under the filename **CHAIN.WPM**.

✔CHECKPOINT

g. Which keystrokes are needed to begin the definition of a macro chain?

h. Which keystrokes are needed to end the definition of a macro chain?

GUIDED ACTIVITY: USING A MACRO CHAIN

Turn your printer on.

1. Begin with a clear screen.

2. Press the **Alt-F10** keys.

Macros   203

3. Type **Chain** Press **<ENTER>**

   The macro chain **CHAIN.WPM** will be executed.

4. Name your file **WRDWRP3**. Exit WordPerfect.

What You Have Accomplished

You have created a macro chain that incorporates three of the macros you previously created. When you typed the name of the macro, your document was retrieved, a header inserted, margins reset, and the revised document printed.

Hint: Should you change your mind after a macro has started, just press Cancel to stop it.

REVIEW QUESTIONS

1. What is a macro?

2. What information can be stored in a macro file?

3. What keystrokes are needed to define a macro?

4. How can you stop the execution of a macro once it has begun?

5. Name several word-processing tasks for which macros can be used.

6. What is a macro chain?

7. How do you Retrieve a macro?

DOCUMENTATION RESEARCH

1. What is the difference in the execution of a chain macro and a nested macro?

2. Which key can be used to repeat a macro a specific number of times?

3. What does the "/m" option do?

4. How can you name a macro with the <ENTER> key? How do you start a macro that was named with the <ENTER> key?

REVIEW EXERCISES

1. Create a macro to Retrieve **EXERCISE.DOC**. Name the macro **RETRIEVE**

2. Use the macro to Retrieve **EXERCISE.DOC**

3. Update the Document Identification Line.

4. Use the macro **PRINT.WPM** that you created in this unit to Print your document.

5. Exit WordPerfect.

APPLICATION D

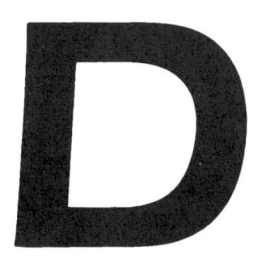

SUPPLIES NEEDED

1. WordPerfect 5.0 program disks 1 and 2
2. WordPerfect 5.0 Learning disk
3. WordPerfect 5.0 Student Data disk
4. printer

ASSIGNMENTS

The assignments to be completed for this application section are:

1. Create **DIL.WPM**
2. Create **ADDRESS.SF**
3. Create **MEETING.PF**
4. Create **MEETING.TXT**

GENERAL DIRECTIONS

Application D contains documents you can use to practice the skills you have acquired. You will need to apply both the fundamentals of Parts 1 and 2 as well as the features of Chapters 10 and 11 to reproduce these documents.

The documents offer you the opportunity to practice to creating primary and secondary files for merge operations. The macro, **DIL.WPM**, gives you a chance to practice macros.

Use your template, Quick Reference card, and the WordPerfect user's manual to find the keystroke commands and menus you need. Remember that there is often more than one keystroke choice that can be used to create and format a document. Your primary task is to find the most efficient way to reproduce the documents.

You may also want to create your own applications - some tasks that are more meaningful to your everyday work. Your WordPerfect Student Data disk should have plenty of space available (use List Files to find out how much) to store additional documents.

Follow the directions below to create the documents in Application D.

Document D-1

1. Name this macro file **DIL**
2. Define a macro to create the Document Identification Line for any document.
3. Retrieve your macro on a clear screen.
4. Print the document.

Document D-2

1. Create a secondary file for a merge operation. Name it **ADDRESS.SF**
2. Enter the names and addresses on the Document D-2 page.
3. Save the document.

Document D-3

1. Create a primary file for a merge operation. Name it **MEETING.PF**
2. Enter the meeting notice on the Document D-5 page.
3. Use the macro created above to add the Document Identification Line to the bottom of the document.
4. Save the document.

Document D-4

1. Merge **ADDRESS.SF** with **MEETING.PF** to create a document named **MEETING.TXT**
2. Type November 20 as the meeting date and 7:00 p.m. as the meeting time when the merge pauses.
3. Save **MEETING.TXT**
4. Print the three personalized documents.

Mary Ann Jensen^R
6952 Charles Street^R
Marine, MN 55029^R
Mary Ann^R
^E
Jennifer Lund^R
2293 Guslander Trail^R
Scandia, MN 55047^R
Jennifer^R
^E
James Hernandez^R
1649 Park Street^R
Forest Lake, MN 55080^R
James^R
^E

Document D-2 **ADDRESS.SF**

^D(current date)

^F1^(name)
^F2^(street address)
^F3^(city, state, and Zip code)

Dear ^F4^(first name):

We are anxious to have a large turnout at our May Strategic Planning meeting. We have two speakers coming whom you may have heard about. We must also finalize next year's budget.

The meeting will be on ^O type date of meeting ^O^C at ^O type time of meeting ^O^C. Please post this date on your calendar.

Sincerely,

(your name)
Chairperson

Document Identification Line

Document D-3 MEETING.PF

UNIT 12 COLUMNS

SUPPLIES NEEDED

1. WordPerfect 5.0 program 1 and 2 disks
2. WordPerfect Student Data disk
3. printer

OBJECTIVES

After completing this unit, you will be able to

1. define a newspaper column;
2. define a parallel column.

IMPORTANT KEYSTROKES

1. Alt-F7   to create text columns

ASSIGNMENTS

1. Create **WORDPER2.COL**
2. Create **PARALLEL.COL**
3. Review Questions
4. Documentation Research
5. Review Exercises

TEXT COLUMNS

Text columns are distinguished from **numeric** columns because they are set up to make it convenient to enter text. Text is entered into one column to the end of the page or until you command the column function to terminate. The following text is then entered into the next defined column, and so on, until the page is filled. In text columns you cannot tab from column to column as you do in numeric columns.

Both parallel columns and newspaper columns can be created with WordPerfect 5.0. In newspaper columns, text flows from the bottom of one column to the top of the next column. In parallel columns, related groups of text are placed side by side (as, for example, in comparison tables).

Two to twenty-four text columns can be defined. Defining columns is much like setting margins, except that the task is done automatically. The column format you have defined appears on your screen as well as on the printed document. After defining columns you can enter text or you can define columns for previously entered text.

To edit newspaper columns use the arrow keys to move around in a column. To move the cursor to another column, use Ctrl-<Home> and the <Right> or <Left> arrow key.

THE MATH/COLUMNS MENU

When you press **Alt-F7**, the Math/Columns menu (figure 12-1) appears on your screen. The first two options on this menu are used to set up numeric columns for mathematical calculations. The last two options are used to define, start, and display text columns. Select an option by typing one of the listed numbers.

---

1 Math On; 2 Math Def; 3 Column On/Off; 4 Column Def: 0

FIGURE 12-1   Math/Columns Menu

Options 1 and 2 apply to math columns and are discussed in Unit 14. The Column feature options are defined as follows:

> 3 Column On/Off   This option is selected when you wish either to begin or end the Column feature. When the Column feature is turned on, a [Col On] code is placed in your document and a "Col" message appears in the status line. When the Column feature is turned off, a [Col Off] code is placed in your text and the "Col" message disappears from your status line. Columns must first be defined before the Column feature can be turned on.

4 Column Def The Text Column Definition submenu (figure 12-2) appears. With this submenu, you can define the style, width, and number of text columns you wish to create.

```
Text Column Definition

    1-      Type                              Newspaper

    2-      Number of Columns                 2

    3-      Distance Between Columns

    4-      Margins

    Column      Left        Right       Column      Left        Right
      1:        1"          4"            13:
      2:        4.5"        7.5"          14:
      3:                                  15:
      4:                                  16:
      5:                                  17:
      6:                                  18:
      7:                                  19:
      8:                                  20:
      9:                                  21:
     10:                                  22:
     11:                                  23:
     12:                                  24:

    Selection: 0
```

FIGURE 12-2 Text Column Definition Submenu

Here are some guidelines for defining text columns:

If you want your columns to be the same width, WordPerfect 5.0 will automatically calculate the margin settings and display them on this submenu. You must designate the number of text columns (2-24) and the distance between columns.

If you would like columns of varying widths, type 4 and reset the right margins.

If you wish to set up parallel columns, type 1 after the prompt "Selection:". The Column Type submenu (figure 12-3) will appear. You can choose parallel columns with or without block protection. A block protection code will be inserted to keep groups of text together.

Column Type: 1 Newspaper; 2 Parallel; 3 Parallel with Block Protect: 0

FIGURE 12-3   Column Type Submenu

GUIDED ACTIVITY: CREATING A NEWSPAPER COLUMN

1. Retrieve **WORDPER2.DOC** from your Student Data disk.

2. Move the cursor to the beginning of the document below the heading.

3. Press the **Alt-F7** keys.

    The Math/Columns menu will appear on the screen.

4. Type **4**

    The Text Column Definition submenu will appear.

5. Type **3** to choose Distance Between Columns

6. Press **<ENTER>** to accept the default distance of one-half inch.

    Notice that the column margins are set automatically.

7. Type **0** (zero) to return to your document and the Math/Columns menu.

8. Type **3** to turn on the Columns feature.

9. Move the cursor to the end of the document. The columns automatically form on the screen. The left column fills to the end of the page before text is entered into the right column.

10. Move the cursor to the blank line above the third paragraph beginning "We think it's because..."

11. Press the **Ctrl-<ENTER>** keys to create a Hard Page break. The remainder of the left column will be moved to the top of the right column.

12. Press **<ENTER>** to align the text in columns 1 and 2.

13. Move the cursor to the bottom of the right column.

14. Press the **Alt-F7** keys.

    The Math/Columns menu will appear on the screen.

15. Type **3** to turn off the Columns feature.

16. Add the Document Identification Line to the bottom of the document.

17. Name this document **WORDPER2.COL**

18. Save and Print **WORDPER2.COL**

✔CHECKPOINT

    a. How do you use the Text Column Definition submenu to create newspaper columns?

---

    b. How do you turn on the Columns feature?

What You Have Accomplished

You have reformatted the text of **WORDPER2.TXT** to print in two newspaper columns. The margins for these columns were calculated automatically. You inserted a [Col On] code to begin the Column feature and a [Col Off] code to end it.

GUIDED ACTIVITY: CREATING PARALLEL COLUMNS

1. Display a clear screen.

2. Press the **Alt-F7** keys to display the Math/Columns menu.

3. Type **4**

    The Text Column Definition submenu will appear.

4. Type **1** to select Type from the submenu.

    The Column Type submenu appears.

5. Type **2** to choose Parallel columns.

    Groups of related information will be kept together on a page.

6. Type **2** to choose Number of Columns.

7. Type **3**

    You have chosen to create three columns. The margins of each column will be calculated automatically and displayed on the Text Column Definition submenu.

8. Press **<ENTER>**

9. Type **0** (zero) to accept the default distance of one-half inch between columns.

    The Math/Columns menu reappears on the screen.

10. Type **3** to turn on the Column feature.

11. Type **Mary O'Ryan**

    Notice that the column number is shown in the status line.

12. Press the **Ctrl-<ENTER>** keys to wrap to the second column.

13. Type the following address in column 2:

    **400 Second Drive
    El Paso, TX 43296**

14. Press the **Ctrl-<ENTER>** keys to wrap to the third column.

15. Type the following telephone number in column 3:

    742-456-9146

16. Press the **Ctrl-<ENTER>** keys to wrap to the beginning of the first column.

17. Repeat steps 11 through 16 to enter the following records in parallel columns:

    **Jerry Jackson
    945 Oak Street
    El Paso, TX 43296
    742-555-6789**

    **Judy Martilla
    456 Myrtle Avenue
    El Paso, TX 43296
    742-796-9221**

18. Press the **Alt-F7** keys.

    The Math/Columns menu will appear on the screen.

19. Type **3** to turn off the Column feature.

20. Add the Document Identification Line at the bottom of the document.

21. Name this file **PARALLEL.COL**

22. Save and Print **PARALLEL.COL**

Hint: Each of the columns you have defined is independent of the others. You can move the cursor to add or delete text in one column without affecting the text in the neighboring columns.

✔CHECKPOINT

c. Which keys are used to wrap to the next column?

d. How do you define parallel columns?

What You Have Accomplished

You have learned that parallel columns are defined in a slightly different manner than are newspaper columns. Block protection codes are placed around related groups of information to protect them from a page break.

REVIEW QUESTIONS

1. Explain the difference between a newspaper column and a parallel column.

2. Which option on the Math/Columns submenu would you choose to turn on the Column feature?

3. Suppose that you have decided to use WordPerfect 5.0 to produce your company newsletter. In what order would you perform the following tasks? (a) Type the articles that will be contained in the newsletter, (b) Turn on the Columns feature, (c) Establish the width of your columns.

4. Which text column style would you choose to display related information side by side? Describe how to select this style.

5. Describe how an existing document is reformatted into text columns.

DOCUMENTATION RESEARCH

1. You can display each column of your document on a separate page. What does this form of display accomplish? How will the columns be printed?

2. How are parallel columns protected from page breaks that could separate related groups of text?

3. Describe how the cursor movement keys are used to edit text columns.

REVIEW EXERCISES

1. Use the Column (parallel type) feature to list the title, a short description, and number of credits of five courses offered at your school.

2. Add the Document Identification Line to the document. Name it **CATALOG.EX**

3. Save and Print the document.

4. On a clear screen copy or create a long newspaper article. Using the Column (newspaper type) feature, arrange the article in four columns.

5. Turn off the Column feature. Add the Document Identification Line to the bottom of the document. Name the document **NEWS.EX**

6. Save and Print the document.

UNIT 13
TABLES OF CONTENTS, LISTS, AND INDEXES

SUPPLIES NEEDED

1. WordPerfect 1 and 2 disks
2. WordPerfect Student Data disk
3. printer

OBJECTIVES

After completing this unit, you will be able to

1. mark text to create a table of contents;
2. create an index.

IMPORTANT KEYSTROKES

1. Alt-F5   to mark text for a list, a table of contents, or an index

ASSIGNMENTS

1. Create a Table of Contents
2. Create an Index
3. Review Questions
4. Documentation Research
5. Review Exercises

TABLES OF CONTENTS, LISTS, AND INDEXES

One of WordPerfect's special features is its capability to generate a table of contents, a list of figures or illustrations, or an index. This is especially useful for very long documents.

A table of contents, list, or index is created by using text from your document. Codes -- [Mark] and [End Mark] -- must be inserted into the document to mark the text you will use. You can generate a table of contents with up to five levels of heads, as many as nine different lists, or an index with both headings and subheadings.

The table of contents, list, or index you generate will most likely require page references. WordPerfect offers five different styles for numbering pages. A code must be placed in the text to define a numbering style.

MARKING TEXT

To mark text, turn Block on, move the cursor-movement keys across each word or words of text you want in your contents, list, or index, then press **Alt-F5** (the Mark Text keys). The Mark Text menu (figure 13-1) will appear on your screen. Select the option that identifies the feature you are creating by typing one of the listed numbers.

Options 3 and 4 are identical to options 3 and 4 on the Mark Text menu (with Block off) and are defined following figure 13-2.

Mark for: 1 ToC; 2 List; 3 Index; 4 ToA;   0

FIGURE 13-1   Mark Text Menu (Block On)

When you press the **Alt-F5** keys with Block off, the Mark Text menu (figure 13-2) has different options. This menu is used to mark a single index word, to define a numbering style, and to generate your contents, list, or index.

---

1 Auto Ref; 2 Subdoc; 3 Index; 4 ToA Short Form; 5 Define; 6 Generate: 0

FIGURE 13-2   Mark Text Menu (Block Off)

The Mark Text menu options (with Block off) are defined as follows:

1. Auto Ref   Automatic reference is used to create and edit references to page numbers, footnote and endnote numbers, figure and paragraph numbers. If you edit a long document, the references are updated automatically.

2. Subdoc   This option inserts into a master document a code that refers to a subdocument file. When the complete document is created, the subdocument file is pulled into the master document.

3. Index   The prompt "Index heading:" appears. The word at the cursor location appears beside the prompt. If you prefer to enter your own heading, type over the one displayed. Then press <ENTER> and the prompt "Subheading:" appears. Type a subheading if you want one. If you entered your own heading after the first prompt, the word at the cursor location appears again. Press <ENTER> to use the displayed text for a subheading or use the <DEL> or <BACKSPACE> key to erase the displayed text, then type your own subheading.

4. ToA Short Form   This option marks text for inclusion in a table of authorities. The prompt "Short Form:" appears. You can block (Mark Text, Block On) or type the text (Mark Text, Block Off) you want to include.

5. Define   The Mark Text Definition submenu (figure 13-3) appears on the screen. With this option, you can define a numbering style for the list, table of contents, table of authorities, or index you are creating. You can also edit a table of authorities (full form).

    The options on this submenu are used to select the feature (contents, list, index, or table of authorities) you wish to create. Each option selection displays a submenu that offers five different numbering styles. The Table of Contents Definition submenu (figure 13-4) offers five levels that can each be numbered in a unique style.

6. Generate   When you select this option, the list, table of contents, or index you have defined is created. This prompt appears: "Have you deleted your old Table of Contents, Lists, and Index? (Y/N) N". A counter at the bottom of your computer screen keeps you informed of the program's progress.

```
Mark Text: Define

    1 - Define Table of Contents

    2 - Define List

    3 - Define Index

    4 - Define Table of Authorities

    5 - Edit Table of Authorities Full Form

Selection: 0
```

FIGURE 13-3   Mark Text Definition Submenu

```
Table of Contents Definition

    1 - Number of Levels                    1

    2 - Display Last Level in              No
        Wrapped Format

    3 - Page Numbering - Level 1    Flush right with leader
                         Level 2
                         Level 3
                         Level 4
                         Level 5

    Selection: 0
```

FIGURE 13-4   Table of Contents Definition Submenu

GUIDED ACTIVITY: CREATING A TABLE OF CONTENTS

1. Retrieve **HUMAN.REL**

2. Block the title of the document.

3. Press the **Alt-F5** keys.

   The Mark Text menu will appear.

4. Type **1**

   The prompt "ToC Level:" will appear on your screen.

5. Type **1** to indicate a first-level heading.

6. Block the topic heading "Human Relations Competencies".

7. Press the **Alt-F5** keys to display the Mark Text menu.

8. Type **1** to select Table of Contents.

   The prompt "ToC Level:" will appear in the status line.

9. Type **2** to indicate a second-level heading.

10. Block the topic heading "Mutual Reward".

11. Press the **Alt-F5** keys to display the Mark Text menu.

12. Type **1** to select Table of Contents.

    The prompt "ToC Level:" will appear in the status line.

13. Type **3** to indicate a third-level heading.

14. Scroll through the document until you find other second- or third-level topic heading. Repeat steps 6 through 13 until all second-level and third-level headings have been marked.

15. To define and generate the table of contents, move the cursor a few lines below the text of **HUMAN.REL**.

16. Press the **Ctrl-<ENTER>** keys to create a Hard Page break.

17. Type **TABLE OF CONTENTS**

18. Press the **<ENTER>** three times to insert two blank lines.

19. Press the **Alt-F5** keys to display the Mark Text menu.

20. Type **5** to display the Mark Text Definition submenu.

21. Type **1** to define the table of contents and display the Table of Contents Definition submenu.

22. Type **1** to choose the Number of Levels option.

224   WordPerfect 5.0

23. Type **3**

    You have indicated that there are three levels of entries in your table of contents.

24. Type **3** to choose the Page Numbering option.

    The Page Numbering submenu appears at the bottom of your screen. Notice that "Flush right with leader" is the default.

25. Type **3** to choose the "(Pg#) Follows" option.

    The page number of each Level 1 table of contents entry will be followed with the page number in parentheses. The cursor has moved to Level 2.

26. Type **3** twice to choose the "(Pg#) Follows" option for Levels 2 and 3.

27. Press **F7** twice to Save your choices and return to your document.

28. Press the **Alt-F5** keys again to display the Mark Text menu.

29. Type **6** to Generate the table of contents. The "Mark Text: Generate" screen will appear.

30. Type **5**

    The prompt "Existing tables, lists and indexes will be replaced. Continue? (Y/N) Yes" will appear on the screen.

31. Type **Y** to continue with the Table of Contents generation.

    The prompt "Generation in progress. Counter:" will appear in the status line while the table is being generated.

    In a few seconds the table of contents for **HUMAN.REL** will appear on the screen.

32. Add the Document Identification Line to the the document.

33. Block and Save the Table of Contents page with the name **CONTENTS**

34. Print the table of contents page.

    ✔**CHECKPOINT**

    a. Which keys are needed to access the Mark Text menu?

Tables of Contents, Lists, and Indexes   225

b. What is the first step in marking text for a table of contents?

_____

c. Which option to generates a table of contents?

_____

What You Have Accomplished

You have used the Block key and the Mark Text menu to create a table of contents. Your table of contents contains three levels of heads. Each header of your table also contains a page reference, which will be printed following the header.

GUIDED ACTIVITY: CREATING AN INDEX

1. Retrieve **HUMAN.REL**

2. Move the cursor to the first heading, "Human Relations Competencies".

3. Block the heading to mark it for inclusion in the index.

4. Press **Alt-F5** to access the Mark Text menu.

5. Type **3** to select the Index option.

    The message "Index heading: Human Relations Competencies" will appear.

6. Press **<ENTER>** twice to bypass the subheading option and to mark the blocked heading for inclusion in the index.

7. Move the cursor to the next heading, "Mutual Reward". Block the heading.

8. Press **Alt-F5** to access the Mark Text menu.

9. Type **3** to select the Index option.

10. Press **<ENTER>** twice to bypass the subheading option and to mark the blocked heading for inclusion in the index.

11. Follow steps 2 - 10 to mark the headings or key words in each headed section for inclusion in the index.

12. Move the cursor to the end of the document (below the table of contents).

13. Press **Ctrl-<ENTER>** to create a Hard Page break.

14. Type **INDEX**

15. Press **<ENTER>** twice to create a blank line.

16. Press **Alt-F5** to display the Mark Text menu.

17. Type **5** to select Define from the Mark Text submenu.

18. Type **3** to select Define Index from the Mark Text submenu.

19. Press **<ENTER>** to indicate that there is no Concordance. The Index Definition submenu will appear.

20. Type **3** to select to choose "(Page Numbers) Follow Entries" from the Index Definition submenu. You are returned to your document.

21. Press **Alt-F5** to display the Mark Text submenu.

22. Type **6** to select Generate from the Mark Text submenu.

23. Type **5** to select Generate Tables, Indexes, Automatic References, etc., from the Generate submenu.

24. Type **Y** (or any other key) to Generate the index.

    The message "Generation in progress. Pass: Page:" appears on the screen as the index is generated.

25. Add the Document Identification Line on the index page.

26. Block and Save the index page. Name this document **INDEX.DOC**

27. Save **HUMAN.REL**

28. Print **INDEX.DOC**

REVIEW QUESTIONS

1. How many headings are available for generating a table of contents?

2. How many lists can be generated from a single document?

3. Explain the procedure you would use to enter a subheading into an index.

DOCUMENTATION RESEARCH

1. For what application is a Table of Authorities most often used?

2. What three basic steps create a List?

3. How could the author of a book use the Master Document and Subdocument features?

4. How is a concordance file used to help create an index?

REVIEW EXERCISES

1. Retrieve **EXERCISE.DOC**

2. Create a table of contents with four levels of heads for **EXERCISE.DOC**.

3. Create an index with at least ten entries for the document **EXERCISE.DOC**. Some of the entries should be typed in as subheadings.

4. Add the Documentation Identification Line to both the index and the table of contents.

5. Block and Print the index and the table of contents.

6. Save **EXERCISE.DOC**

7. Exit WordPerfect.

UNIT 14 MATH

SUPPLIES NEEDED

1. WordPerfect 1 and 2 program disks
2. WordPerfect Student Data disk
3. printer

OBJECTIVES

After completing this unit, you will be able to

1. calculate subtotals, totals, and grand totals in a vertical column;
2. define numeric and calculation columns.

IMPORTANT KEYSTROKES

1. Alt-F7   to use the Math feature

ASSIGNMENTS

1. Create a Math Document
2. Review Questions
3. Documentation Research
4. Review Exercises

THE MATH FEATURE

With WordPerfect's Math feature, you can add, subtract, multiply, and divide up to twenty-four columns of numbers. When you create a math document, you need both text columns and numeric columns. Text columns are used for descriptions and labels. Numeric columns contain numbers that are used in calculations.

The first step in establishing numeric columns is to set tabs. Keep in mind that the columns must be wide enough to contain all the digits of your longest number. Most calculations are done in vertical columns, but columns can also be set so that calculations are performed across columns horizontally.

The process of setting up columns for math calculations is tedious, but once the columns are set up, they can be used for both macros and merges. Although WordPerfect's Math feature is sophisticated, it cannot substitute for a spreadsheet. Therefore, carefully consider the applications for this feature before going through the effort of setting it up.

THE MATH DEFINITION MENU

When the Math/Columns key (Alt-F7) is pressed, the Math/Columns menu (figure 14-1) appears. Select an option by typing one of the listed numbers.

---

1 Math On; 2 Math Def; 3 Column On/Off; 4 Column Def: 0

FIGURE 14-1   Math/Columns Menu

The Math options on this menu are defined as follows:

    1 Math On   A [Math On] code is placed in your document. A "Math" message appears in the status line. This message must always be present when you wish to create, edit, or calculate a math document. Columns must first be defined before Math is turned on.

    2 Math Def   The Math Definition (figure 14-2) submenu appears on your screen. With this submenu, you can define numeric and text columns.

```
Math Definition          Use arrow keys to position cursor

Columns                  A B C D E F G H I J K L M N O P Q R S T U V W X

Type                     2 2 2 2 2 2 2 2 2 2 2 2 2 2 2 2 2 2 2 2 2 2 2 2

Negative Numbers         ( ( ( ( ( ( ( ( ( ( ( ( ( ( ( ( ( ( ( ( ( ( ( (

Number of Digits to      2 2 2 2 2 2 2 2 2 2 2 2 2 2 2 2 2 2 2 2 2 2 2 2
  the Right (0-4)

Calculation     1
  Formulas      2
                3
                4

Type of Column:
     0 = Calculation   1 = Text     2 = Numeric    3 = Total

Negative Numbers
     ( = Parentheses (50.00)        - = Minus Sign   -50.00



Press Exit when done
```

FIGURE 14-2 Math Definition Submenu

Guidelines for Defining Columns follow:

You can set up as many as twenty-four numeric columns, but only four can be designated as calculation columns. It is important to make the columns wide enough to contain your longest number. If the columns overlap, the calculations will not be correct.

Four types of columns can be defined. **Numeric columns** are used to add constants, totals, subtotals, and grand totals. **Text columns** are used for descriptions and labels. **Total columns** are used for displaying only totals from the column to the left. **Calculation columns** contain equations to calculate data across columns. The default setting is numeric: unless you designate otherwise, all columns are treated as numeric columns except for the first column, which is reserved for labeling your math document.

Negative numbers may be displayed either in parentheses or with a minus sign. The default is set for parentheses.

There may be from zero to four digits to the right of a decimal point. The default setting is two.

Options 3 and 4 on the Math/Columns menu are used to set up newspaper columns or parallel columns.

GUIDED ACTIVITY: SETTING TABS

The first step in preparing a math document is to set the tab stops. These tab stops determine the width of each column you will later define.

1. Display a clear screen.

2. Access the Line Format menu (Shift-F8, 1) to change the tab stops. Set the tab stops at 4, 6, and 8 inches.

3. Return to your document.

GUIDED ACTIVITY: DEFINING COLUMNS

1. Press the **Alt-F7** keys.

   The Math/Columns menu will appear on your screen.

2. Type **2**

   The Math Definition submenu will appear.

3. Move the cursor to the Type row in the A column if it is not already there.

4. Type **2**

   You have defined a numeric column. Notice the type definitions under the header Type of Column on this submenu.

5. Move the cursor to "Number of Digits to the Right (0-4)" in the A column.

6. Type **0**

   You have indicated that there will be no digits to the right of the decimal point in column A.

7. Move the cursor to the Type row in the B column.

8. Type **0**

   You have defined a calculation column. The cursor on this submenu will automatically move to Calculation Formulas and a "B" will appear after the "1".

Math   233

9. Type **A*1.1**

   You have specified the mathematical formula to be used in the calculation column, column B. All of the numbers in column A will be multiplied by 1.1 (110%).

10. Press **<ENTER>** to enter the formula.

11. Press **F7** to Exit the Math Definition submenu.

12. Type **0** or press **<ENTER>** to clear the screen.

13. Save your definition. Name it **BUDGET.DOC**

✔CHECKPOINT

a. Which keys are used to access the Math/Columns menu?

b. Explain how to define a numeric column on the Math Definition submenu.

c. How does the cursor respond when a calculation column is selected?

d. Which key do you press when you have completed the task of defining columns?

What You Have Accomplished

You have used the Math Definition submenu to define two columns, a numeric column and a calculation column. You have also determined the width of these columns by changing the tab stop settings. Column A (the numeric column) begins at the first tab stop; column B (the calculation column) begins at the second tab stop. The first column (the space between the left margin and the first tab stop) is reserved for labeling your math document.

GUIDED ACTIVITY: CREATING A BUDGET WORKSHEET

This Guided Activity for creating a Math document is a lengthy one. Refer to figure 14-3 to enter the values and labels required.

234   WordPerfect 5.0

Retrieve **BUDGET.DOC** if necessary.

1. With the cursor at Ln 1 of the clear screen, type   **ABC Corporation**

2. Press **<ENTER>**

3. Type **Budget Report for 1989**

    You have entered a title for your budget worksheet.

4. Press **<ENTER>** twice.

5. Type **Budget Items**

    You have labeled the first column (the labels column).

6. Press **<SPACEBAR>** thirteen times.

7. Type **Total**

    You have labeled column A.

8. Press **<SPACEBAR>** fifteen times.

9. Type **Next Year 110%**

    You have labeled column B.

10. Press **<ENTER>** twice.

11. Press the **Alt-F7** key.

    The Math/Columns menu will reappear on the screen.

12. Type **1**

    You have turned the Math feature on. The message "Math" appears in the status line.

13. Type **Advertising**

    You have identified your first budget item and labeled the first row.

14. Press **<TAB>**

15. Type **2,000**

    You have identified the value of your first budget item, which has been placed in column A (the numeric column).

Math   235

16. Press <TAB>

    An ! has been automatically inserted into column B because you defined it as a calculation column.

17. Press <ENTER>

✔CHECKPOINT

e. Which column in your math document is reserved for labels?

---

f. How is the Math feature turned on?

---

g. How does the WordPerfect program signal that a column has been defined as a calculation column?

---

18. Type **Travel**

    You have identified the second budget item and labeled the second row.

19. Press <TAB>

20. Type **800**

    You have identified the second value to be placed in column A.

21. Press <TAB>

    An ! will appear in column B.

22. Press <ENTER> twice.

23. Press <SPACEBAR> twice.

24. Type **Subtotal**

25. Press <TAB>

26. Type **+** (plus).

    You have inserted an operator. The numbers above the operator in column A will be added and displayed in the row labeled Subtotal.

236   WordPerfect 5.0

27. Press **<TAB>**

28. Press **<ENTER>** twice.

29. Refer to figure 14-3. Enter the next two budget item labels and their corresponding values. Also enter "Subtotal" and the operator "+".

30. Press **<ENTER>** twice.

    The cursor should be in the first column.

31. Type **Total**

32. Press **<TAB>**

33. Type **=** (equal sign).

    You have inserted an operator.

34. Press **<TAB>**

    An **!** will appear in column B.

35. Press **<ENTER>** twice.

36. Press the **Alt-F7** keys.

    The Math/Columns menu appears on the screen.

37. Type **2** to choose Calculate.

    The subtotals and totals (the results of the "+" and "=" operators will be calculated and displayed. Your printed document will look like that in figure 14-4. The document on your screen displays the symbols representing the math operations. However, the budget report will not when printed contain those symbols.

    ✔**CHECKPOINT**

    h.   What happens when the operator "=" is inserted into your math document?

Hint: WordPerfect does not perform calculations in text columns. Therefore you may use numbers as labels in the first column. Keep in mind that the Math feature (option 1 on the Math/Columns menu) must be turned on before you can create or edit a math document. As long as the "Math" message is displayed at the bottom of your screen, your math calculations will take place as they should.

GUIDED ACTIVITY: TURNING OFF THE MATH FEATURE

1. Press the **Alt-F7** keys.

2. Type **1**

   The Math feature has been turned off and the "Math" message has disappeared from your screen. You can insert additional text if you like, but any time you wish to make changes to the budget report, Math must be turned on again.

3. Add the Document Identification Line to the document.

4. Save and Print **BUDGET.DOC**

✓CHECKPOINT

i. What menu option must you choose to insert results into a calculation column automatically?

---

j. What two steps are needed to turn off the Math feature?

What You Have Accomplished

You have created a Math document (a budget report). Your document contains both text columns for labels and numeric columns for numbers and mathematical formulas. You calculated the numbers in the numeric columns by inserting operators. Then you chose an option from the Math/Columns menu that automatically performed calculations using the formula you placed in column B when you defined your columns. You now have a completed budget report.

```
ABC Corporation
Budget Report for 1987

Budget Items        Total           Next Year 110%

Advertising         2,000                               !
Travel                      800                         !

  Subtotal                   +                          !

Printing                    500                         !
Education                   700                         !

  Subtotal                   +                          !

Total                        =                          !
```

FIGURE 14-3   Uncalculated Budget Report

```
ABC Corporation
Budget Report for 1989

Budget Items        Total           Next Year 110%

Advertising                         2,000           2,200.00
Travel                                800             880.00

  Subtotal                          2,800           3,080.00

Printing                              500             550.00
Education                             700             770.00

  Subtotal                          1,200           1,320.00

Total                               4,000           4,400.00
```

FIGURE 14-4   Calculated and Printed Budget Report

Math 239

REVIEW QUESTIONS

1. What is the main purpose of WordPerfect's Math feature?

2. Explain how the Math feature is turned on.

3. Describe the contents of each of the four types of columns that can be defined.

    a. _____

    b. _____

    c. _____

    d. _____

4. What is a calculation column? How many can be set up?

5. What is a numeric column? How many can be set up?

6. What is the major difference between text columns and numeric columns?

7. Describe how an operator functions.

8. How do you turn off the Math feature?

9. How do you set column widths?

DOCUMENTATION RESEARCH

1. What are the two ways to display negative values in a math document?

   _____

2. What operator is needed to calculate a grand total?

   _____

3. How can you insert extra totals and subtotals?

   _____

REVIEW EXERCISES

1. Display a clear screen.

2. Define a Math document to add the following columns:

395.45	460.65
600.00	600.00
50.00	75.98
201.78	143.87

   Total

3. Calculate the totals. Turn off the Math feature. Add the Document Identification Line.

4. Name the document **MATH.EX**

5. Save and Print **MATH.EX**

UNIT 15
GRAPHICS

SUPPLIES NEEDED

1. WordPerfect 5.0 disks 1 and 2
2. WordPerfect 5.0 Fonts/Graphics disk
3. WordPerfect 5.0 Student Data disk
4. graphics printer

OBJECTIVES

After completing this unit you will be able to

1. Create horizontal and vertical lines;
2. Create a box containing text;
3. Create a box containing a graphic image.

IMPORTANT KEYSTROKES

Alt-F9   to display the Graphics menu

ASSIGNMENTS

1. Create **WORDPER3.COL**
2. Create **WORDPER4.BOX**

GRAPHICS

WordPerfect 5.0 has many graphics features that may be incorporated into text to enhance it. Businesses are producing their own newsletters, advertisements, presentation documents and many other types of copy which are enhanced by graphic images. Producing this type of document is often referred to as desktop publishing.

In this unit you will learn to enhance your documents with horizontal and vertical lines, boxes and graphic images. You will learn to incorporate into your document graphic images that are saved in separate files.

To take full advantage of the Graphics feature you will need some specific hardware. To see the graphic images you will need a graphics card installed in your microcomputer. Even with the graphics card installed you will only be able to see the graphic images and lines (other than a box outline) with the View feature. To print lines, boxes and other graphic images, you will need a graphics printer. If you do not have a graphics card available but do have a graphics printer, you can print the graphics images.

GRAPHICS MENU

When the Graphics key (Alt-F9) is pressed, the Graphics menu (figure 15-1) appears. The first four options on the Graphics menu are used to define a type of box. The fifth option is used to create lines. Select an option by typing one of the listed numbers or highlighted letters.

---

1 Figure; 2 Table; 3 Text Box; 4 User-Defined Box; 5 line: 0

FIGURE 15-1   Graphics Menu

The options on the Graphics menu are defined as follows:

1 Figure		This box type might be used for graphic images, diagrams and charts. The graphic images may be created with other application software and saved in a separate file (e.g., Lotus 1-2-3 graphs.)
2 Table		This box type might be used for tables of numbers, statistical data, and maps.
3 Text Box		The text box might be used to set off quotes or other special text from the rest of the document. When you choose this option the Text Box submenu appears. This and the other submenus used for creating a box will be covered later in this unit.

Graphics 243

4 User-Defined Box   This box type would be used for any image or type of text that does not fall into one of the first three categories.

5 Line   This option allows you to place horizontal and vertical lines in your document. When you choose this option the Line submenu (figure 15-2) appears.

---

1 Horizontal Line;   2 Vertical Line: 0

FIGURE 15-2   Line Submenu

The option on the Line Submenu are defined as follows:

1 Horizontal Line   The Graphics: Horizontal Line submenu (figure 15-3) appears. With this submenu you can set the position and size of the horizontal line.

2 Vertical Line   The Graphics: Vertical Line submenu (figure 15-5) appears. With this submenu you can set the position, size, and length of the vertical line.

Graphics: Horizontal Line

    1 -   Horizontal Position   Left & Right

    2 -   Length of Line

    3 -   Width of Line   0.01"

    4 -   Gray Shading (% of black)   100%

Selection: 0

FIGURE 15-3   Graphics: Horizontal Line Submenu

The options on the Horizontal Line submenu are defined as follows:

1 Horizontal Position — When you choose this option, the Horizontal Position submenu (figure 15-4) appears. The Horizontal Position (horizontal line) submenu allows you to position the horizontal line against the right or left margin, centered between the margins, or at the cursor location.

2 Length of Line — You may choose any length (e.g., 1.5"). The default length of the line is from the cursor position to the margin specified in the horizontal position option. If the horizontal position is left and right the line is drawn from margin to margin.

3 Width of Line — This option allows you to choose how thick you want the line. The default width is .01".

4 Gray Shading (% of black) — This option allows you to choose how dark (a percent of black) the line should be. The default 100% is black.

```
Horizontal Pos:   1 Left  2 Right  3 Center  4 Both Left & Right  5 Set Position:0
```

FIGURE 15-4 Horizontal Position Submenu (horizontal line)

```
Graphic:  Vertical Line

    1 -  Horizontal Position              Left Margin

    2 -  Vertical Position                Full Page

    3 -  Length of Line

    4 -  Width of Line                    0.01"

    5 -  Gray Shading (% of black)        100%

Selection:  0
```

FIGURE 15-5 Graphics: Vertical Line Submenu

The option on the Graphics: Vertical Line submenu are defined as follows:

1 Horizontal Position — When you choose this option, the Horizontal Position submenu (figure 15-6) appears. The Horizontal Position (vertical line) submenu allows you to position the vertical line slightly outside the right or left margin, between columns or any specified position from the left margin. The default setting is at the left margin.

2 Vertical Position — When you use this option the Vertical Position submenu (figure 15-7) appears. The Vertical Position submenu allows you to position a vertical line against the top or bottom margin, centered between the top and bottom margins, or at a specific distance from the top margin. The default is from top to bottom margin.

3 Length of Line — You may specify the length of the line (e.g., 2"). If you have used the default setting Full Page for the Vertical Position option, the Length of Line will automatically be set to the length of the page.

4 Width of Line — This option allows you to choose how thick you want the line. The default width is .01".

5 Gray Shading (% of black) — This option allows you to choose how dark (a percent of black) the line should be. The default (100%) is black.

Horizontal Position: 1 Left; 2 Right; 3 Between Columns; 4 Set Position: 0

FIGURE 15-6 Horizontal Position Submenu (vertical line)

Vertical Position: 1 Full Page; 2 Top; 3 Center; 4 Bottom; 5 Set Position: 0

FIGURE 15-7 Vertical Position Submenu

Hint: You cannot edit a line. If you make a mistake, delete the codes from your document and recreate the line.

GUIDED ACTIVITY: CREATING A HORIZONTAL LINE

1. Retieve **WORDPER2.COL** from your WordPerfect 5.0 Student Data disk.

2. Position the cursor on the blank line under the left-column heading "Practice makes WordPerfect."

3. Press the **Alt-F9** keys.

   The Graphics menu will appear.

4. Type **5** to choose the Line option from the Graphics menu.

   The Line submenu appears.

5. Type **1** to choose the Horizonital Line option from the Line submenu.

   The Graphics: Horizonital Line submenu appears.

6. Type **1** to choose the Horizonital Position option.

   The Horizontal Position (horizontal line) submenu appears.

7. Type **3** to choose the Center option.

   The Graphics: Horizonital Line submenu appears. "Center" has been entered as the Horizontal Position.

8. Type **2** to choose the Length of Line option.

   The cursor will move to the typing area.

9. Type **2** to set the Length of Line at two inches.

10. Press **<ENTER>**

    The inch (") symbol is added for you and the cursor returns to the Selection area.

11. Press **<ENTER>** to accept the default settings for the Width of Line and Gray Shading options.

    You are returned to your document. The line does **not** appear on the screen.

12. Use the View Document (Shift-F7) feature to see the line in your document.

13. Save your document with the name **WORDPER3.COL**.

Graphics 247

✔CHECKPOINT

a.   Which keys access the Graphics menu?

GUIDED ACTIVITY: CREATING A VERTICAL LINE

1. Retrieve **WORDPER3.COL** if necessary. Position the cursor anywhere in the right column.

2. Press the **Alt-F9** keys to access the Graphics menu.

3. Type **5** to choose the Line option. The Line submenu appears.

4. Type **2** to choose the Vertical Line option. The Graphics: Vertical Line submenu appears.

5. Type **1** to choose the Horizontal Position option. The Horizontal Position (vertical line) submenu appears.

6. Type **2** to choose the Right margin option. The Right Margin is entered as the Horizontal Position on the Graphics: Vertical Line submenu.

7. Type **4** to choose the Width of Line option.

8. Type **.02** to change the width of the line.

9. Press **<ENTER>** twice to return the cursor to the Selection area and to accept the options you have set and the default settings for the Vertical Position, Length of Line, and Gray Shading options.

10. Use the View document feature to look at the vertical line you created.

11. Print your docment. The vertical line will be wider than the horizontal line.

12. Save your document. Replace **WORDPER3.COL.**

GUIDED ACTIVITY: CREATING A VERTICAL LINE BETWEEN COLUMNS

1. Retrieve **WORDPER3.COL** if necessary. Place the cursor in the left column on the first line of text "From a good idea..."

2. Press the **Alt-F9** keys to access the Graphics menu.

3. Type **5** to choose the Line option. The Line submenu appears.

4. Type **2** to choose the Vertical Line option. The Graphics: Vertical Line submenu appears.

5. Type **1** to choose the Horizontal Position option. The Horizontal Position (vertical line) submenu appears.

6. Type **3** to choose the Between Columns option. The prompt "Place line to right of column: 1" appears.

7. Press **<ENTER>** to accept the default. The line is placed to the right of the left column or between the two columns. "Column 1" is entered as the Horizontal Position.

8. Type **2** to choose the Vertical Position option. The Vertical Position submenu appears.

9. Type **5** to choose the Set Position option.

10. Press **<ENTER>** to accept the vertical position. The measurement is the distance from the top of the page to the cursor position.

11. Type **3** to choose the Length of Line option.

12. Type **4** then press **<ENTER>** to indicate the length of the vertical line as four inches.

13. Press **<ENTER>** to accept the options on the Graphics: Vertical Line submenu.

14. Use the View document feature to look at the vertical line you created between the columns.

15. Print your docment. Your document will look like figure 15-8 depending on the capabilities of your printer.

16. Save your document. Replace **WORDPER3.COL**.

WordPerfect

Practice makes WordPerfect.
From a good idea, a great product can evolve. But it takes people with vision who can nurture and refine it. And it requires users who appreciate it. Loyal users who call with questions and suggestions.

In the case of WordPerfect word processing, we're fortunate to have both exceptional product designers and users. So fortunate, in fact, that we've produced the number-one selling word processor for two years running.

We think it's because we listen to our users, and we respond with products that reflect their needs. And by doing more of the same--by **practicing** what we know best--we'll continue to make WordPerfect the leader in sales, service and customer satisfaction.

For more information, write to WordPerfect Corporqation, 1555 North Technology Way, Orem, Utah 84057.

WordPerfect Corporation Advertisement in P C Magazine, Vol 7, Number 15, September 13, 1988.

FIGURE 15-8 WORDPER3.COL

BOXES

The first four options on the Graphics menu are used to define boxes. WordPerfect saves a list of each type of box. You can retrieve a graphic image or text into any of the four types of boxes. The box type does not refer to the contents of the box but to which list of boxes it belongs. A list of each type of box can be generated with the List feature.

Boxes containing text or graphic images are very useful for enhancing your documents. WordPerfect 5.0 supplies several clip-art graphic images on the Fonts/Graphics disk. You can also Retrieve graphic images created with other software packages.

When you define a box, the options chosen stay in effect for the rest of the document unless you redefine.

Only the outline and number of the box type will be visable on your screen. Use the View document feature to see a rough image of the contents of the box. You will need a graphics printer to print boxes.

When you choose a box type from the Graphics menu, a box type submenu will appear. This submenu is the same for all box types. The Text Box submenu is shown in figure 15-9.

Text Box: 1 Create; 2 Edit; 3 New Number; 4 Options: 0

FIGURE 15-9 Text Box Submenu.

The options for the types of boxes are defined as follows:

1 Create   When you choose this option the Definition: Text Box submenu (figure 15-10) appears. The Create submenus help you define the contents of the box and its position in the document.

2 Edit   If you choose the Edit option, four options will be available for editing the contents of a box. These options allow you to move the move the contents in the box, enlarge or reduce the contents, rotate the contents a number of degrees in a circle, and switch the contrast of a graphic image (e.g., The dark image switches to light while the light parts of the image become dark.)

3 New Number   Boxes are automatically numbered in consecutive order by box type. You can change the number with this option.

4 Options   When you choose this option Options: Text Box (figure 15-11) submenu appears. The Options submenus help you define the appearance of the box. Once the options are set they will stay in effect for the rest of the document or until changed.

```
Definition: Text Box

    1 - Filename

    2 - Caption

    3 - Type                         Paragraph

    4 - Vertical Position            0"

    5 - Horizontal Position          Right

    6 - Size                         3.25" wide x 0.59" (high)

    7 - Wrap Text Around Box         Yes

    8 - Edit




Selection: 0
```

FIGURE 15-10   Definition: Text Box Submenu

Options on the Definition: Text Box submenu are defined as follows:

- 1 Filename   This option allows you to retrieve a text or graphics file into a box.

- 2 Caption   This option allows you to enter a caption to be printed under the box.

- 3 Type   This option allows you to choose how the box will be treated in regard to the text on the page. If you choose Paragraph, the box will stay with the paragraph of text that surrounds it. If you choose Page, the box will stays at a fixed position on the page. If you choose Character, the box is treated as part of a line. When the line containing the box is wrapped the next line will start below the box.

- 4 Vertical Position   The options available for the Vertical Position of the box depend on your choices for the Type option. In general, this option allows you to change the position of the box in relation to the surrounding text or the top margin.

- 5 Horizontal Position   The options available for the Horizontal Position of the box depend on your choice for the Type option. In general, this option allows you to change the position of the box in relation to the surrounding text or the margins.

252 WordPerfect 5.0

    6 Size   This option allows you to change the width and height of the box.

    7 Wrap Text Around Box If you change from the default setting of "Yes" the text will be written over the box from margin to margin rather than around the box.

    8 Edit   This option allows you to edit the text or graphic image in the box.

Hint: While the menu and submenu structure for the Graphics feature may seem very complicated, the feature is easier to use than to explain. Complete the Guided Activities in this unit then go back and experiment with more of the available options and combinations of options and you will soon be an expert.

```
Options:     Text Box

     1 - Border Style
             Left                              None
             Right                             None
             Top                               Thick
             Bottom                            Thick
     2 - Outside Border Space
             Left                              0.16"
             Right                             0.16"
             Top                               0.16"
             Bottom                            0.16"
     3 - Inside Border Space
             Left                              0.16"
             Right                             0.16"
             Top                               0.16"
             Bottom                            0.16"
     4 - First Level Numbering Method          Numbers
     5 - Second Level Numbering Method         Off
     6 - Caption Number Style                  [BOLD]1[bold]
     7 - Position of Caption                   Below box, Outside borders
     8 - Minimum Offset from Paragraph         0"
     9 - Gray Shading (% of black)             10%

Selection: 0
```

FIGURE 15-11 Options: Text Box Submenu

The options available on the Options: Text Box submenu are available for each type of box. The options on this submenu are defined as follows:

    1 Border Style   When you choose this option the Border Style submenu (figure 15-12) appears. The options on the Border Style

submenu allow you to choose a style for each of the four box borders.

2 **Outside Border Space** Use this option to set the amount of space between the outside of the box border and the text in the document.

3 **Inside Border Space** Use this option to set the amount of space between the inside of the box border and the text or figure inside the box.

4 **First Level Numbering Method** This option allows you to set the numbering style and level for the box caption. The first level numbers will be in uppercase.

5 **Second Level Numbering Method** This option allows you to set the second level numbering style. The second level numbers will be in lowercase.

6 **Caption Number Style** Use this option to add text and codes to caption. For example, you can add Font attributes such as large or small letters to the box caption.

7 **Position of Caption** This option allows you to position the caption above or below or inside or outside the box.

8 **Minimum Offset from Paragraph** Set this option to specify how far a box can be moved up toward the top of a paragraph rather than moved to the next page of text.

9 **Gray Shading (% of black)** This option sets the shading intensity of the inside of a box. Enter the desired intensity as a percent of black.

```
1 None; 2 Single; 3 Double; 4 Dashed; 5 Dotted; 6 Thick; 7 Extra Thick: 0
```

FIGURE 15-12 Border Style Submenu

GUIDED ACTIVITY: CREATING A BOX WITH ENTERED TEXT

1. Retrieve **WORDPER3.COL** Place the cursor to the bottom of the document below the [Col Off] code.

2. Press the **Alt-F9** keys to access the Graphics menu.

254 WordPerfect 5.0

3. Type **3** to choose the Text Box option.

   The Text Box submenu appears.

4. Type **4** to choose the Options option.

   The Options: Text Box submenu appears.

5. Type **1** to choose the Border Style option.

   The Border Style submenu appears.

6. Type **6** to choose the Thick option for the Left Border.

7. Type **6** to choose the Thick option for the Right Border.

8. Press **<ENTER>** three times to accept the default settings for the rest of the options and to return to your document.

9. Press the **Alt-F9** keys to access the Graphics menu.

10. Type **3** to choose the Text Box option. The Text Box submenu appears.

11. Type **1** to choose the Create option. The Definition: Text Box submenu appears.

12. Type **3** to choose the Type option. The Type submenu appears.

13. Type **2** to choose the Page option.

14. Type **4** to choose the Vertical Position option. The Vertical Position submenu appears.

15. Type **5** to choose the Set Position option.

16. Press **<ENTER>** to accept the current position of your cursor.

17. Type **5** to choose the Horizontal Position option. The Horizontal Position submenu appears.

18. Type **1** to choose the Margins option.

19. Type **3** to choose the Center option.

    The box will be centered between the current margin settings.

20. Type **8** to choose the Edit option.

    The prompt "Press Exit when done, Graphics to rotate text" appears.

21. Type **WordPerfect 5.0 is a sophisticated word-processing program.**

Graphics 255

22. Press **F7** twice to accept your text and return to your document.

23. Press **<ENTER>** to extend the bottom of the page so that you can see the Text box. The text you entered will not be visable on the screen.

21. Use the View Document feature to view the box placement on the page.

22. **Print the document.**

23. Save your document. Name it **WORDPER4.BOX**

GUIDED ACTIVITY: CREATING A BOX WITH A RETRIEVED FILE

1. Retrieve **WORDPER4.BOX** if necessary. Move the cursor to the top of the right-hand column.

2. Press **Alt-F9** to access the Graphics menu.

3. Type **1** to choose the Figure Box option.

    The Figure Box submenu appears.

4. Type **4** to choose the Options option.

    The Options: Figure submenu appears.

5. Type **1** to choose the Border Style option.

    The Border Style submenu appears.

6. Type **3** four times to choose the Double option all four borders.

7. Press **<ENTER>** to accept the default settings for the rest of the options and to return to your document.

8. Press the **Alt-F9** keys to access the Graphics menu.

9. Type **1** to choose the Figure option. The Figure submenu appears.

10. Type **1** to choose the Create option. The Definition: Figure submenu appears.

11. Type **1** to choose the Filename option. The prompt "Enter filename:" appears.

12. Remove your Student Data disk from Drive B and insert the WordPerfect 5.0 Fonts/Graphics disk.

13. Type **B:PC.WPG**

14. Press <ENTER>

    The prompt "Please wait - Loading WP Graphics File" appears. In a moment the filename **PC.WPG** appears on the Definition: Figure submenu.

15. Press **F7** to accept the Definition: Figure submenu settings and to return to the document. The blank Figure box is at the cursor position. Use the <down> arrow key to move the cursor to see the box outline.

16. Print the document.

17. Remove the Fonts/Graphics disk from Drive B and insert your Student Data disk.

18. Save your document. Replace the previous version.

What You Have Accomplished.

You have enhanced **WORDPER3.COL** with horizontal and vertical lines. You added two boxes to the document. You entered text in one box and retrieved a graphics file into another box. Hopefully you are anxious to experiment with all the options available to you when you use the Graphics feature.

REVIEW QUESTIONS

1. Which keystrokes are needed to access the Graphics menu?

   ___

2. You can enclose any type of text or graphic image in any type of box. Why would you want to decide on different types of boxes for different types of information?

   ___

3. You have prepared a graph with your favorite type of spreadsheet software. List the steps needed to enclose this graph in a box in your WordPerfect 5.0 document.

   ___

4. If you want all the boxes in a document to look alike, must you set the options more than once?

   ___

DOCUMENTATION RESEARCH

1. WordPerfect 5.0 has another feature (other than the Graphics feature) that allows you to draw lines. What is that feature and what keystrokes access the feature's menu?

2. Can you Retrieve a complete document into a box?

3. Can you place graphics boxes in a header or footer?

4. Where can you find a list of the graphics software programs that WordPerfect supports?

5. If your printer does not support different levels of box shading, how should you set the Gray Shading option on the Options submenu?

REVIEW EXERCISES

1. Retrieve **INVITE.TXT** from your Student Data disk.

2. Add a horizonital line above and below the text.

3. Add the WordPerfect5.0 clip-art file **PHONE.WPG** at the bottom of the invitation.

4. Save the document as **INVITE2.TXT**

5. Print your document.

APPLICATION E

SUPPLIES NEEDED

1. WordPerfect 5.0 program disks 1 and 2
2. WordPerfect 5.0 Learning disk
3. WordPerfect 5.0 Fonts/Graphics disk
4. WordPerfect Student Data disk
5. graphics printer

ASSIGNMENTS

The assignments to be completed for this application section are:

1. Create **MINUTES.TXT**
2. Create **CLINIC.TXT**
3. Create **NEWS.LTR**
4. Create **WORDPERF.COL**
5. Create **NEWS2.LTR**

GENERAL DIRECTIONS

Application E contains documents you can use to practice the skills you have acquired. You will need to apply the skills you acquired in Parts 1 and 2 as well as the special features of Part 3 to reproduce these documents.

The documents offer you the opportunity to practice writing reports, creating parallel columns, and writing newsletters. You will also add graphic images to a newsletter.

260   WordPerfect 5.0

Use your template, Quick Reference card, and the WordPerfect user's manual to find the keystroke commands and menus you need. Remember that there is often more than one keystroke choice that can be used to create and format a document. Your primary task is to find the most efficient way to reproduce the documents.

You may also want to create your own applications - some tasks that are more meaningful to your everyday work. Your WordPerfect Student Data disk should have plenty of space available (use List Files to find out how much) to store additional documents.

Follow the directions below to create the documents in Application E.

Document E-1

1. Name this document **MINUTES.TXT**
2. Type the text as shown.
3. Use the Math feature to calculate the tree and price columns.
4. Add the Document Identification Line to the bottom of the document.
5. Save and Print the document.

Document E-2

1. Name this document **CLINIC.TXT**
2. Type the text as shown.
3. Use the Math/Column feature to create the parallel columns.
4. Add the Document Identification Line to the bottom of the document.
5. Save and Print the document.

Document E-3

1. Name this document **NEWS.LTR**
2. Use the Math/Column feature to create newspaper columns with .25" between the columns.
3. Type the text as shown.
4. Add the Document Identification Line to the bottom of the document.
5. Save and Print the document.

Document E-4

1. Retrieve **WORDPERF.TXT** from your WordPerfect 5.0 Student Data disk.
2. Use the Math Column feature to arrange the text into three newspaper-style columns.
3. Name this document **WORDPERF.COL**
4. Add the Document Identification Line to the bottom of the document.
5. Save and Print the document.

Document E-5

1. Retrieve **NEWS.LTR** from your WordPerfect 5.0 Student Data disk.
2. Use the Graphics feature to add vertical lines at the left and right margins and between the columns.
3. Add horizontal lines between the newsletter articles.
4. Create a box at the upper left corner of the newsletter.
5. Retrieve the WordPerfect 5.0 clip-art file **NEWSPAPR.WPG** into the box.
6. Name this document **NEWS2.LTR**
7. Update the Document Identification Line.
8. Save and Print the document.

LAKEWOOD SCHOOL
LAND DEVELOPMENT COMMITTEE

MINUTES
MARCH 22, 1990

Present: Don Lord, Jeff Albert, Glenn Maki, John Nelson, Bob White, Les Carlson, Tom Bryant, John Richards

We discussed covering the nature path with wood chips. We may have to use a chemical spray to kill weeds. We will check into the Wild Life Packet (7 or 8 bushes) that is supposed to attract and keep birds.

Plantings (seedlings)

Norway Pine	500	$215.00
White Spruce	500	230.80
Scotch Pine	500	210.00
Green Ash	100	68.35
Norway Spruce	500	240.00
Black Walnut	100	112.75
Total		

Dates: Saturday, April 20   Clearing and chipping
Saturday, April 27   Planting of trees

Bring: Chain saws, planting bars, wheelbarrows, shovels, rakes, sprayers

Document E-1 MINUTES.TXT

CEDAR HILLS MEDICAL CLINIC
2631 CEDAR LANE
MORRIS, MICHIGAN 56031
621/456-3189

September 3, 1986

The following physicians have recently joined our full-time medical staff:

Theresa F. Schmitt, M.D. — Pediatrician. Earned her medical degree at Stanford University in 1971. Interned at Ramsey County General Hospital. Board-certified by the American Board of Pediatrics.

John M. Clark, M.D. — Obstetrician and Gynecologist. Received his medical degree from the University of Minnesota in 1978. Junior Fellow of the American College of Obstetrics and Gynecology.

Brian T. Tuma, M.D. — Internist. Earned his medical degree at Duke University. Completed advanced training in California. Board-certified by the American Board of Internal Medicine.

Document E-2 CLINIC.TXT

HORIZON NEWSLETTER

SHARE YOUR IDEAS

Parents, do you have some special things you do with your children, or do you know of some "neat" places to visit as a family that you can share with us? We would like to publish some ideas in the coming issues -- things to do with children. If you can share ideas with us, please send them to Horizon Newsletter at the Lakewood School. We appreciate your help and support.

ADVISORY COUNCIL NOTES

February 22nd meeting: A brief meeting was held at Lakewood School. The field trip to the Children's Theatre was canceled because not enough people had signed up to go. March 11th is the date for the next general meeting, on the topic of creativity. Possible dates considered for the next meeting are the first or second week in May. Suggestions from the parents for topics are welcome. Other discussion centered around the need for more parental input to the newsletter and the need for parental awareness of changes taking place in the district.

March 10th meeting: Mr. Johnson reported that programs for the gifted on the elementary- and middle-school levels are going well. He hopes to have a formal program for the high school on paper and in operation by next fall.

Articles and drawings are coming in slowly for the literary magazine "Beyond the Horizon." If not enough material is submitted, publication will probably be through the monthly newsletter.

HORIZON CHESS INVITATIONAL

The Horizon Program will sponsor an invitational tournament on Saturday, March 20th, at the Lakewood School. The tournament will be divided into three sections:
1. Unrated Juniors (under 18)
2. Rated Juniors
3. Unrated Adults (over 18)

We will play 40 moves an hour and individuals are encouraged to bring their own boards and clocks with them.

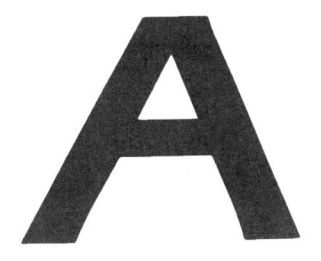

APPENDIX A
GETTING STARTED ON YOUR MICROCOMPUTER

Laura B. Ruff
Mary K. Weitzer
Steve C. Ross

This appendix covers the knowledge necessary to use application software for the IBM PC or compatible microcomputers along with the disk operating system (DOS). It is not intended to make you an expert in DOS, but rather to provide some level of competence in the necessary operations external to the software discussed in this manual.

PART I: THE KEYBOARD

The IBM and other personal computers have over eighty keys, about forty more than most typewriters. An illustration of the keyboard appears inside the back cover. Many of the "extra" keys have symbols or mnemonics rather than characters. This illustration includes the WordPerfect 5.0 template which identifies the purpose of each function key. To minimize confusion, the following conventions are used in **Understanding and Using WordPerfect 5.0**.

Conventions

Several typographical conventions have been established to improve readability and understanding. They were established to clearly communicate each WordPerfect 5.0 function. They are as follows:

When a keystroke activates a single command, it is designated like this: <KEYNAME> (e.g., <ENTER>, <SPACEBAR>).

The keys that direct cursor movement are for example, designated like these: <Up>, <Down>, <Left>, <Right>, <Home>, <End>, <PgUp>.

When one key is used in combination with another, the first one must be held down while the other is pressed. Combination keys are separated by a hyphen (e.g., Alt-F4).

When keys are pressed one after another but not in combination, they are separated by a comma (e.g., <Home>,<Home>,<Right> arrow).

All functions begin with a capital letter (e.g., Exit, Save, Cancel).

FUNCTION KEYS

These ten keys are located in two columns along the left edge of the keyboard. Most application software packages make special use of these keys. Although these keys also have special meanings when used by DOS, we ignore those uses here to avoid confusion with the application program that is the subject of this book.

MULTIPLE KEY COMBINATIONS

On a typewriter, the Shift is used in conjunction with a letter key to produce a capital letter. The same is true on a computer. On a computer, the Ctrl and Alt keys act as modifying keys; if either of these keys is used in conjunction with another key, the original letter is modified. These keys are manipulated in the same manner as the Shift key; for example, to type **Alt-M**, hold down the Alt key and type M.

WHAT IS A TOGGLE KEY?

Toggle keys act as on-off switches. Press them once and they are activated; press them a second time and they are deactivated. Examples of toggle keys include the <NUM LOCK> key (activates the numeric keypad), the Ctrl-<PrtSc> combination (prints the current screen when in DOS), and the <CAPS LOCK> key.

CAPS LOCK KEY

The <CAPS LOCK> key shifts all alphabet (A...Z) keys to uppercase but has no affect on any key that does not contain a letter. (In this it is unlike the shift lock key of a typewriter, which locks all keys into shifted characters.) The <CAPS LOCK> key is a toggle key.

NUMERIC KEYPAD KEYS

The numeric keypad keys on the right side of the keyboard are configured as a ten-key pad. The keys with arrows on them are referred to as arrow keys or as <Up>, <Left>, <Down>, and <Right>. The other keypad keys are referred to by the text that appears on them: <Home>, <PgUp>, <PgDn>, <End>, <DEL>, and <INS>. The numeric function of the keys can be activated by using the <Num Lock> key (a toggle key). Most of these keys have no effect in DOS, but they are used to control movement on the screen by many application programs.

PART II: GETTING STARTED

LOADING DOS

Loading DOS means that some of the DOS programs are read from the DOS disk to load the system before loading the application program. Other application software gives you instructions on how to install DOS onto the software program disk in order to make it self-loading, and how to attain some system capabilities without switching disks.

DOS PROMPT

The DOS or system prompt (A> with a single or dual drive system or C> with a hard disk) tells you that it is your turn to type information; that is, you must tell DOS what to do by entering a command.

The system prompt's letter also indicates the default drive. The default drive is the disk drive that DOS goes to automatically if you do not type a drive specification. On a single or dual drive system, the default drive is usually A>; on a hard disk system, the default drive is usually C>. Simply typing the drive letter followed by a colon overrides the default. If you intend to perform a number of operations on the files in the drive that is not the default, you may wish to change the default disk drive. In **THE MICROCOMPUTING SERIES** all drive specifications are indicated.

STARTUP PROCEDURES IF MICROCOMPUTER SYSTEM IS TURNED OFF

Single or Dual Drive System

1. The door on Disk Drive A should be open. Insert the DOS disk or a program disk on which DOS has been installed.

A-4   Appendix A

2. When the disk is fully inserted, close the drive door.

3. If you have dual disk drives and have a second disk for data, insert it into Disk Drive B.

4. When the disk is fully inserted, close the drive door.

5. Make sure that the printer is turned on and that the power, ready, and online lights (or their equivalent) are on.

6. Turn on the power switch.

7. When the red in-use disk drive lights go off, the program should be loaded.

8. Adjust the contrast controls on the monitor to a comfortable level.

9. If you have a single disk drive and a data disk, remove the program disk from Drive A.

10. Insert the data disk into Drive A.

11. When the disk is fully inserted, close the drive door.

Hard Disk System

1. Make sure that the printer is turned on and that the power, ready, and online lights (or their equivalent) are on.

2. Turn on the power switch.

3. When the red in-use disk drive lights go off, the program should be loaded.

4. Adjust the contrast controls on the monitor to a comfortable level.

5. After the program has loaded, you may insert a data disk into Drive A.

STARTUP PROCEDURES IF MICROCOMPUTER SYSTEM IS TURNED ON

Single or Dual Drive System

1. Adjust the contrast controls on the monitor.

2. The door on Disk Drive A should be open. Insert the DOS disk or a program that has been set up with DOS.

3. When the disk is fully inserted, close the drive door.

Getting Started on Your Microcomputer   A-5

4. If you have a second disk for data, insert it into Disk Drive B.

5. When the disk is fully inserted, close the drive door.

6. Make sure that the printer is turned on and that the power, ready, and online lights (or their equivalent) are on.

7. Load the program by pressing and holding the Ctrl-Alt keys; then press the <DEL> key. RELEASE ALL THREE KEYS.

8. When the red in-use disk drive lights go off, the program should be loaded. Continue with the procedures related to the program being used.

Hard Disk System

1. Make sure that the printer is turned on and that the power, ready, and online lights (or their equivalent) are on.

2. Load the program. Press and hold the Ctrl-Alt keys; then touch the <DEL> key. RELEASE ALL THREE KEYS.

3. When the red in-use disk drive lights go off, the program should be loaded.

4. Adjust the contrast controls on the monitor.

5. After the program has loaded, you may insert a data disk into Drive A.

6. Continue with the procedures related to the program being used.

SETTING THE DATE AND TIME

It is strongly recommended that you allow the system to "time stamp" the files you are using by setting the date and time whenever you begin a work session. (Some microcomputers have special boards with clocks that automatically set the time. If your system has this feature, you may skip these procedures.)

1. When DOS asks for the current date, type the current date using one of the following formats: xx/xx/xx or xx-xx-xx. Fill in appropriate numbers where x's appear. Do not type the name of the day; this would result in an "invalid date" prompt. (For example: April 30, 1986 is entered as 4-30-86 or 4/30/86.)

2. Press <ENTER>

3. When DOS asks for the time, type the current time using this format: xx:xx. Fill in appropriate numbers where x's appear using 24-hour time to distinguish a.m. from p.m. Do not type "a.m." or "p.m." (For example, 10:15 a.m. is simply typed as 10:15 -- no other time indicators are required. If you are starting at 1:15 in the afternoon, you would type 13:15.)

Appendix A

4. Press <ENTER>

   The DOS prompt will appear on the screen (A> with a single or dual drive system or C> with a hard disk).

Resetting the Date

If you enter the wrong date or forget to enter the date at system startup or reset, you can reset the date with the Date command:

1. Type **Date**

2. Press <ENTER>

3. Type in the appropriate date according to the format discussed above.

Resetting the Time

If you enter the wrong time or forget to enter the time at system startup or reset, you can reset the time with the Time command.

1. Type **Time**

2. Press <ENTER>

3. Type in the appropriate time according to the format discussed above.

SHUTDOWN PROCEDURES

1. Make sure that you have followed the proper escape or exit procedures for the software program you are using. Failure to follow such precautions may result in lost data.

2. When the red in-use disk drive lights are off for both drives, remove the disk from one of the drives. Do not close the drive door.

3. Follow the same procedure and remove the disk from the other drive. Do not close the drive door.

4. If you know that you or someone else will be using the system within a short time, leave the system turned on in order to minimize wear and tear. In order to protect your display, however, turn down the contrast.

PART III: ISSUING COMMANDS

TO ISSUE COMMANDS

1. Commands must be typed exactly as described in this appendix, including any spaces within the command.

2. Commands may be typed in upper- or lowercase letters. DOS reads them as upper-case letters.

3. If the command you type contains a typographical error, a missing space, or an extra space, the prompt "Bad command or file name" appears after you press <ENTER>. If this prompt appears, simply retype the command correctly.

4. Be sure to press <ENTER> after you have typed in any command in order to tell the system to begin the procedure.

TO CORRECT A TYPING MISTAKE BEFORE YOU TOUCH <ENTER>

1. The <BACKSPACE> key may be used to correct errors made while in DOS. Characters are erased as you backspace. The <Left> arrow also moves the cursor to the left; however, characters are not erased as the cursor moves to the left.

2. If a line has many errors, just touch the <ESC> key. A backslash (\) will appear. The cursor moves down one line on the screen, and even though the error-filled line still appears on the screen, it is deleted from memory. The system then waits for your corrected command.

TO STOP A COMMAND IN PROGRESS

1. Hold down the Ctrl-<BREAK> keys.

    The Break key has Scroll Lock on the top and Break on the forward edge.

2. Release both keys. Execution of the command will halt.

3. The system command (A> or C>) will reappear and you can type your next command.

PARAMETERS

Parameters are items that can be included in DOS command statements in order to specify additional information to the system. Some parameters are required, others are optional. If you do not include some parameters, a default value is provided by

A-8   Appendix A

the system. Examples of some of the parameters you will be working with frequently when using DOS follow.

Parameter	Explanation

[filespec]   A filespec will appear as [d:][filename][.ext]

　　　　　　Example: B:myfile.doc
　　　　　　　　　　　A:yourfile
　　　　　　　　　　　anyfiles.bas
　　　　　　　　　　　thisfile

　　　　　　An explanation of each part of the filespec follows.

[d:]   This parameter is the drive indicator. Enter the drive letter followed by a colon to indicate the intended drive.

is   For example to display a directory of the disk in Drive B (when B not the default drive), type **Dir B:**. After you press **<ENTER>**, the system displays the directory of the disk in Drive B.

　　　　　　If you do not specify a drive in the command, the system assumes that the default drive is intended. For example, if the default drive is Drive A, type Dir. When you press **<ENTER>**, the system gives you a directory of the disk in Drive A.

[filename]   You may assign any name to a file as long as it meets the following criteria: The name assigned to the file can have from one to eight characters. Valid characters: A to Z   0 to 9 $ & @ % / \ _ - ( ) " { } # !

　　　　　　The filename parameters are in force even when you are using application software, but some software does not accept all the characters listed above.

[.ext]   You may assign an optional filename extension of from one to three characters. If you specify the optional three-character extension, it must be separated from the filename by a period. Sometimes you cannot specify the filename extension because the application program does so automatically. Again, the characters listed are the only valid characters. If an extension is assigned, you must include it as part of the filespec whenever you want the system to locate the file.

CHANGE DEFAULT DRIVE

Change the default drive to B>

1. Type **B:**

2. Press **<ENTER>**

Change the default drive to A>

1. Type **A:**

2. Press **<ENTER>**

Change the default drive to C>

1. Type **C:**

2. Press **<ENTER>**

   The last command does not work unless you have a hard disk drive or some other special configuration.

CHECKDISK

The Checkdisk command produces a disk and memory status report. The report tells you how much space your files are using on the disk, how much space is still available on the disk, and whether the disk has any bad sectors. (If a disk does have bad sectors, you may want to use the Copy *.* command to copy all your files to another formatted disk.) Checkdisk also indicates how much memory is available in the system unit you are using.

1. The DOS disk should be in the default drive (either A> or C>) and the disk to be checked should be in Drive B (single or dual drive system) or Drive C (hard disk).

2. Type **Chkdsk B:, Chkdsk A:** or **Chkdsk C:**

3. Press **<ENTER>**

COPY

The Copy command allows you to transfer a copy of files from one disk to another without erasing any data on the disk to which you are copying. This is one method that can be used to back up your data disks.

The disk that contains the files you wish to copy is called the **source disk**. The disk to which you are copying is called the **target** or **destination disk**.

A-10   Appendix A

In order to use this command, the target disk must already have been formatted. The name of the file to be copied must be spelled correctly and the complete filespec (drive designation [if not default drive], file name, and any optional extension) must be included.

1. DOS must be loaded.

2. Place the source disk in one of the drives and the target disk in the other drive.

3. Type Copy, enter the source drive, followed by a colon and filename, and then enter the target drive followed by a colon. The command is terminated by **<ENTER>**.

   a. If the file you wish to copy is in Drive A and the target disk is in Drive B, type the command as follows:

   Copy A:filename.ext **B:**

   Since the new filename is not specified, DOS assumes that you want the filename to stay the same.

   b. If the file you wish to copy is in Drive B and the target disk is in Drive A, type the command as follows:

   Copy B:filename.ext **A:**

   Since a new filename is not specified, DOS assumes that you want the filename to stay the same.

   c. If the file you wish to copy is in Drive C (root directory) and the target disk is in Drive A, type the command as follows:

   Copy C:filename.ext **A:**

   Since a new filename is not specified, DOS assumes that you want the filename to stay the same.

   With any form of the command, you are specifying that you want to copy the named file from the first drive designated to the disk located in the second indicated drive.

4. If the system cannot find the file, it indicates "0 Files copied". Check the spelling of the filename. Be sure you have included any extension that has been assigned to the file. If you made a mistake in typing the command, just retype it at the DOS prompt as described previously.

Getting Started on Your Microcomputer A-11

COPY USING GLOBAL CHARACTER (*)

When you wish to copy more than one file and there is some common element in the names of the files you wish to copy, you can use the global character (*) to expedite the process.

1. DOS should be loaded.

2. Remove the DOS disk from Drive A.

3. Insert the source and target disks into the disk drives.

   a. If the source disk is in Drive A, the target disk is in Drive B, and the files you wish to copy have a common extension, type

      Copy A:*.ext B:

      Press <ENTER>

      Since a new filename is not specified, DOS assumes that you want the filename to stay the same.

   b. If the source disk is in Drive B, the target disk is in Drive A, and the files you wish to copy have a common extension, type

      Copy B:*.ext A:

      Press <ENTER>

      Since a new filename is not specified, DOS assumes that you want the filename to stay the same.

   c. If the source disk is in Drive C (root directory), the target disk is in Drive A, and the files you wish to copy have a common extension, type

      Copy C:*.ext A:

      Press <ENTER>

      Since a new filename is not specified, DOS assumes you want the filename to stay the same.

   d. If the source disk is in Drive A, the target disk is in Drive B, and the files you wish to copy have the filename in common, type

      Copy A:filename.* B:

      Press <ENTER>

e. If the source disk is in Drive B, the target disk is in Drive A, and the files you wish to copy have the filename in common, type

   Copy B:filename.* A:

   Press <ENTER>

f. If the source disk is in Drive C (root directory), the target disk is in Drive A, and the files you wish to copy have the filename in common, type

   Copy C:filename.* A:

   Press <ENTER>

4. If the system cannot find the files, it indicates "0 Files copied". Check the spelling of the filename. Be sure you have included any extension assigned to the file. If you made a mistake in typing the command, just retype it at the DOS prompt as described previously.

COPY *.* (FILE BY FILE)

With this command you copy the entire contents of the source disk onto a formatted target disk without erasing any data on the target disk.

1. DOS must be loaded.

2. Remove the DOS disk from Drive A.

3. Insert the source disk and the target disk in the drives.

   a. If the source disk is in Drive A and the target disk is in Drive B, type

      Copy A: *.* B:

      Press <ENTER>

   b. If the source disk is in Drive B and the target disk is in Drive A, type

      Copy B: *.* A:

      Press <ENTER>

   c. If the source disk is in Drive A and the target disk is Drive C, type

      Copy A: *.* C:

Getting Started on Your Microcomputer A-13

    Press <ENTER>

4. When the copy is complete, the number of files copied (or a message that there is insufficient disk space) appears on the screen.

DELETE (ERASE FILE)

This command is used to delete a specified file from a disk in the designated drive.

1. DOS must be loaded, but the DOS disk does not have to be in the drive when the command is given.

2. Make sure the disk containing the file to be deleted is in the drive before you press <ENTER>.

    a. If the disk containing the file(s) to be deleted is in Drive B, type

        Del B:filename.ext or **Erase B:filename.ext**

        Press <ENTER>

    b. If the disk containing the file(s) to be deleted is in Drive A, type

        Del A:filename.ext or **Erase A:filename.ext**

        Press <ENTER>

    c. If the disk containing the file(s) to be deleted is in Drive C, type

        Del C:filename.ext or **Erase C:filename.ext**

        Press <ENTER>

3. If the file is successfully erased, there is no message. The global character can be used with the Delete (or Erase) command just as it was used with the Copy command. However, the file-by-file delete is not recommended. Formatting is the preferred method of erasing all files from a floppy disk.

4. If the system cannot find the file, it gives you an error message. Check the spelling of the filename. Be sure you have included any extension that has been assigned to the file. If you made a mistake in typing the command, just retype it at the DOS prompt.

DIRECTORY

The directory is a listing of all files located on the disk in the specified drive. It is possible to display a directory on a disk in any drive in the system.

1. DOS must be loaded.

   a. If you wish to see a directory on the disk in Drive B, type

      Dir B:

      Press <ENTER>

   b. If you wish to see a directory on the disk in Drive A, type

      Dir A:

      Press <ENTER>

   c. If you wish to see a directory of the disk in Drive C, type

      Dir C:

      Press <ENTER>

      A listing of the names of the files located on the disk in the designated drive will appear.

DIRECTORY (PAUSE)

With this form of the Directory command, the listing pauses so that you can read the first lines of the directory. When you are ready, press any key to continue the listing.

1. Type **Dir/P A:**, **Dir/P B:**, or **Dir/P C:**

2. Press <ENTER>

DIRECTORY (WIDE)

This form of the Directory command produces a wide display that lists only the file names.

1. Type **Dir/W A:**, **Dir/W B:**, or **Dir/W C:**

2. Press <ENTER>

DIRECTORY (PRINT)

If you would like to print the directory rather than have it appear on screen, use the following command.

1. Type **Dir A:>Prn**, **Dir B:>Prn**, or **Dir C:>Prn**

2. Press **<ENTER>**

   The directory will be printed.

DISKCOPY

With the Diskcopy command you can copy the entire contents of a disk onto another disk. The Diskcopy command also formats the target disk. Be careful when you use this command; any files on the target disk will be erased.

1. Type **Diskcopy A: B:** or **Diskcopy B: A:**

2. Press **<ENTER>**

TO STOP THE SCREEN FROM SCROLLING

Information sometimes appears on the screen and then scrolls off before you can read it, as frequently happens when you display a long directory. The following procedure stops the scrolling until you are ready for it to continue.

1. Press the **Ctrl-<NUM LOCK>** keys.

2. Release both keys.

   The scrolling will stop.

3. Press any key to restart the scrolling.

FORMAT

The Format command can be used to format a blank disk (a disk cannot be used on the system until it is formatted) or to erase an entire disk that contains data you no longer need (such a disk can then be reused). Unless you wish to use the Format command to erase a disk, you will have to format each disk only once.

Caution. This command erases the entire contents of disk. If you have any doubts about the contents of the disk you are going to format, display a directory of the disk to make sure that it does not contain any files you want to keep (see Directory in this appendix).

1. DOS should be loaded and the DOS disk should be in Drive A.

2. Type **Format B:**

3. Press <ENTER>

4. When the system prompts you to insert a new disk in the designated drive, make sure that the disk you wish to format is in the designated drive.

5. Touch any key to begin the formatting process.

6. When the formatting process is complete, you will be asked if you wish to format another disk. If you wish to format another disk, type the letter "Y" for "yes" and follow the screen prompts to insert a blank disk. If you do not wish to format another disk, type the letter "N" for "no." Your data disk is now ready to be used with the system.

FORMAT WITH VOLUME LABEL

By using the V option of the Format command you put an electronic label on your disk. When you use the Directory or Checkdisk commands, this electronic volume label is displayed.

1. DOS should be loaded and the DOS disk should be in Drive A. A blank disk should be in Drive B.

2. Type **Format B:/V**

3. Press <ENTER>

4. When the system prompts you to insert a new disk in the designated drive, make sure that the disk you wish to format is in the designated drive.

5. Touch any key to begin the formatting process.

6. Part of the process will be completed when the following appears on the screen:

```
Formatting...Format complete

Volume label (11 characters, ENTER for none)?
```

7. Type in the label you want to use, for example, your name, social security number, or the disk number. Review the filename parameters for a list of valid characters.

8. Press <ENTER>

9. When the formatting process is complete, you will be asked if you wish to format another disk. If you wish to format another disk, type the letter "Y"

for "yes" and follow the screen prompts to insert a blank disk. If you do not wish to format another disk, type the letter "N" for "no." Your data disk is now ready to be used with the system.

PRINT SCREEN FUNCTION

The Print Screen function is available through DOS. It allows you to print an exact copy of what appears on the screen.

1. Be sure DOS is loaded and the printer is turned on and is online.

2. Press the **Shift-<PrtSc>** keys.

3. Release both keys.

    The contents of the screen will print.

OUTPUT TO PRINTER FUNCTION

When the Output to Printer or Echo function is activated, anything that is typed on the keyboard appears on both the screen and on paper.

1. Be sure DOS is loaded.

2. Make sure that the printer is turned on and is online.

3. Press and hold the Ctrl key and then just touch the <PrtSc> key. When you use these keys to activate the Output to Printer function, it will appear that nothing has happened.

4. Release both keys.

5. In order to see if the function has been activated, press the **<ENTER>** key a few times. The paper will advance one line and print the command prompt (e.g., A>) each time you press **<ENTER>**.

6. If there is no printer response, repeat the procedure.

HOW TO DEACTIVATE OUTPUT TO PRINTER

Until you deactivate the Output to Printer function, everything that appears on the display will also appear on paper.

1. Make sure the printer is on line. Press the Ctrl-<PrtSc> keys.

2. Release both keys.

3. This stops the output to the printer. In order to be sure that the function is no longer active, press the <ENTER> key a few times. If the paper does not advance one line and print the command prompt each time you press <ENTER>, the Output to Printer function is deactivated.

APPENDIX B
ANSWERS TO CHECKPOINT QUESTIONS

Unit 2

a. B> will appear
b. Drive B
c. to end one line and begin another; to create blank lines
d. 3.07" depending on your hardware
e. 2.07" (if typing began on Ln 1 and depending on your hardware)
f. F10
g. <Home>, <Down> arrow keys
h. <Home>, <Home>, <Up> arrow keys
i. <Down> arrow key; twice
j. <Home>, <Home>, <Down> arrow keys
k. <Up> arrow key
l. <Right> arrow key
m. Ctrl-<Right> arrow keys; four times
n. <Home>, <Home>, <Right> arrow keys
o. <Home>, <Home>, <Left> arrow keys
p. F7
q. Your revised document can be saved in the original file or placed it in a new file with a new filename.
r. Shift-F10

UNIT 3

a. <CR>
b. 7
c. <DEL>
d. Ctrl-<End>
e. 2.5"
f. Retrieve the document if necessary, press Shift-F7, type "1"

UNIT 4

a. the number next to Pos appears in a contrasting color or intensity
b. F8
c. F6
d. <CAPS LOCK>
e. Shift-F6
f. press <CR>
g. it jumped to the right margin
h. Alt-F4
i. the text appears in a contrasting color or intensity; the change is indicated in the status line
j. the text appears in a contrasting color or intensity; the change is indicated in the status line
k. Block, Ctrl-F4, option 1 twice, move the cursor to the new location, press <ENTER>
l. Alt-F4, Shift-F3
m. Alt-F3
n. [CNTR],[UND]
o. [C/A/FLRT]
p. [UND],[BOLD]

UNIT 5

Section 1
a. the Font menu
b. Ctrl-F8,1,2
c. Ctrl-F8,3 or press the <right> arrow key

Section 2
d. Shift-F8,1
e. text is formatted within the new margin settings
f. The text appears double-spaced on the screen. The Ln number in the status line identifies the line on which the cursor is resting.
g. Shift-F8,1,8
h. move the cursor to the first tab stop, press Ctrl-<End>
i. F7 twice
j. Shift-F8,2
k. Shift-F8,2,3,1,4
l. Shift-F8,2,7, then choose placement
m. Shift-F8,2,1
n. Shift-F8,3,5

Section 3
o. Alt-F8

UNIT 6

a. Shift-F7
b. press Shift-F7,N,2
c. press Shift-F7,2
d. Alt-F4
e. 1
f. Shift-F7,4,5
g. Shift-F7,4,4
h. Shift-F7, 3, document name, select page(s) (e.g.,2,3,5)
i. Pages (All) prompt after the document selection allows you to select specific pages to be printed
j. type "1" from the Printer Control submenu

UNIT 7

a. Shift-F5
b. name of month, the date, and the year
c. F4
d. it is indented from both margins
e. F4, Shift-<TAB>
f. <ESC>
g. <ESC>, type number after the prompt, type character
h. F2
i. a "Not found" message appears on the screen
j. Shift-F2
k. Alt-F2, N
l. Ctrl-F3, 1, answer the prompt, "# Lines in this Window"
m. press Ctrl-F3, type "1", answer the prompt by typing a number greater than the number of lines on the screen (e.g., >24)

UNIT 9

a. 10
b. option 1

UNIT 10

a. F9
b. Shift-F9, E
c. Shift-F9
d. Ctrl-F9
e. a message is displayed to remind you of the information you would like to enter from the keyboard
f. the printer pauses
g. Format menu and Page and Paper Size submenus
h. the Format Line submenu

UNIT 11

a. Ctrl-F10
b. press Ctrl-F10 again
c. when the prompt "Macro Def" appears on the screen
d. when the "Define Macro" message appears on the screen, hold down the Alt key while typing a single letter from A-Z
e. press Alt-F10, then type the name of the macro file
f. press Alt and the file letter
g. Ctrl-F10
h. Ctrl-F10

UNIT 12

a. from the Text Column Definition submenu, choose "1" from the Column Type submenu
b. select option 3 from the Math/Columns menu
c. Ctrl-<CR>
d. from the Text Column Definition submenu, choose "2" from the Column Type submenu

UNIT 13

a. Alt-F5
b. Block the text for each heading
c. option 6 from the Mark Text menu (Block off)

UNIT 14

a. Alt-F7
b. type "2" in the Type row on the Math Definition submenu
c. it automatically jumps to Calculation Formulas on the Math Definition submenu
d. F7
e. the first one
f. by selecting option 1 from the Math/Columns menu
g. "!" appears in the calculation column
h. subtotals above the operator in the numeric column are added
i. option 2 from the Math/Columns [Math on] menu
j. Alt-F7, option 1

UNIT 15

a. Alt-F9

INDEX

A

Advance, 93
Appearance submenu, 68
Arrow keys, 19

B

Backspace, 30
Backup, 61
Block and Switch, 57
Block text, 51
Boldface, 48
Boxes, Graphic, 249

C

Calculation columns, 231
Cancel a print job, 106
Cancel key, 21
Capitalization, 48
Carriage Return, 16
Center text horizontally, 49
Center page vertically, 85

Columns, 210-215
Copy blocks of text, 54
Copy for backup, 61
Cursor, 15
Cursor, horizontal movement, 19
Cursor, vertical movement, 20

D

Date menu, 126
Date and Time feature, 126
Decimal characters, 93
Default values, 16
Delete a file, 151
Directory, change, 152
Document identification line, 30
Document summary, 90
Double Word submenu, 160

E

Editing, 32
Endnotes, 129
Envelopes, 189
Exit WordPerfect, 21

F

Field, 176, 179
File management, 150-154
Flush Right, 51
Font menu, 67
Footers, 85
Footnotes 137
Footnote/Endnote menu, 139
Format a disk, 13
Format Document submenu, 90
Format Line submenu, 76
Format menu, 75
Format Other submenu, 92
Format Page submenu, 84
Format, text, 66

G

Go To key, 21
Graphics, 242-256
Graphics menu, 242

H

Hanging paragraph, 130
Hard disk, 14
Hard page, 17
Hard space, 16
Headers, 85
Help function, 23
Horizonital lines, graphics, 244
Hyphenation, 76

I

Indenting, 128
Index, 220
Insert key, 35
Insert mode, 35

J

Job List, 106
Justification, 77

K

Keys, 177

L

Lines, 176, 242-249
Line spacing, 77
Line submenu, 244
Lists, 220
List Files menu, 151
Loading WordPerfect 5.0, 13, 14
Locked documents, 154

M

Macros, 196-203
Mailing labels, 191
Margin Release, 80
Margins, 77
Margins, top/bottom, 85
Math, 230-238
Math/Columns menu, 210, 230
Math Definition submenu, 231
Mark Text menu, 220
Menus, 6, 36
Merge Codes menu, 182
Merge/Sort menu, 177
Merging, 175-192
Move a block of text, 54
Move menu, 54

N

Name a document, 18
Newspaper columns, 210
Not Found submenu, 159, 160
Numeric columns, 231

O

Outline, 205
Overstrike, 93

P

Page Format menu, 84
Page numbering, 85
Paper size/type, 85
Parallel columns, 210
Pitch, 90
Primary file, 181-184
Print a document, 105
Print a page, 105
Print menu, 36, 37, 104
Printer control, 105
Printer Control submenu, 106
Printing, 104
Printing a block of text, 108
Printing a document stored
    on a data disk, 105, 151
Print, change print options, 93
Print Format menu, 63
Print menu, 100

Q

Quick Reference Card, 6

R

Records, 176, 179
Redline, 90
Rename files, 151
Repeat a character or feature, 131
Replace, 133
Retrieve, 23, 151
Rewrite feature, 34
Reveal codes, 60
Right justification, 77

S

Save a document, 18
Save and Exit, 21
Search and Replace, 133
Search for text 133
Secondary file, 175-181
Selecting, 177
Size submenu, 67
Soft page, 17

Sort menu, 178
Sorting, 186-189
Sorting and Selecting, 177
Speller, 158-161
Split screens, 144
Status line, 15
Subscript, 68
Superscript, 67
Switch feature, 57

T

Tab, 32
Table of contents feature, 220-224
Tab Ruler, 142
Tabs Set submenu, 77
Template, 4, 5
Text columns, 210, 231
Thesaurus, 162-164
Thesaurus menu, 162
Totals column, 231
Toggle keys, 34

U

Undelete, 38
Underline, 48
Underline spaces/tabs, 93
User's manual, 6

V

Vertical lines, graphics, 244
View Document feature, 112

W

Widow/Orphan lines, 78
Windows, 142
Words, 177
Word Pattern, 152
Word Search, 152
Workbook, 6

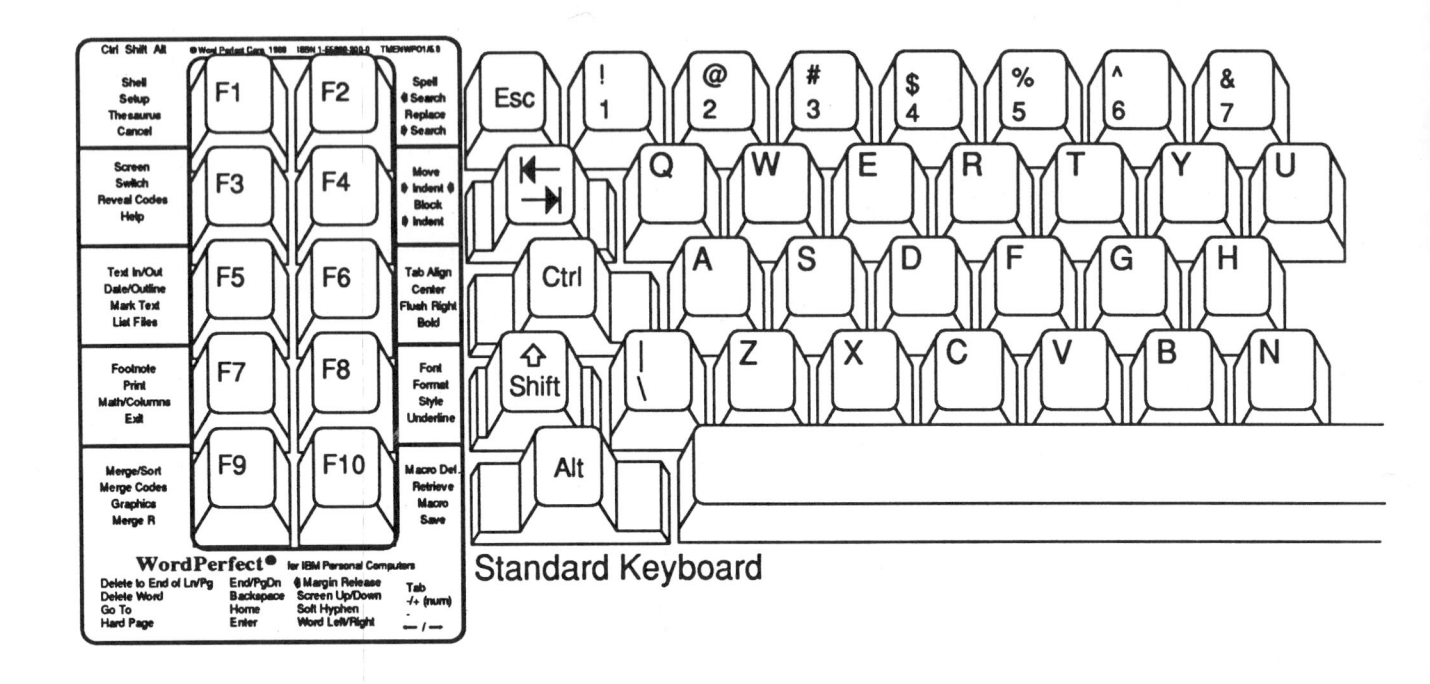

Ctrl	Shift	Alt			
		Shell	F1	F2	Spell
		Setup			Search
		Thesaurus			Replace
		Cancel			Search
		Screen	F3	F4	Move
		Switch			Indent
		Reveal Codes			Block
		Help			Indent
		Text In/Out	F5	F6	Tab Align
		Date/Outline			Center
		Mark Text			Flush Right
		List Files			Bold
		Footnote	F7	F8	Font
		Print			Format
		Math/Columns			Style
		Exit			Underline
		Merge/Sort	F9	F10	Macro Def.
		Merge Codes			Retrieve
		Graphics			Macro
		Merge R			Save

WordPerfect® for IBM Personal Computers

Delete to End of Ln/Pg	End/PgDn	Margin Release	Tab
Delete Word	Backspace	Screen Up/Down	-/+ (num)
Go To	Home	Soft Hyphen	
Hard Page	Enter	Word Left/Right	— / —

Standard Keyboard

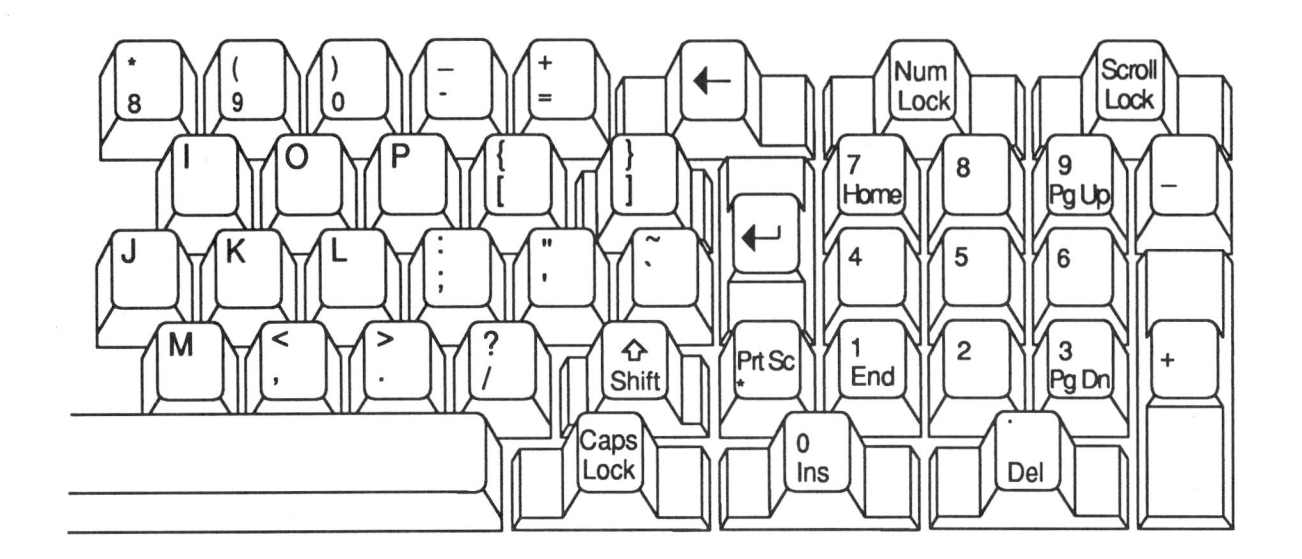

IBM PC™ Abbreviations

Esc—Escape Key
Ctrl—Control Key
Alt—Alternate Key
Num Lock—Number Lock Key
Pg Up—Page Up Key

PrtSc—Print Screen Key
Pg Dn—Page Down Key
Ins—Insert Character
Del—Delete Character

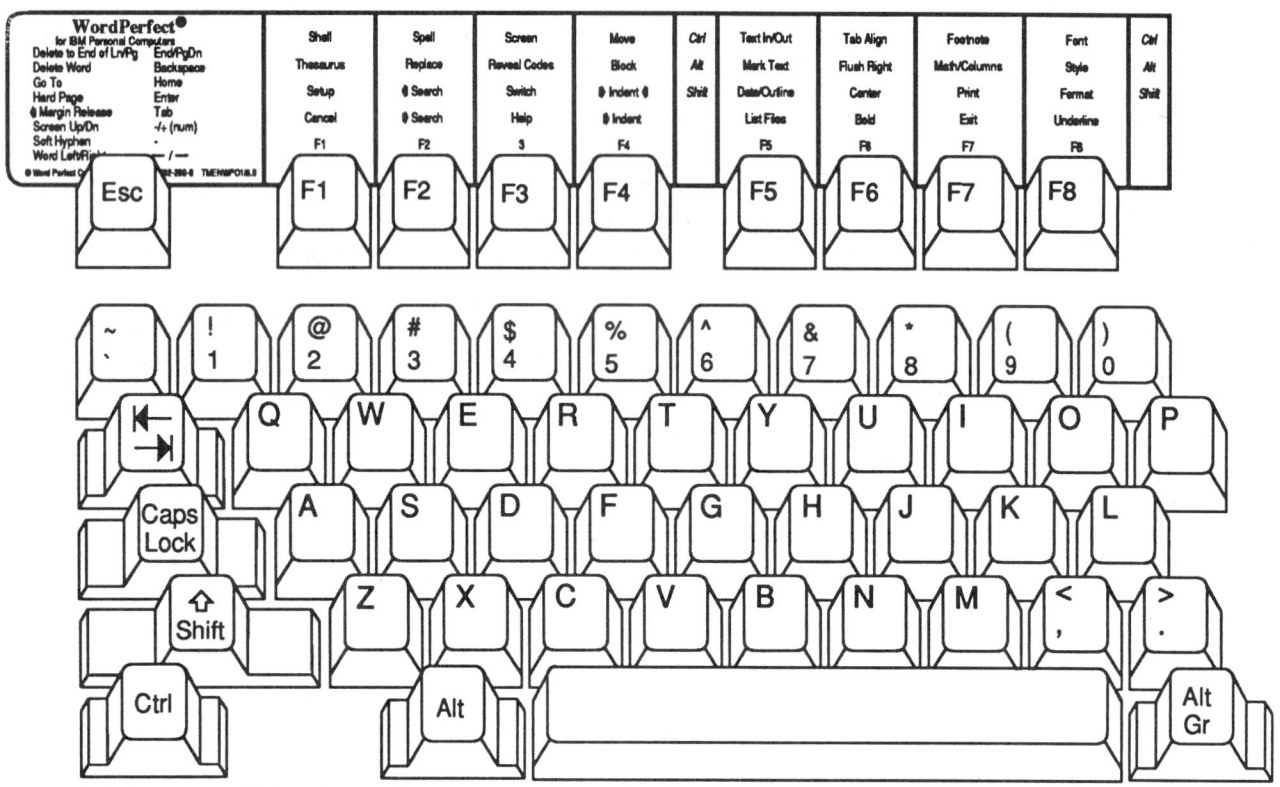

Enhanced Keyboard

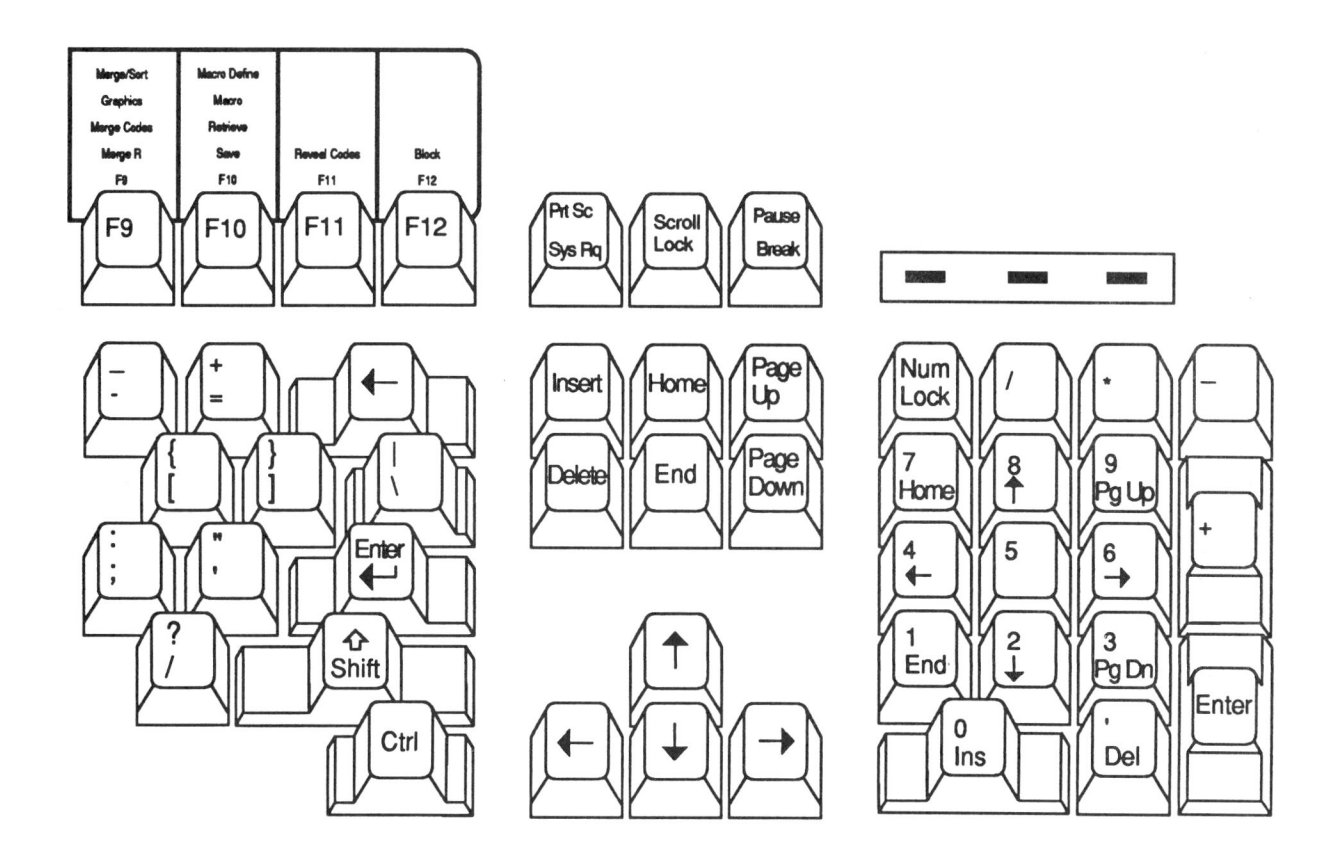

IBM PC™ Abbreviations

Esc—Escape Key   PrtSc—Print Screen Key
Ctrl—Control Key   Pg Dn—Page Down Key
Alt—Alternate Key   Ins—Insert Character
Num Lock—Number Lock Key   Del—Delete Character
Pg Up—Page Up Key

Notes

Notes

Notes

Notes

Notes

Notes

Notes

Notes

Notes